The Significance of Interpersonal Forgiveness in the Gospel of Matthew

The Significance of Interpersonal Forgiveness in the Gospel of Matthew

ISAAC KAHWA MBABAZI

◆PICKWICK *Publications* • Eugene, Oregon

THE SIGNIFICANCE OF INTERPERSONAL FORGIVENESS IN THE GOSPEL OF MATTHEW

Copyright © 2013 Isaac Kahwa Mbabazi. All rights reserved. Except for brief quotations in critical publications or reviews, no part of this book may be reproduced in any manner without prior written permission from the publisher. Write: Permissions, Wipf and Stock Publishers, 199 W. 8th Ave., Suite 3, Eugene, OR 97401.

Pickwick Publications
An Imprint of Wipf and Stock Publishers
199 W. 8th Ave., Suite 3
Eugene, OR 97401

www.wipfandstock.com

ISBN 13: 978-1-62564-177-9

Cataloging-in-Publication data:

Mbabazi, Isaac Kahwa

    The significance of interpersonal forgiveness in the Gospel of Matthew / Isaac Kahwa Mbabazi.

    xii + 256 p. ; 23 cm. —Includes bibliographical references and index(es).

    ISBN 13: 978-1-62564-177-9

    1. Bible. Matthew—Criticism, interpretation, etc. 2. Forgiveness of sin—Biblical teaching. I. Title.

BS2575.6 F64 M25 2013

Manufactured in the U.S.A.

Contents

Foreword by Peter Oakes | vii
Preface | ix
Abbreviations | xi

1 General Issues, History of Scholarship, and Method | 1
2 The Centrality of Interpersonal Forgiveness in Matthew | 30
3 The Rhetoric of Interpersonal Forgiveness in First-Century Secular Literature | 62
4 The Rhetoric of Interpersonal Forgiveness in Jewish Literature in Greek | 88
5 The Rhetoric of Interpersonal Forgiveness in Matt 6:9–15 | 117
6 The Rhetoric of Interpersonal Forgiveness in Matt 18:21–35 | 148
7 Forgiveness and Connected Aspects of Matthew's Theology | 190

Bibliography | 223
Index of Subjects | 237
Index of Authors | 245
Ancient Document Index | 249

Foreword

ISAAC CAME TO RESEARCH on this topic with an interest in tackling it as a way of helping people in his home area, the eastern Democratic Republic of Congo, to handle issues of reconciliation following bouts of civil war. In these conflicts, all the participants tend to profess some sort of Christian allegiance, so biblical resources can provide key ground for enabling dialogue and helping people and groups move forward after violence.

The tendency for many students whose interests are as highly contextual as those of Isaac is to produce a type of reader-response study of the biblical text in question, where the readers are those in the current contextual situation. The resulting work can be of great value for such readers but the level of interest among other kinds of reader can sometimes be somewhat limited. Isaac has not gone down this reader-response route but has instead produced a more directly exegetical study of the topic in Matthew that he is interested in for contextual reasons.

As Isaac's study progressed I was increasingly impressed that he has indeed drawn out a major theme in Matthew, the significance of which has not been properly recognized by previous scholarship. In fact, interpersonal forgiveness could possibly be seen as one of the key drivers of the distinctive shape of Matthew's Gospel. Isaac sets the evidence out clearly and draws in a range of illuminating ancient comparative material to show how interpersonal forgiveness was handled in other texts. His argument is one that anyone studying Matthew's Gospel will find interesting.

Isaac was a joy to supervise, both because of his character and because of his unremitting commitment to surmounting the range of challenges involved in turning his passion for his subject into successful PhD work. Isaac's dissertation was passed, as one of the last academic acts of the great Matthean scholar, R. T. France. He was my own first academic

New Testament teacher and I owe him a great debt for key foundations that he laid for future study. He combined great scholarship, great graciousness, and great commitment to the Christian faith. Knowing also his commitment to biblical scholarship in Africa, I am sure that this book too would also have given him some delight.

Peter Oakes
Greenwood Senior Lecturer in the New Testament
University of Manchester

Preface

THIS BOOK IS THE published version of a PhD dissertation studied at The University of Manchester, in the United Kingdom. An interest in the theme of interpersonal forgiveness in Matthew's Gospel arose in 2002, when a series of teaching on the significance of the theme was given by Rev. Dr. David Langford[1] at the Institut Supérieur Théologique de Bunia (ISTB), in Congo. Later, the interest in researching this subject as a doctoral topic emerged. Dr. Peter Oakes became my supervisor, guiding my work through to its completion. Other scholars also came in at different stages of the project with diverse contributions. The following names are worth mention in this respect: first, the members of the Ehrhardt Seminar (i.e., Centre for Biblical Research of The University of Manchester), particularly Prof. George J. Brooke, Rev. F. Gerald Downing, and Rev. Dr. Jack McKelvey; second, the members of Tyndale Fellowship, particularly Dr. David J. Reimer, Dr. David Wenham, Rev. Dr. John Nolland, Prof. Donald A. Hagner, and Prof. I. Howard Marshall; and third, the members of the British New Testament Society. It has been a great honor to learn from each of them.

Special thanks are due to the late Dr. R. T. France and Dr. Todd Klutz, who examined my dissertation and gave reasonable comments and suggestions. These have been very helpful and have been taken into consideration in the process of producing the present monograph. A vote of thanks is also due to the Université Shalom de Bunia (USB) for kindly granting me a period of leave to undertake my doctoral studies

---

1. David Langford was a missionary in the Democratic Republic of Congo (DRC) for several years. He taught at Institut Supérieur Théologique de Bunia (ISTB), as it was then. Later he became the Principal of ISTB for a few years. Currently, he is in the United States of America and is an adjunct professor of Practical Theology at Université Shalom de Bunia (USB), in the DRC.

that has culminated in a dissertation that has now become a monograph. I am extremely grateful to Langham Partnership International (LPI), to Educating Africans for Christ (EAFC), to Mylne Trust, and to Ministers' Relief Society for sponsoring the project.

I am also extremely grateful to Pickwick Publications for the acceptance of my monograph proposal for publication, thus making my dissertation more widely available.

In the process of writing this monograph, I have received tremendous support from friends—these I came to consider my extended family—for moral, spiritual, and practical support. I feel indebted particularly to Revd Kenneth and Mary Habershon, Dr. Steve and Mrs. Jane Hawes, Dic and Phyllis Lawson, Pastor Nyakufa Bagota, Cley and Jane Crouch, Mrs Elizabeth Johnston, Miss Ruth Johnston, Dr. Suseela Mathias, Margaret Habershon, Carl and Michelle Bucknor, Sarah Nativel, Montunrayo Ogunyinka, Lorna Lindsay, Lore and Colin Chumbley, Zarina Karmali, Andy and Katina Williams, Les and Christina Hampstead, David and Emma Peppiatt, Phil and Barbara Hawksley, Adrian and Madalen Haines, Martin and Faida Austin, Jon and Jude Witt, and many other friends around the world. Thank you for your love and companionship, which always keeps me both humble and joyful.

I owe many thanks to Downing, Miss Katharina Keim, and Miss Emily Innes, for their whole-hearted assistance in reading the manuscript, correcting and helping improve my English, and to Dr. Chris Spinks for editing the manuscript and bringing the project to its completion. It was great pleasure working with Christian Amondson, Ian Creeger, Jim Tedrick, Matthew Stock, and Raydeen Cuffe.

And last, but far from least, I am grateful to my wife, Jeannette Bugurwenda Mbabazi, for shouldering all the laborious work at home and taking care of our daughters (Grâce Komwinsingo Mbabazi, Georgine Kyakuhaire Mbabazi, and Vanessa Kabasinguzi Mbabazi), when I was away doing research, and for the family for their patient support throughout. I owe a lifelong debt to my mother Kezia Rubito Kahwa, and to my brothers and sisters, for their encouragement for their son and brother to pursue his lengthened study in England.

Isaac Kahwa Mbabazi

Abbreviations

Ant.	*Jewish Antiquities*
Ant. Rom.	*Roman Antiquities*
BAGD	*Greek-English Lexicon of the New Testament and Other Early Christian Literature*
BASOR	Bulletin of the American Schools of Oriental Research
CBQ	*Catholic Biblical Quarterly*
CBQMS	Catholic Biblical Quarterly Monograph Series
EDNT	*Exegetical Dictionary of the New Testament*
ISBE	*International Standard Bible Encyclopedia*
JBL	*Journal of Biblical Literature*
JIS	*Journal of International Studies*
JRE	*Journal of Religious Ethics*
JSNT	*Journal for the Study of the New Testament*
JSNTSup	*Journal for the Study of the New Testament Supplement Series*
JSOT	*Journal for the Study of the Old Testament*
JSOTSup	*Journal for the Study of the Old Testament Supplement Series*
JSPR	*Journal of Social and Personal Relationships*
NICNT	New International Commentary on the New Testament
NIDB	*New Interpreter's Dictionary of the Bible*

NIDNTT	*New International Dictionary of the New Testament Theology*	
NIGTC	New International Greek Testament Commentary	
PSPR	*Personality and Social Psychology Review*	
PSTJ	*Perkins School of Theology Journal*	
SNTSMS	Society for New Testament Studies Monograph Series	
TDNT	*Theological Dictionary of the New Testament*	
TLG	Thesaurus Linguae Graecae	
WUNT	Wissenschaftliche Untersuchungen zum Neuen Testament	

1

General Issues, History of Scholarship, and Method

THE PRESENT STUDY EXPLORES the theme of interpersonal forgiveness in Matthew.[1] By "interpersonal forgiveness" I mean giving up or letting go resentment for an injury (or wrongdoing) caused, or for failure to meet one's obligation. It is a sort of "moving past" transgression or failure by ceasing to harbor bitterness and refraining from taking revenge, with the ultimate aim of potentially restoring a disrupted (or broken) relationship between a wrongdoer and a wronged person.

I argue that this idea of interpersonal forgiveness is more central to the message in the First Gospel than scholars have previously appreciated. I also venture an understanding of the nature of interpersonal forgiveness in this gospel. I do not engage in the study of the systematic theology of "conditionality," although conditionality in forgiveness is considered. I focus on what this conditionality means for the people. (By "conditionality" I mean the condition to forgive others that is expected from the Christian before he or she can ask for God's forgiveness.)

The structure of this first chapter takes the form of four main sections. The first section states the problem and the aim of the study; the second section discusses the history of scholarship; the third section describes the method of interpretation used in this study in handling the

---

1. "Matthew" is used in this study to refer either to the *author* of the first canonical gospel or to his *work*.

Matthean material and the fourth describes what was covered in the first chapter and what will be done in each succeeding chapter along with the respective tasks of each.

PROBLEM, AIM, AND RELEVANCE OF THE STUDY

This investigation takes up the issue of interpersonal forgiveness in the First Gospel. However, insufficient attention seems to have been given to this theme in this gospel. No attempt has been made to consider its centrality, or to explore its nature and understand better Matthew's passages related to it. Although the subject is inevitably considered by almost every commentator on Matthew, to the knowledge of the present author, the above mentioned aspects of this theme have not been given adequate attention in published exegesis.

A number of issues have characterized scholarly debate in Matthean studies for the last four decades. They can be grouped into five categories: first, Matthew's relation to formative Judaism; second, the literary structure of the gospel and moral instruction; third, Matthew's view of salvation history; fourth, his Christology; fifth, the place of Matthew in the development of early Christianity and Judaism.[2] This study is a potential contribution to the debate concerning the latter issue. The main question of concern here is twofold. First, what contribution did he expect it to make to the internal problems that his community was facing? Second, what then are possible values which he commends to his community? Engaging in this involves inquiring into the situation of Matthew's group.[3] There are some clues within Matthew, which clearly reflect its possible situation to do with conflicts. Several items have been proposed as possible aspects of the situation of this community in later first-century Antioch. Because of their prominence in the gospel, they have been considered as the prominent themes in it. First is the role of the Torah in its relation to Jesus and his teaching. Second is hostility toward

---

2. Excellent updated critical surveys of Matthean studies include the following: Senior, "Directions in Matthean Studies," 5–21; Sim, "The Social Setting of the Matthean Community," 268–80; Riches, *Matthew*; Hurtado, "New Testament Studies in the 20th Century," 43–57.

3. "Matthean community" or "Matthew's community" is used in this piece of work in a generic way to refer to the recipients of the First Gospel understood as a cluster of communities located in the region of Antioch of Syria. Stanton was the first to suggest this (cf. Stanton, *Gospel for a New People*, 50).

the Jewish leadership. Third are identity, self-definition and the future of God's covenant people. Fourth is righteousness, and fifth forgiveness of sins.[4] Discipleship, community, reward and judgment have sometimes also been suggested to be prominent in the gospel.[5]

There are sound reasons to believe that these are prominent issues in the First Gospel; for most of them are to a greater or less extent subjects of a full scale discussion—some running throughout. The law and its right interpretation and correct application to life, as well as the hostility toward the Jewish leadership, are evident from the so-called fulfillment citations[6] (Matt 2:13 cp. Exod 2:15; Matt 2:16 cp. Exod 2:23; Matt 2:19 cp. Exod 4:19; Matt 2:12 cp. Exod 4:20, etc.), from the conflict stories (12:1–8; 15:1–20; 22:34–40) and from the section 5:17–48. As to identity, self-definition and the future of God's covenant people, it is also possible to derive them from and relate them to the Matthean fulfillment citations and conflict story texts. As J. Andrew Overman has written, "The rejection of the Jewish leadership and the conviction that they are faithless and have corrupted the will and law of God lead naturally to the question about the future of God's people . . . The exclusive nature of these communities and the claims they made led inevitably to the conclusion that the community constituted God's new . . ., God's *true* people."[7] The righteousness theme is directly stated in the gospel by means of the noun δικαιοσύνη (7x: 3:15; 5:6, 10, 20; 6:1, 33; 21:32) and the corresponding adjective δίκαιος (17x). As Graham N. Stanton has stated, discipleship and community themes in the context of the whole gospel are intertwined and interdependent[8] (Matt 6; 18).

Each of these themes has been given due attention in scholarship. Overman, for example, has thoroughly explored these motifs in his monograph *Matthew's Gospel and Formative Judaism*. Interpersonal forgiveness, however, never appears on his list of themes in Matthew which

---

4. For some of these suggestions, see, e.g., Przybylski, *Righteousness in Matthew and His World of Thought*; France, *Matthew: Evangelist and Teacher*; Luz, *The Theology of the Gospel of Matthew*; Overman, *Matthew's Gospel and Formative Judaism*; and Deines, "Not the Law but the Messiah."

5. E.g., Stanton, "Matthew as Interpreter of the Sayings of Jesus," 257–72; M. Brown, "Matthew," *NIDB*, 3:839–52, esp. 3:844.

6. As is widely recognized, roughly half of the fulfillment quotations are concentrated in the Matthean birth narrative; cf. Overman, *Matthew's Gospel and Formative Judaism*, 77.

7. Ibid., 151; emphasis original.

8. Stanton, "Matthew," 271.

he regards as central themes. To his mind, this is clearly a prominent theme in Matt 18—but not necessarily one of outstanding topics in the entire gospel—being stressed in that chapter.[9] Under the subsection "ordering the life of the community," Overman discusses five items, among which are righteousness, community life in Matt 5–7 and community discipline in Matt 18. Interpersonal forgiveness is referred to in two of them, only in passing.[10] In the paragraph in which a few Matthean forgiveness texts (6:12, 14; 9:8; 16:19; 18:15; 26:28) are involved in the discussion, Overman focuses his attention on the object (ὀφειλήματα/ ἁμαρτίας) of the verb, but not on the verb itself (ἀφίημι).[11]

Indeed, themes listed above are central to the message in the First Gospel. It is not unreasonable that they have received considerable attention. The prominence of interpersonal forgiveness has not been completely ignored, of course, but most tend to discuss it either in general terms, or under the topic of forgiveness of *sins*. Roland Deines' statement below may serve to illustrate this:

> The prominence of the forgiveness motif is visible throughout the whole gospel (3:6 [only confession of sins, no mentioning of forgiveness as in Mark 1:4, because only Jesus can forgive]; 9:2–6, 13; 12:31; 20:28; 26:28; cf. also Jesus' taking care of the sinners, 9:10f.; 11:19) . . .[12]

The evidence provided in Deines's statement speaks strongly in favor of the prominence of the theme of forgiveness in the First Gospel. The same evidence has been used by Ulrich Luz in an attempt to make a similar point.[13] Affirming forgiveness of *sins* as a prominent theme in Matthew is not the same as affirming the prominence of the *interpersonal* forgiveness theme in it. These are obviously two distinct notions; and each of them probably deserves to be studied as a theme on its own right.

Up to the present, as far as the present author is aware, insufficient attention has been given to the theme at hand. A few scholars, it has to be noted, have come close to examining the subject of this study; but they have not addressed the very concern of this study. To begin with, P.

---

9. Overman, *Matthew's Gospel and Formative Judaism*, 103.
10. Ibid., 90–113.
11. Ibid., 108.
12. Deines, "Not the Law but the Messiah," 71.
13. Luz, *Matthew* 2:28–29.

Ellingworth has aptly stated the importance of interpersonal forgiveness in Matthew as follows:

> God's forgiveness cannot be effectively received except by those who are ready to forgive others. This is given special emphasis in Matthew's version of a unique comment: "If you do not forgive others, then your father will not forgive the wrongs you have done (6:15)."[14]

This statement recognizes the significance of the theme in Matthew by pointing to the special emphasis given to it in 6:15. Ellingworth uses the saying in 6:15 as evidence. He could have also used the saying in 6:14 so as to include the whole package of the antithetical parallelism found in 6:14–15. Davies and Allison have used this rhetorical device as evidence for the significance of interpersonal forgiveness in Matthew.[15] Donald A. Hagner has made a useful comment in this regard:

> Vv 14–15 form a logion that the evangelist appends to the prayer because of its close association to the content of the fifth petition. The fact that it interrupts the flow of the larger passage (vv 1–18) suggests that the evangelist regarded its content as of great importance, not only for the offering of acceptable prayer but perhaps for its practical relevance for certain tensions with his Jewish-Christian community (cf. 5:23–24).[16]

Hagner's observation has two great merits. It connects harmoniously with the forgiveness texts within the Sermon on the Mount[17] (5:23–24 + 6:12 + 6:14–15), therefore adding something to the evidence. It also recognizes the importance of interpersonal forgiveness embodied in these passages at two levels. At the vertical relation level, it connects the notion of interpersonal forgiveness to the ideas of prayer and sacrifice; at the horizontal relation level, it recognizes the practical relevance of interpersonal forgiveness within the community. In this way, Hagner spells out quite clearly the practical relevance of the interpersonal forgiveness motif in Matthew.

This relevance has also attracted Luz's attention. He has commented that, with the *logion* of 6:14–15, Matthew repeats the forgiveness petition

---

14. Ellingworth, "Forgiveness of Sins," 242.

15. Davies and Allison, *A Critical and Exegetical Commentary on the Gospel according to Saint Matthew* 1:616–17.

16. Hagner, *Matthew* 1:145–46.

17. Hereafter the Sermon.

of the Lord's Prayer[18] and puts it in parenetic form; both the conditional wording and the "negative" (v. 15) make clear that human forgiving is a condition for divine forgiving. He then argues that, with this statement, the first evangelist emphasizes precisely the part of the Prayer where human activity is most directly involved.[19] Luz's comment spells out explicitly two aspects of the rhetorical device which emerge in 6:14–15 (the conditional wording and the negative statement) as evidence for the significance of interpersonal forgiveness in the Prayer and beyond. John Nolland has expressed the importance of this theme in Matthew by using a contrast:

> [I]n the explanation in vv. 14–15 clearly Matthew thinks of forgiveness of others as a necessary condition for seeking God's forgiveness. This is not to say that the source of our whole understanding of forgiveness is not in the mercy of God . . ., but it is to say that failure to forgive closes the door to ongoing forgiveness (cf. Mt. 18:23–35).[20]

What is most relevant for our purposes in Nolland's statement is the fact that he relates the understanding of Matthew's teaching about the issue of interpersonal forgiveness to God's mercy; he does no more than that. Hans D. Betz sees *not forgiving someone* as both a fault on the part of the unforgiving person and an act leading to God's refusal to forgive the "faithful," an act which has exacting eschatological consequences.[21] He does not elaborate on these consequences nor suggest their possible implications.

Warren Carter has identified four items as possible aspects of the situation of the Matthean community in later first-century Antioch, which he describes as follows: a minority community, a community recently separated from a synagogue because of a recent and bitter dispute with it, a community in transition trying to build a new identity and lifestyle, and an alternative community on the cultural margins of society.[22] The discussion about forgiving appears under "a community in transition, building a new identity." Claiming the *authorial audience* reading of Matthew, Carter argues that mercy and forgiveness are hallmarks in

---

18. Hereafter the Prayer.
19. Luz, *Matthew* 1:327.
20. Nolland, *The Gospel of Matthew*, 291.
21. Betz, *The Sermon on the Mount*, 416–17.
22. Carter, *Matthew*, 66–91.

this gospel (5:21–26; 9:17; 18:21–35), which he considers as evidence for a lifestyle in which each member cares for the others, a fact which is emphasized throughout the gospel.[23] He further argues that treating others with mercy and forgiveness is a consequence of and continuing condition for experiencing God's mercy and forgiveness (6:14–15; 18:21–35).[24] Carter, like the scholars discussed so far, recognizes the centrality of the theme under scrutiny. He points out the evidence, which unfortunately he does not explore.

David J. Reimer has also recognized its prominence in Matthew. He has fairly discussed the most relevant Matthean forgiveness texts.[25] Some of his conclusions will be discussed in detail later in this chapter. Although Reimer recognizes the fact, having his own agenda to do with the examination of this theme in the Apocrypha and Pseudepigrapha, he fails to supply enough evidence for this.

A few of the scholars surveyed above have recognized the prominence of the topic, but they have not given it the attention it deserves. Each of their treatments is not only short of details on the use of interpersonal forgiveness in ancient literature of the world of Matthew; it also lacks detailed exegesis of human forgiving in Matthew. Because of a clear gap in this regard in Matthean scholarship, a more complete study of this topic is required. This study will be carried out within the broader context of the First Gospel. The main purpose is to demonstrate that the concept of interpersonal forgiveness is much more central to the message in this gospel than has been previously seen. It also ventures an understanding of the nature of human forgiving and Matthew's texts related to it, focusing on conditionality in forgiveness and the emphasis on the responsibility of the offended person to forgive. There are a string of references to this theme across the Sermon (5:7, 21–26, 38–42, 43–48; 6:12, 14–15; 7:1–2, 12), which is developed in two sections outside the Sermon (18:15–17, 21–35). These texts altogether offer a significant forgiveness pattern, which can be used as evidence for the hypothesis to be probed in this piece of work.

An interest in these aspects of the subject is compelling, particularly for church life and practice in all contexts. Undertaking such a study would help understand better what forgiveness is and to suggest

---

23. Ibid., 84.
24. Ibid.
25. Reimer, "The Apocrypha and Biblical Theology," 268–71.

how Matthew should be read in a post-conflict period context. In order to form just an estimate of the contribution made by Matthew to a fuller understanding of the significance and nature of this theme for the church in the wider world, Matt 6:12, 14–15 and 18:21–35 will be examined in detail. These are the most relevant texts to this study because they are the only Matthean texts in which the notion of interpersonal forgiveness is stated directly by using ἀφίημι to describe the interpersonal interrelationships.

HISTORY OF SCHOLARSHIP

The purpose of this section is to situate this study in recent NT scholarship. The aim is to identify possible areas of discussions over the interpersonal forgiveness theme in Matthean scholarship to which a contribution would be of value. This survey looks for the main lines of research and to find how major scholars (biblical scholars and systematicians) see issues related to forgiveness. Literature to be surveyed includes books, commentaries, essays, and articles on forgiveness, on forgiveness and conditionality (or both), on aspects of each of them (or of both), deemed relevant for this study; but the publications on either 6:9–15 or 18:21–35 (or both) will mostly claim our attention. The organization of this survey is not chronological, as the data are examined with the main purpose of finding what eminent scholars think and say about the issues just described, as affirmed in Matt 6:12, 14–15 and 18:21–35. Significant gaps in the work of scholars will be made evident, which will lay the ground for thorough investigation of such relevant issues in the following section and again later in this work (chs. 5 and 6).

There have been numerous attempts to produce accounts of forgiveness in recent years.[26] However, the discussion over forgiveness in scholarly discourse is carried out in general terms. The two key Matthean forgiveness texts are referred to sometimes only in passing, or are discussed in a small section of only a couple of paragraphs. There are, however, scholars who have sharpened the discussion over the subject to

26. E.g., Quanbeck, "Forgiveness," 314–16; Bultmann, "Ἀφίημι, ἄφεσις, παρίημι, πάρεσις, κτλ.," *TDNT*, 1:509–12; Morro, "Forgiveness," *ISBE*, 340–44; Vorländer, "Forgiveness," *NIDNTT*, 1:697–703; Westerholm, "Forgiveness," *NIDB*, 2:480–85; Carmignac, *Recherches sur le "Notre Père"*; Reimer, "The Apocrypha and Biblical Theology," 259–82; Reimer, "Stories of Forgiveness," 359–78; Jones, *Embodying Forgiveness*; Volf, *Exclusion and Embrace*.

concentrate the debate on 6:12, 14-15 and 18:21-35, engaging with the study of forgiveness exegetically using these two texts. One may think, for example, of Israel Abrahams, R. A. Guelich, C. F. D. Moule, and Hans D. Betz. The rhetoric of forgiveness in contemporary discussions tends to concentrate on relationships between the rhetoric of forgiveness in the OT and its rhetoric in the NT, between the role of grace over against the Matthean ethical demands, between forgiveness and repentance, between forgiveness and justice, as well as on the meaning of forgiving in the First Gospel and on the motivations in forgiveness.

Jewish Background to Forgiveness

The context of Matthew's teaching about interpersonal forgiveness has extensively been studied. As has become well known, this is set in the first-century ce, when some of Christianity's fundamental claims about forgiveness came to be articulated and perhaps slowly differentiated from those of Judaism.[27] As a Jew and someone raised within a Jewish culture, Jesus surely knew that God is gracious and forgiving, notions which are plain in the OT. Controversy, however, surrounds the description of the rhetoric of forgiveness in the OT and its rhetoric in the NT, and particularly in Matthew. Some scholars have claimed that the First Gospel presents essentially the same understanding of forgiveness as the OT.[28] David J. Reimer, however, has argued for the possibility of a gap between forgiveness in the OT and in the NT. Having studied carefully Jesus' statements on forgiveness in Matt 6:12, 14-15 and 18:21-35, he notices that, unlike Matthew where Jesus' statements on forgiveness place pivotal importance on interpersonal forgiveness, interpersonal forgiveness is virtually absent from the OT.[29] His essay published in 2007[30] examines carefully the relevant forgiveness texts in the LXX: stories of Jacob and Esau (Gen 32-33), Joseph and his brothers (Gen 45; 50:15-21), Saul and Samuel (1 Sam 15:24-31), David and Abigail-Nabal (1 Sam 25), and

---

27. Cf. for example the Pauline tradition (Rom 4:7; Eph 1:7; 4:32; Col 1:14; 2 Cor 2:7, 10), the Markan tradition (Mark 11:25-26), and the Lukan tradition (Luke 11:2-4; 17:3-4).

28. E.g., Fensham, "The Legal Background of Mt. vi 12," 1-2; Quanbeck, "Forgiveness," 319.

29. Reimer, "The Apocrypha and Biblical Theology," 271-72.

30. Reimer, "Stories of Forgiveness," 359-78.

Shimei and David (2 Sam 16:5–14; 19:16–23; 1 Kings 2:8–9, 36–46), together with the narrative in Sir 28:1–7.

To the question of how to bridge the gap between the OT and NT (Matthew in particular) on the teaching about interpersonal forgiveness, Reimer proposes the so-called "intertestamental period" (Apocrypha and Pseudepigrapha) as a possible place where theological sense could be made of the two Testaments.[31] Most relevant in these materials to the subject under enquiry is Sirach (28:1–7, cp. 5:4–7; 17:25–32; 18:8–14). In his treatment of the Sirach text, Reimer makes a reasonable connection between Sir 28:1–4[32] and other Sirach texts. He clearly shows, for example, how in Sir 5:4–7; 17:25–32; 18:8–14, notions of death and judgment sharpen the consideration of divine forgiveness. He points out that in Sir 28:1–2, this combination of traditional Jewish concepts of death as punishment for sin, obedience to the commandments of the law and loyalty to the covenant produces the conclusion that divine judgment can be influenced by human activity. Those who lack mercy, he argues, obstruct forgiveness from God when they seek it.[33] Aspects of the teaching about forgiveness contained in Sir 28:1–4 are similar to its teaching in Matt 6:12, 14–15; 18:23–35 (cp. Mark 11:25; Luke 11:14; Jas 2:13). Matt 18:23–35 particularly links forgiving to judgment quite explicitly. On the ground of this thematic connection between 18:23–35 and 6:12, 14–15, one may think of the idea of "not being forgiven by the Father" in 6:15 to mean punishment. Roger Mohrlang has the same opinion. Matt 6:14–15 is listed among the texts in which he thinks judgment is implicit.[34] The parallelism between Sir 28:1–4 and Matt 18:23–35 has made Reimer think of Sir 28:4 as a possible basis for the parable of the unmerciful debtor (18:23–35).[35] He suggests this from the conceptual structure of the two texts. This proposal is persuasive enough, and the present author endorses it. As an additional comment, because of the underlying idea of conditionality in them, a possibility that Reimer fails to notice, one may also think of Sir 28:1–7 as a possible basis for the teaching in 6:12, 14–15 (cp. 5:7; 7:1–2).

---

31. Reimer, "The Apocrypha and Biblical Theology," 276–77.

32. The content of this text is provided in ch. 4 of this work where it is discussed at length.

33. Reimer, "The Apocrypha and Biblical Theology," 279.

34. Mohrlang, *Matthew and Paul*, 51.

35. Reimer, "The Apocrypha and Biblical Theology," 277–79.

Two observations need to be noted here. Firstly, in both Sir 28:1–7 and Matt 6:12, 14–15, the concept of conditionality in forgiveness emerges in the context of prayer, a phenomenon which can also be observed in Mark 11:25[–26] and in Luke 11:2–4. The situation described in Sir 28:1–7 is closer to the one in Matt 6:9–15. In both texts, the connection between forgiveness and prayer seems to stress the importance of the horizontal and vertical relationships. Secondly, both passages connect the notion of reluctance in forgiveness to that of judgment. As will be shown later (ch. 4), in Sir 28:1–7, more than just being defined as disgrace, anger, and wrath are connected with the unforgiving people. This has a parallel in Matt 5:22 where anger with an ἀδελφός makes one liable to judgment. The emphasis here is clearly on God's vengeance over those who eventually fail to forgive others. This same emphasis obviously underlies the teaching in Matt 18:23–35 (cp. 7:1–2) and is probably alluded to in 6:15 through the statement "not being forgiven by the Father." Reimer concludes his reflexion as follows:

> In the world of early Judaism and nascent Christianity, notions of interpersonal forgiveness overlap almost entirely. Despite the claims that have been made for the radical nature of Jesus' teaching on this subject, he was heir to an interpretative tradition which had already linked the love command to the idea of forgiveness and had begun to draw out some of the implications of this move. When Jesus' teaching is seen side by side with the Hebrew Bible, the distance between them is great. However, the *noncanonical* literature I have cited reflects the process of interpreting authoritative texts for their communities. And the range of concerns displayed by *these* communities—Jews and Christians around the turn of the era—on this issue are very similar (we might even say, the same).[36]

Reimer's careful analysis of the theme of interpersonal forgiveness in the Apocrypha and Pseudepigrapha is a valuable enterprise. His handling of these data in an attempt to establish the place where theological sense could be made of the two Testaments is quite reasonable. With regard to the interpersonal forgiveness theme in Matthew, Reimer's handling of the Matthean text is generally fair. He states the responsibilities of each party in the forgiveness processes; that is, responsibility of granting forgiveness and that of seeking forgiveness. He notes, for example, the fact that in 5:23–24, it is the offender's obligations which are in view. He contrasts

---

36. Ibid., 281; italics original.

this text with its parallel in Mark 11:25, and points to the fact that in Mark it is the offended party's obligations which are in view. He then stresses the reality that this teaching in Mark 11:25 is very much of a piece with that concluding the Matthean Prayer (6:14–15), with the exception that here the onus is placed on the offended person to freely forgive so as not to impede divine forgiveness.[37] Regarding Matt 18:23–35, Reimer accurately locates the story of the unmerciful debtor in its immediate context of Peter's question (18:21) and of its wider context of Jesus' teaching on reconciliation between the community members (18:15–20), in the framework of Jesus' teaching on the maintenance of relationships in the community (Matt 18). He then notes that the picture given is of an offended party going to the offending party to point out the fault, eventually to return with one or two others in the case of a negative response by the offending party, before they are ostracized (as he conceives it).[38]

There is, however, a point of uncertainty with Reimer's reading of the Matthean material: his interpretation of the fate of the potential unrepentant offender of 18:15–17. He seems to think that here forgiveness can be denied. He imagines that given a potential unrepentant offender, Jesus positively recommends forgiveness denial, although he also recognizes that this appears to be in tension with the subsequent counsel to Peter (18:22) that forgiveness knows no limits.[39] One wonders whether in 18:15–17 the focus of the Matthean Jesus' teaching is on the denial of forgiveness. This would contradict not only Jesus' subsequent counsel to Peter, as Reimer himself also recognizes, but also the teaching in Matt 18 as a whole, in which the emphasis is clearly on the responsibility of the offended person, as will be shown in chapter 6.

Grace and Matthean Conditionality

Matthew's vision of the role of grace over against his ethical demands—including the demand for interpersonal forgiveness—has been heatedly discussed. It is, therefore, not out of place to consider aspects of this question here. Querying Matthew's vision on this subject would mean clarifying our understanding of the role of grace over against the demand for forgiveness in Matthew's perspective.

37. Ibid., 269.
38. Ibid., 270–71.
39. Ibid., 271.

In the First Gospel, there is a strong emphasis upon the *doing*. The obvious importance that Matthew has given to the idea of righteousness and that of *eschatological* reward and punishment is an excellent illustration of this. This fact has caused some scholars to see Matthew as the antipode to Paul[40]—Paul is taken as a paradigm for interpreting Matthew, a phenomenon known as the "reading of Matthew through the eyes of Paul." The main question is to what extent are the differences between Matthew and Paul to be drawn, while also listening to each?

Roger Mohrlang's monograph, *Matthew and Paul*, arguably provides a good answer. This monograph is an excellent attempt to correct the disproportionate polarization. Dealing with the issues of eschatological reward and punishment in Matthew, he has shown their significance and how, by using them, Matthew seeks to motivate ethical behavior whether by enticement or by threat. His overall argument in this regard is that Matthew uses the notions of reward and punishment to underscore the fact that what one does matters for the kingdom.[41] In an attempt to secure his argument, Mohrlang begins by noticing the fact that Matthew has more material related to rewards and punishment than any other evangelist.[42] He then argues that the idea of eschatological recompense and punishment pervades Matthew and functions significantly in Matthew's motivation of ethical behavior, whether more or less explicitly.[43] He appeals, for example, to the way the initial summaries of the preaching of both John and Jesus (3:2; 4:17; cp. 10:7) are programmatic for the teaching that follows in the Sermon. He shows how Matthew is clear that a radical change of heart and life is essential if one is to gain the kingdom. He also notes the prominence of this concept in Matthew's thinking, visible in the beatitudes especially, which are significantly placed at the beginning of the Sermon (5:3–12). He points to the fact that here it is the promise of the kingdom, above all else, in which appeal is made for a moral life.[44]

Fascinatingly, Mohrlang points out that it is the negative side of this issue that the first evangelist is most concerned to stress, that is, the danger of failing to attain the kingdom and the fearful prospect of judgment that is implied. He then cautiously suggests that it is the threat of judgment

---

40. Hagner, "Righteousness in Matthew's Theology," 101.

41. Mohrlang, *Matthew and Paul*, 48.

42. For statistics, see Houlden, *Ethics and the New Testament*, 52; and Barth, "Matthew's Understanding of the Law," 58–59.

43. Mohrlang, *Matthew and Paul*, 48.

44. Ibid., 48n3.

that underlies the warnings about not achieving the kingdom (5:20; 18:3) and reasonably makes the connection with the emphasis on judgment which is evident in the immediate contexts of 5:21–30 and of 18:6–10. He then makes the point that for Matthew, eschatological judgment is a corollary of the coming of the kingdom and references to the latter therefore often indirectly express the threat of the former. He concludes that, in general, it is the threat of judgment and loss of the kingdom that serves as the dominant motivating force for ethics throughout Matthew.[45] Other evidence in support of interpreting judgment as ethical motivation includes 5:22–26, where the threat of judgment is declared against specific behavior such as anger, or any abuse toward one's ἀδελφός. The seriousness with which the evangelist takes the matter is apparent in his references to γέεννα (5:22, 29, 30; cf. 18:8–9).[46] Mohrlang further notes that the theme of judgment returns toward the end of the Sermon, where passing judgment on others is prohibited on the grounds that it renders one liable to the judgment of God (7:1–5, cp. 7:13–14, 21–27; 8:12, 29; 10:15, 26–28; 11:20–24; 12:41–42; 13:42, 50; 18:3, 10; 21:28–32; 22:13; 25:30, many of which occur in Matthew's own material). He then highlights the fact that the fear of judgment is a major element in Matthew's thought, and plays a crucial role in his ethics (10:26–28).[47]

Mohrlang's overall argument on eschatological reward and punishment in Matthew and the explanation of the *raison d'être* and purpose of such a teaching by the evangelist to his community is reasonable because of the weight of the biblical evidence used and the handling of it. Mohrlang, as far as I can see, seems to have maintained a good balance between Matthew's theology and his ethics, for he recognizes the central role of grace in Matthew: grace is implicit in the *whole story* of Jesus told by Matthew.[48] The difficulty with Mohrlang's argument, however, is that he believes that Matthew does not exploit the assumed structure of grace, and that for the most part it remains only in the background, simply taken for granted. Put differently, for Mohrlang, in Matthew the imperative is not *simply* built upon or derived from the indicative.[49] But when

---

45. Ibid., 49n4.
46. Ibid., 49.
47. Ibid., 51.
48. Ibid., 80; the entire section on "the role of grace" (pp. 78–81) is worth reading.
49. Ibid., 80.

one turns to the gospel itself, as will be shown in a moment, one finds just the opposite.

Unlike Mohrlang, Hagner has argued that in the First Gospel, the indicative is basic to the imperative; that is, for all of its emphasis on the ethical imperative, the gospel gives far more place to the indicative, to gift, and grace.[50] With regard to our interpersonal forgiveness and related texts, this would mean understanding them within the framework of the whole gospel—and not in isolation. As Davies and Allison have reasonably stated, the Sermon "is in the middle of a story about God's acted love, his gracious overture to his people through his Son, the Messiah Jesus. The story, read in its entirety, is about Jesus, not just ethics, a story which brings together gift and task, grace and law, benefit and demand."[51] Most significantly, Hagner points out the fact that the Sermon is preceded by a statement of grace in the Beatitudes, which is a clear indication of the fact that the kingdom is the gift of God, a matter of grace, not of human accomplishment.[52] This reading of the role of grace in Matthew is to be preferred because it is more plausible; for when we turn to the gospel, this is precisely what we find (i.e., a strong emphasis on gift and grace). The evidence for this can be summed up in the following points: the traditional Jewish assumption of God's mercy and forgiveness, as evident from the recurrence of these themes (6:12, 14–15; 9:2–8; 12:31–32; 18:23–27, 32–35; 21:31); the references to the soteriological significance of Jesus' life and death (1:21; 6:12, 14–15; 9:1–8; 12:31–32; 18:15–17, 21–35; 26:28); the gospel of the kingdom (4:23; 9:35; 24:14); the selection of the individual disciple (4:18–22) and God's fatherly care and aid for all needs (6:6–13, 25–30; 7:7–11; 10:20, 29–32; 18:10–14, 19–20; 24:20; 26:36–44). This evidence will be discussed in more detail in chapter 7.

Motivations in Forgiving

Why do people forgive? Research has shown that the motives underlying decisions to forgive are varied. These motives tend to depend on individuals, categories of people (e.g., philosophers, psychologists, theologians, etc.) and their respective worldviews of forgiveness. E. L. Worthington

---

50. For a more detailed argument on the role of grace in Matthew, see Hagner, "Righteousness in Matthew's Theology," 102–7.

51. Davies and Allison, "Reflections on the Sermon on the Mount," 299.

52. Hagner, "Righteousness in Matthew's Theology," 103n1.

Jr., J. W. Berry, and L. Parrott's grouping of these motives is striking. They have suggested that, in general, people forgive out of either *warmth-based virtues* (e.g., compassion, empathy, and altruism) or *conscientiousness-based virtues* (e.g., responsibility, honesty, accountability, and duty).[53] Julie J. Exline, E. L. Worthington Jr., P. Hill, and M. E. McCullough seem to agree with this proposal, adding only a brief comment to suggest that in many situations, *warmth-based virtues* and *conscientiousness-based virtues* should complement each other.[54]

This category, as formulated by Worthington, Berry, and Parrott, has some merits. It sees forgiving as altruistic, a moral duty and an act motivated with a sense of accountability. An aspect of this seems to be in line with what one study has demonstrated recently, claiming that when compared to those who forgave out of a sense of religious obligation, individuals who forgave out of love for the injurer showed less elevation in systolic and diastolic blood pressure when recalling the event.[55] This shows one of the positive outcomes of forgiving for other-oriented reasons. The category articulated by Worthington, Berry, and Parrott also suggests one of the significant features of forgiving also affirmed in Matthew, accountability. However, how forgiveness is viewed by these authors (and many others) tends to give the impression that the altruistic aspect of forgiveness has the lion's share; self-orientated reasons for forgiving appear to be less important for them.

Self-oriented reasons for forgiving have been paid careful attention to by J. W. Younger, R. L. Piferi, R. L. Jobe, and K. A. Lawler. They argue that primary motives for forgiving are largely self-focused rather than altruistic.[56] Their conclusions may be useful for the study of the theme of interpersonal forgiveness in Matthew, where both features of forgiveness mentioned above seem to be present, with perhaps the self-focused feature being the more predominant.[57]

Forgiveness as a *gift* emerges essentially in Matthew in the context of divine-human relation (8:2, 6; 18:27, 32). This most likely echoes the OT teaching about the nature of forgiveness. W. A. Quanbeck has also

---

53. Worthington, Berry, and Parrott, "Unforgiveness, Forgiveness, Religion, and Health," 107–38.

54. Exline et al., "Forgiveness and Justice," 343.

55. Huang and Enright, "Forgiveness and Anger-related Emotions in Taiwan," 71–79.

56. Younger et al., "Dimensions of Forgiveness," 837–55.

57. Attention will be paid to this in chs. 5 and 6.

observed that in the Bible, forgiveness is primarily God's act and benefit (gift). First, this divine act consists of God himself taking away graciously the barriers that separate man from his presence. Second, forgiveness is a free and sovereign gift of the loving God. As an act and a gift, forgiveness is an expression of the religious relationship between God and man.[58] W. C. Morro has more intensely enforced this possible twofold meaning of forgiveness. He sees forgiveness as always a matter of divine privilege, rather than human right. It is a privilege because the price of sin must first be paid before the conditions can exist for forgiveness to become a reality, he argues.[59] Additionally, in Matthew, forgiveness also appears as a moral duty most particularly in interpersonal relationship (cf. 6:12b, 14–15; 18:33). On the other hand, a sense of accountability also seems to motivate the acts of showing mercy and of forgiving. This is apparent in 6:12b, 14–15; 18:33; 7:1–2 and 5:7 (by implication), where the ultimate goal of the acts described above is the merciful person's or the forgiver's relationship with their heavenly Father. Therefore, for the first evangelist, neglecting an aspect of either relationship has potentially severe consequences.

Forgiveness and Repentance

Current discussions on forgiveness, ranging from popular treatments to theological analyses, seem to have taken quite seriously the relationship between forgiveness and repentance. The discussions tend to focus on whether or not repentance is a prerequisite for forgiveness; and if so, to what extent. The significance of repentance in forgiveness is a widely acknowledged fact in biblical scholarship. About eight decades ago, J. F. Bethune-Baker noted that in nearly all instances where the idea of forgiveness appears in the OT, the context implies repentance for the offence and an intention to avoid a repetition of it (as condition of forgiveness).[60] Two decades later, Quanbeck argued that, in the OT, forgiveness is realized through repentance and the intention to avoid a repetition of the offence.[61] These two representative observations indicate the belief that, whether in divine-human or in interpersonal forgiveness, repentance

---

58. Quanbeck, "Forgiveness," 314–15.
59. Morro, "Forgiveness," *ISBE*, 340–44, esp. 340.
60. Bethune-Baker, "Forgiveness," *Dictionary of the Bible*, 56–58; esp. 56.
61. Quanbeck, "Forgiveness," 316.

is fundamental for forgiveness to take place; that is, something is required on the part of the offender before they can be the beneficiary of forgiveness.

A tendency in the forgiveness discourse to overemphasize the centrality of repentance has also been observed. R. Swinburne, for example, extending the logic of Immanuel Kant's argument for the prior requirement of repentance to forgiveness,[62] has argued that repentance along with reparation, apology, and penance to victims are all necessary prerequisites for a person to expunge their guilt and to make atonement for the past. Of these elements, he singles out forgiving as belonging to the victim.[63] What Swinburne has suggested may be taken as an evidence for the common contemporary assumption of a causal priority for repentance to forgiveness.

Speaking more broadly, those who give much weight to repentance (and acts attached to it) as a prerequisite for forgiveness, seem to do so as a way of compelling the offender to acknowledge their responsibility and accountability for their wrongdoing and thus to break potential cycles of violence. There may be sound reasons to advocate the causal priority of repentance for forgiveness, for it seems to take the gospel as a way of ensuring that people take questions of culpability and accountability seriously.

L. G. Jones has proposed the need to recognize the logical and theological "priority" of God's forgiveness to various dimensions of human forgiveness as a possible way for appropriately understanding the relationship between forgiveness and repentance. This would imply that, for a Christian account, we can only know how to understand appropriately the relationship between forgiveness and repentance in the dynamics of interpersonal forgiveness if we *first* understand their relationship in God's forgiveness, insofar as God's forgiveness provides the paradigm for how we are to understand our own vocation to be forgiven and forgiving people.[64] The question is what this logical and theological "priority" of God's forgiveness consists of. In Jones' view, the answer could be something like this: being disposed to forgive without requiring prior repentance, because God in Christ forgave without requiring prior repentance. This position is open to debate.

---

62. Kant, *Religion within the Limits of Reason Alone*, 106–7.

63. Swinburne, *Responsibility and Atonement*, 84.

64. Jones, *Embodying Forgiveness*, 153n15.

It has been claimed that one of the crucial differences between Jesus and the Judaism of his day was his willingness to forgive in God's name without requiring prior repentance and, more determinatively, his authorization for his disciples to do likewise. Sanders, for example, has stated that Jesus invited sinners into the kingdom without requiring them to repent in the way that repentance was understood within Judaism—that is, without requirements of restitution, sacrifice, and obedience to the law.[65] Jones has criticized Sanders for seeming to imply that Jesus' message abandoned repentance.[66] Whether or not Jones' criticism is reasonable, what is clear is that in the Synoptics, Jesus' ministry is inaugurated with Jesus' announcement of the kingdom and his call to repentance. Matthew does not overlook repentance. He stresses it as a necessary condition to enter the kingdom of heaven (3:2, 8, 11; 4:17). In 5:21–26, he underscores the urgency to be reconciled with an ἀδελφός in order to avoid eventual punishment. In this text, the onus is placed on the offender. So it is possible to read from it the idea of repentance in the process of seeking reconciliation.

To the central question of whether or not repentance is a prerequisite for forgiveness, Volf has argued that repentance is not so much a prerequisite of forgiveness, especially in the first step in the process of forgiveness; in which case, forgiveness is not predicated on repentance on the part of the wrongdoer or on their willingness to redress the wrong committed. Repentance, it is suggested, is the kind of result of forgiveness whose absence would amount to a refusal to see oneself as guilty and therefore a refusal to receive forgiveness as forgiveness.[67] This viewpoint parallels Jones' proposal for the need to recognize the logical and theological "priority" of God's forgiveness to various dimensions of human forgiveness, as was discussed earlier in this subsection. As we shall see, it seems to be in line with Matthew's understanding of forgiveness and repentance.

Forgiveness and Justice

Current discussions of forgiveness have considered the relationship between forgiveness and justice. There is controversy about the approach

---

65. Sanders, *Jesus and Judaism*, 207.
66. Jones, *Embodying Forgiveness*, 110.
67. Volf, "Forgiveness, Reconciliation, and Justice," 875–76.

the victim should use in the process of granting forgiveness. Should one follow the principle of "first justice, then forgiveness" or that of "first forgiveness, then justice"? Differently stated, should forgiveness be offered after or before the demands of justice have been satisfied? Most scholars tend to favor the former; only a minority argues toward the latter. Volf is among the minority advocates of the "first forgiveness, then justice" principle.[68] What Volf actually proposes is forgiveness—justice—then reconciliation. As the discussion of the subject develops, he now makes a connection between the "first justice, then reconciliation" and "first justice, then forgiveness" statements. He makes it clear that "forgiveness is an element in the process of reconciliation, a process in which the search for justice is an integral and yet subordinate element."[69] He dismisses the view of "justice, then forgiveness," which to his mind sounds practically illogical:

> If forgiveness were properly given only after strict justice has been established, then one would not be going beyond one's duty in offering forgiveness; one would indeed wrong the original wrongdoer if one did not offer forgiveness. "The wrong has been fully redressed," an offender could complain if forgiveness were not forthcoming, "and hence you owe me forgiveness." But this is not how we understand forgiveness. It is a gift that the wronged gives to the wrongdoer. If we forgive we are considered magnanimous; if we refuse to forgive, we may be insufficiently virtuous. . ."[70]

The "justice, then forgiveness" principle is problematic. It fails to recognize the magnanimous character of forgiveness, a character which is stressed in Matt 18:22–35. Volf is probably right in reasoning that forgiveness *after* justice is not much different from forgiveness *outside* justice. Forgiveness outside justice, he argues, means treating the offender as if they had not committed the offence. Forgiveness after justice, on the other hand, means doing the same, only that the demand that justice be satisfied before forgiveness can be given is meant to redress the situation so that one can rightly treat the wrongdoer as if they had not committed the deed. He then makes the point that in both cases, it is to treat the offender as if they had not committed the offence or as if it were not

---

68. Ibid., 861–77.
69. Ibid., 876.
70. Ibid., 871.

theirs.⁷¹ He then proposes a few elements which he summarizes in six points that he thinks best illustrate the relation between forgiveness and justice. Following is a summary of these points.

First, forgiveness does not stand outside of justice; on the contrary, forgiveness is possible only against the backdrop of a tacit affirmation of justice. Second, forgiveness presupposes that justice—full justice in the strict sense of the term—has not been done. If justice were fully done, forgiveness would not be necessary, except in the limited and inadequate sense of being vindictive; justice itself would have fully repaid for the wrongdoing. Third, forgiveness entails not only the affirmation of the claims of justice but also their transcendence. Fourth, since it consists in forgiving the affirmed claims of justice, forgiveness, like any instantiation of grace, involves self-denial and risk; one has let go of something one had a right to, while not fully certain whether one's magnanimity will bear fruit either in one's inner peace or in a restored relationship. Fifth, the first step in the process of forgiveness is unconditional; it is not predicated on repentance on the part of the wrongdoer or on their willingness to redress the wrong committed. Repentance is not so much a prerequisite of forgiveness. It is the kind of result of forgiveness whose absence would amount to a refusal to see oneself as guilty and thus a refusal to receive forgiveness as forgiveness. Sixth, forgiveness is best received if in addition to repentance some form of restitution takes place.⁷²

These points are presented with such a compelling logic that critics may find it hard to squeeze in eventual criticism. Yet, what is probably not persuasive enough is Volf's final point where he states that "forgiveness is best received if in addition to repentance there takes place some form of restitution."⁷³ This statement raises the question of whether there ought to be an action seeking compensation or reparation after the offender is forgiven. Although what Volf suggests does have some logic in it and has apparently support in the gospels (e.g., Luke 19:1–10 where Zacchaeus is said to have repaid all those debts he owed to the people he exploited), it probably does not find support in Matthew. As we shall see in chapters 5 and 6, to demand reparation or compensation would stand in contrast with Matthew's intended meaning of ἀφίημι τὰ ὀφειλήματα/τὸ δάνειον/ τὴν ὀφειλὴν (6:12; 18:27, 32). In all three instances, this expression is

---

71. Ibid.
72. Ibid., 875–76.
73. Ibid., 876.

best understood to mean something like "forgive a debt" in the sense of cancelling it. The notion of forgive with this sense in Matthew seems to drive away the possibility that the demand for reparation or compensation be expected from the offender. Aspects of this will be dealt with in chapters 5 and 6.

Forgiving as Ability

C. F. D. Moule is probably the first to have taken seriously the problematic nature of forgiving in the First Gospel. He has suggested that in 6:12, 14–15, forgiving is about the ability to receive God's forgiveness. Moule begins his reflection by wondering whether there is a conflict between the conditional terms of the Prayer and the unconditional terms of Jewish liturgy. He then suggests that the key to answering this question lies in distinguishing between earning forgiveness and adopting an attitude which makes forgiveness possible—the distinction that is between deserts and capacity.[74]

Moule's observation brings out the notion of capacity. He interprets human forgiving in the context of its Matthean forgiveness discourses (6:12, 14–15; 18:21–35) to mean the believer's capacity to receive God's forgiveness. Moule, however, is not the first to have formulated the idea of capacity with regard to the meaning of forgiveness. Israel Abrahams is probably the pioneer of this understanding. He wrote three essays in which he carefully studied the relationship between God's forgiveness and interpersonal forgiveness. In the first two essays, Abrahams discusses God's forgiveness and interpersonal forgiveness respectively; in the third, he contrasts the conditional clause in the Prayer with the unconditional forgiveness of God as it is affirmed in Jewish liturgy.[75] In the latter essay, he argues that the conditional element in divine-human forgiveness is absent in the actual Jewish liturgy where, according to him, the unconditional generosity of God is allowed to stand alone. He goes on to contrast with this the conditionality of the clause in the Prayer, and points to the difference as a mark of the distinctiveness of that prayer.[76]

---

74. Moule, "As We Forgive," 281.

75. Abrahams, "God's Forgiveness," 1:139–149; "Man's Forgiveness," 1:150–167; "The Lord's Prayer," 2:94–108.

76. Abrahams, "The Lord's Prayer," 2:98.

Moule, in his criticism of aspects of Abrahams' thesis, notes that Abrahams more than once formulates the idea of capacity, but seems to also entertain the idea of deserts.[77] Moule's criticism is pertinent. It spots a few problematic phrases which Abrahams has used in his attempt to describe the responsibility of each party in the giving and the receiving forgiveness processes. Moule finds in these phrases some confusion. The apparent confusion is to make forgiveness conditional on repentance the same as to say that forgiveness can be earned by the recipient.[78] In fact, Moule agrees with Abrahams that forgiveness is conditioned by repentance. But he departs from Abrahams on the view that forgiveness is earned by repentance which, according to Moule, Abrahams seems to entertain.[79] Moule's own thesis is that forgiveness, though not conditional on merit, is nevertheless conditional; it is conditional on human response to the gift, the capacity to receive it.[80] Moule's argument has at least two clear advantages. Firstly, it helps draw a fundamental distinction between deserts and capacity, and states clearly forgiving as a necessary condition for receiving God's forgiveness. Secondly, it states what conditionality in forgiveness in Matthew seems to represent: ability to receive God's forgiveness. Moule, however, shows no interest in the significance of interpersonal forgiveness in Matthew. This reinforces the impression that this theme is a neglected one in Matthean scholarship, and further underlines the worthwhileness of this present enquiry.

Summarizing, the foregoing survey aimed at situating this study in recent NT, theological and philosophical scholarships. It has shown five most important lines of research in contemporary debate about forgiveness. This debate has focused on the relationship between the rhetoric of forgiveness in the OT and its rhetoric in the NT, between Matthew's view on the role of grace over against his ethical demands, between forgiveness and repentance, between forgiveness and justice, as well as on the meaning of forgiving in Matthew and on the motivations in forgiveness. As was shown, these lines altogether seem to be not well informed by the evidence about the centrality of the interpersonal forgiveness theme in Matthew.

---

77. Moule, "As We Forgive," 281.
78. Ibid., 281–82.
79. Ibid., 282.
80. Ibid., 284.

METHOD

This section describes the method for the interpretation of Matthew's texts and other materials surveyed in this work. It also defines key terms used in this work in regard to discourse analysis.

Discourse Analysis as a Model

This study uses discourse analysis. There are many models employed in NT exegesis, and each model has its strength and its limitations. However, discourse analysis is not exempt from limitations. The main reason which lies behind the choice of this model for this study is that discourse analysis probably offers a better way of drawing attention to the text; it proceeds from the detail to the whole discourse. In this way, I hope that this model will enable discerning the first evangelist's point of view on the nature of interpersonal forgiveness. Two fundamental assumptions underlying the interpretation of Matthean material need noting at this point. First, I presuppose the narrative critical reading of Matthew. Matthew's text will be addressed as units and coherent texts; the meaning of interpersonal forgiveness texts in it will be sought in the dynamic interplay between 6:12, 14–15; 18:21–35 (or other texts under consideration) and their respective larger literary units as a whole. Second, I assume the two-source theory (2ST [Mark and Q]) because of the importance of this theory in scholarship and what it offers as a solution to the Synoptic Problem. (This is discussed in chapter 5.)

Various systems of discourse analysis have complex features. But these will not be used in this study; only areas of concern in this model will be considered. The first is the text; that is, the details of the structure and language of Matt 6:12, 14–15 and 18:21–35. The second area is the co-text; that is, how other parts of Matthew affect the interpretation of 6:12, 14–15 and 18:21–35 (or other Matthean texts under scrutiny). In an attempt to make sense of this, structural and conceptual analyses, as part of discourse analysis, will be used. Conceptual analysis will be used in chapters 2 and 6 for explaining the concept of reciprocity and the link between mercy and forgiveness, together with the link between reluctance in the *praxis* of them and judgment. It is also used in these chapters for explaining the emphasis on the offended person's responsibility in forgiving and the link of this with concept of *spiritually mature* and *immature* Christians. Structural analysis is used in chapter 2 for showing the strategic rhetorical positioning of interpersonal forgiveness and related texts within the Matthean text, together with the proportion they occupy within their respective discourse. The third area is the inter-text; that is, what other texts outside Matthew relate to 6:12, 14–15 and 18:21–35 (or other texts under consideration). The fourth area is the context; that is, the setting of Matthew and the wider Graeco-Roman socio-cultural setting.

It is with all this in mind that the structure for an interpretative model which I use will be constructed as a sequence of these four distinct and connected parts, although they will not appear as titles *per se* in the work itself. They will be included in the interpretation of the two Matthean texts for my purposes. In discussing them, the focus will be on personal *deixis*, social *deixis*, temporal *deixis*, and discourse *deixis*. Every particular word, expression or idea in 6:12, 14–15 and 18:21–35 will be taken seriously as part of the entire discourse. More precisely, the study will be concerned with how a particular word, expression or concept in these two texts functions in their whole respective discourse. Further, the study will be concerned with how these texts relate to (or differ from) each other, and how both fit Matthew's flow of thought in the First Gospel. The study of interpersonal forgiveness in Matthew, based on the discourse meaning of ἀφίημι in 6:9–15 and 18:21–35, falls into the area of NT exegesis. By choosing discourse analysis, it is the intent of the present author to be among those few African NT scholars who happen to use this model in the hope that this will contribute toward the wider use of such methodology in African NT exegetical scholarship.

Clarifying Terms

There are five key technical terms pertaining to the method of interpretation used in this study for handling the Matthean material. First is the "text." This can be defined as "a monological stretch of written language that shows coherence."[81] As T. and J. Sanders have written, it is "more than a random set of utterances: it shows connectedness."[82] It is quite possible to think of the text as the actual words used in a passage. In this work, "text" will be used to refer to the actual Greek words of 6:12, 14–15 and 18:21–35 (or other texts under consideration), the Greek words in

81. Sanders and Sanders, "Text and Text Analysis," 598.
82. Ibid.

the selected texts from the LXX, Dionysius, Philo and Josephus, as well as the Latin words in the selected texts from Seneca.

Second is "co-text." It may refer to what comes before as well as after a text. This can be sentences, paragraphs, pericopes, sections or chapters. Whether they are any of these, they are to surround and relate to the text. This relationship is emphasized by J. B. Green. Defining the co-text, Green states that it refers to the string of linguistic data within which a text is set; the relationship of, say, a sentence to a paragraph or a pericope to a larger narrative.[83] In this work, thus, "co-text" points to the body of the text which surrounds and relates to the passages identified above. As far as the "context" is concerned, this may refer to the historical and socio-cultural setting of the text. In this study, "context" will be used to refer mainly to the socio-historical context of the first-century Graeco-Roman world from which Matthew emerged.

Third is *deixis*. It is one of the major features of discourse analysis. According to D. Crustal, *deixis* is a term used in linguistic theory to subsume those features of language which refer directly to the personal, temporal or locational characteristics of the situation within which an utterance takes place, whose meaning is thus relative to that situation.[84] In this study, *deixis* refers to the features of language to be pointed out in the definitions below. Fourth is "discourse." It can be defined as a specimen of linguistic material displaying structural and semantic coherence, unity, and completeness, and conveying a message.[85] In the light of this, a discourse can be any form of either oral or written communication. Fifth is "discourse analysis," also known as "text-linguistics." According to J. C. Richards, J. Platt, and H. Platt, the "analysis of spoken discourse is sometimes called 'conventional analysis.' Some linguists, however, use the term 'text linguistics' for the study of written discourse."[86] To be sure, discourse analysis has not been satisfactorily defined. Two difficulties seem to underlie the attempt to define this expression. The first difficulty arises from the fact that discourse is being studied by scholars from various fields, and therefore with different perspectives.[87] The other difficulty seems to

---

83. Green, "Discourse Analysis and New Testament," 183.

84. Crystal, ed., *A Dictionary of Linguistics and Phonetics*, 127.

85. Nida, *Componential Analysis of Meaning*, 229.

86. Richards, Platt, and Platt, *Longman Dictionary of Language Teaching and Applied Linguistics*, 111.

87. Snyman, "A Semantic Discourse Analysis of the Letter to Philemon," 83.

be the newness of discourse analysis as a model in NT interpretation.[88] Though very difficult to define, several definitions have been proposed, including the following two. M. McCarthy sees discourse analysis as the analysis of connected speech and writings, and their relationship to the contexts in which they are used.[89] The second definition has been formulated by J. C. Richards, J. Platt, and H. Platt; it sees discourse analysis as the study of how sentences in spoken and written language form larger meaningful units such as paragraphs, conversations, interviews, etc.[90] These two definitions are not mutually exclusive; they both strongly view discourse analysis as an analysis of connected sentences, whether in spoken or written language, in their relationship to the contexts in which they are used. Clearly, discourse analysis is an analysis of a discourse.

OUTLINE OF THE STUDY

This study is structured around seven related chapters, each of which has a specific function. The first chapter has introduced this study, stating the problem and the aim of the study. It has also discussed the history of scholarship and described the method of interpretation used in handling the Matthean material. The second chapter outlines the evidence for the significance of interpersonal forgiveness in Matthew, using conceptual and structural analyses as part of discourse analysis. One of the main tasks of it is to sketch the interpersonal forgiveness texts and related texts; that is, all Matthean passages which contain interpersonal forgiveness narratives and references using the technical term ἀφίημι and related concepts (such as mercy, reconciliation, love, and non-retaliation). The third and the fourth chapters explore the interpersonal forgiveness theme in Graeco-Roman material and in Jewish literature in Greek respectively, as the background against which Matthew's text will be read. In reality, most of these materials relate more to political amnesty (which is not automatically the case with those in Matthew) or (in the case of the Jewish material) to divine forgiveness than to *interpersonal* forgiveness *per se*. In bringing in secular and Jewish materials in these chapters, the present

---

88. Porter, "Discourse Analysis and New Testament Studies: An Introductory Survey," 18.

89. McCarthy, "Discourse Analysis," 316.

90. Richards, Platt, and Platt, *Longman Dictionary of Language Teaching and Applied Linguistics*, 111.

author is mainly trying to achieve three main things. Firstly, to understand the nature of interpersonal forgiveness and to discover the place of this topic in the first-century CE discourse in Graeco-Roman and Jewish writings of the time (in the case of the Jewish material, to also understand the character of God, the forgiver *per excellence* to be emulated in practicing forgiveness). Secondly, to illustrate the distinctiveness of the gospel material (i.e., to find out how the act of forgiving is viewed in secular and Jewish writings of that time, and whether this act is associated with any form of demands as seems to be the case in Matthew). Thirdly, to discern possible motivations underlying forgiving and whether what will happen to the unforgiving person is a concern in these materials.

The fifth and sixth chapters examine the rhetoric of interpersonal forgiveness in 6:12, 14–15 and in 18:21–35 respectively, using discourse analysis. These are the key interpersonal forgiveness passages and the only Matthean passages in which the idea of interpersonal forgiveness is stated quite directly by using ἀφίημι to describe the interpersonal interrelationships. Also, in them some aspects of each of the four pieces of evidence to be probed in this piece of work are concentrated. The seventh chapter discusses the dynamics of forgiving in 6:12, 14–15 and in 18:21–35, and ventures an understanding of how this relates to the overall Matthean theology. To do so, a synthesis of these texts and other Matthean related texts is presented. This is followed by a discussion of the forgiveness teaching and Matthew's theology. Then four implications of the study for the Church in all contexts are presented.

Alongside the LXX, writings of four authors (Dionysius, Seneca, Philo, and Josephus) were selected as representing secular and Jewish sources respectively. These authors are first-century or roughly first-century ce, thus near contemporaries of Matthew. Moreover, and most importantly, a number of the forgiveness texts in their writings are relevant to the interest of the present study. Four means were employed to find this out. Firstly, Hebrew words and well-known LXX texts about interpersonal forgiveness and related topics were considered. Secondly, the TLG database was used to find the Greek equivalent terms for forgiveness in Dionysius. Thirdly, the present author read right through the relevant Dionysius and Seneca books, looking for interpersonal forgiveness texts and related texts, and took note of the relevant vocabulary. With regard to Seneca, finding these texts was not too complicated. Being aware of his *De clementia*, it was reasonable to suppose that it could be related to the subject under scrutiny. In fact, it happens to discuss, among other things, the notion of forgiveness in relation to that of mercy. Fourthly, theological dictionaries and dictionary-based introductions were also used to find Greek and Latin terms for forgiveness and related concepts. Liddell and Scott[91] and Lewis and Short[92] proved particularly helpful in this regard. Unless otherwise stated, biblical quotations in this work are taken from NRSV. The translations of the LXX interpersonal forgiveness texts and texts related to this topic are this author's own. The Dionysius and Philo texts followed Loeb. For the Josephan texts, on the other hand, William Whiston's translation (in its 1987 new updated edition) was followed. For the Senecan texts, S. M. Braund's translation was adopted because it is quite recent.

---

91. *A Greek-English Lexicon.*
92. *A Latin Dictionary.*

2

The Centrality of Interpersonal Forgiveness in Matthew

THIS CHAPTER PRESENTS THE evidence for the significance of the interpersonal forgiveness theme in Matthew. The emphasis on this theme in it is expressed in five ways. First is through the concept of reciprocity and the link between mercy and forgiveness, together with the link between reluctance in the *praxis* of them and judgment; second is through the emphasis on the offended person's responsibility to forgive and the link with the concept of *spiritually mature* and *immature* Christians; third is through a reinforcement of the forgiveness concept by the use of related ideas; fourth is through the strategic rhetorical positioning of interpersonal forgiveness and related texts within the Matthean text; and fifth is through the proportion these texts occupy within the Sermon and the Community Discourse. This chapter is mainly structured around these five features.

THE CONCEPT OF RECIPROCITY AND THE LINK BETWEEN MERCY AND FORGIVENESS

The concept of reciprocity and the link between mercy and forgiveness is evident from the gospel. In the fifth Matthean beatitude (5:7), this idea is embodied in the "mercy for mercy" axiom: "Blessed are the merciful (οἱ ἐλεήμονες), for they will receive mercy (ἐλεηθήσονται)." The "mercy for mercy" principle is used here to describe divine-human and interpersonal relationships: the disciples are to show mercy to their fellow humans if they are to expect to receive mercy from God. This principle comes to fuller expression in 6:12, 14–15 and in 18:23–35, as the outline below shows:

5:7   μακάριοι οἱ ἐλεήμονες . . . ἐλεηθήσονται

6:12 ἄφες . . . ὡς καὶ ἡμεῖς ἀφήκαμεν

6:14 Ἐὰν γὰρ ἀφῆτε . . . ἀφήσει καὶ ὑμῖν ὁ πατὴρ ὑμῶν ὁ οὐράνιος

6:15 ἐὰν δὲ μὴ ἀφῆτε . . . οὐδὲ ὁ πατὴρ ὑμῶν ἀφήσει

18:32b πᾶσαν τὴν ὀφειλὴν ἐκείνην ἀφῆκά σοι, ἐπεὶ παρεκάλεσάς με·

18:33 οὐκ ἔδει καὶ σὲ ἐλεῆσαι τὸν σύνδουλόν σου, ὡς κἀγὼ σὲ ἠλέησα;

This outline highlights the key terminology in the relationship between the conditioned mercy and the conditioned forgiveness in the Sermon and in the Community Discourse. From the outline, it is possible to equate the conditioned mercy of 5:7 with the conditioned forgiveness of 6:12, 14–15. The idea of conditioned mercy embodied in 5:7 is apparently echoed in 6:12 (ἄφες . . . ὡς καὶ ἡμεῖς ἀφήκαμεν), in 6:14 (Ἐὰν γὰρ ἀφῆτε . . . ἀφήσει καὶ ὑμῖν ὁ πατὴρ ὑμῶν ὁ οὐράνιος) and in 6:15 (ἐὰν δὲ μὴ ἀφῆτε . . . οὐδὲ ὁ πατὴρ ὑμῶν ἀφήσει). Most interestingly, both ideas of conditioned mercy and conditioned forgiveness are juxtaposed in 18:23–35 (v. 32b: πᾶσαν τὴν ὀφειλὴν ἐκείνην ἀφῆκά σοι, ἐπεὶ παρεκάλεσάς με; v. 33: οὐκ ἔδει καὶ σὲ ἐλεῆσαι τὸν σύνδουλόν σου, ὡς κἀγὼ σὲ ἠλέησα; v. 35: Οὕτως καὶ ὁ πατήρ μου . . . ποιήσει ὑμῖν ἐὰν μὴ ἀφῆτε . . .).

On this basis, one can strongly suggest a thematic connection between the Beatitudes and the Prayer (plus 6:14–15), and between the Beatitudes and the parable in 18:23–35, and vice versa. David Hill was probably right when he suggested that 5:7 ("Blessed are the merciful, for they shall obtain mercy") echoes the approach of Jesus in the Prayer ("Forgive . . . as we have forgiven") which the first evangelist makes explicit in the comment on the Prayer in 6:14–15.[1] R. T. France has gone further to include three texts: first, 7:1–2 in which the reciprocal judgment principle is stated directly and indirectly using the metaphor of measuring out commodities in the market[2]; second, 7:12 where the reciprocal principle,

---

1. Hill, *The Gospel of Matthew*, 108; so also Gore, *The Sermon on the Mount*, 38–39.

2. France, *The Gospel of Matthew*, 168, 275; so also Couroyer, "'De la mesure dont

broadly conceived, seems to be established; third, 18:21–35 where mercy and forgiveness are juxtaposed.³ The call to be perfect (τέλειός) as the heavenly Father is perfect (5:48) also supports this proposal. But neither France nor Hill and Gore see the link between mercy and forgiveness as one of possible strategies of the first evangelist to stress the importance of the interpersonal forgiveness theme in the gospel. Having indicated that, these passages may now be considered more closely.

Matt 5:7

As was indicated earlier, in 5:7 the idea of interpersonal forgiveness is stated indirectly by way of the reciprocal principle of "mercy for mercy." It is noteworthy that the term ἐλεήμων used in its nominal form here in 5:7 is a *hapax legomenon* in Matthew; the adjectival form appears elsewhere in the NT only in Heb 2:17, where it applies to Jesus. Luke's equivalent of this verse has a different term: οἰκτίρμων (Luke 6:36). Davies and Allison have aptly brought to our attention how significant the idea of mercy is to Matthew and to his first readers and hearers:

> Matthew's Jesus . . . gives the demand for mercy renewed emphasis and vividness by placing it at the centre of his proclamation (9.13; 12.7; 23.23; 25.31–46) and by making it plain that mercy should be shown to all . . ., including not only those on the fringes of society but even enemies (5.43–8; cf. Luke 10.29–37).[4]

The Matthean call to practice mercy, as suggested by the literary frame of the Sermon, is based upon God's nature and character. In the Sermon and elsewhere in the First Gospel, God is depicted as a merciful, loving and forgiving king and father.[5] God's mercy is linked with his perfection, a perfection which the disciple is called to practise; this is stated indirectly in 5:7 using the divine passive and more directly in 5:48 (cp. Luke 6:36). This is a clear example of the *imitatio Dei* in Matthew. In 5:7 this idea includes being merciful: as God is merciful to all, including his adversaries and enemies (5:47), so must his children and people be to one another.

---

vous mesurez il vous sera mesuré,'" 366–70.

3. France, *The Gospel of Matthew*, 707–8.

4. Davies and Allison, *Saint Matthew*, 1:455.

5. The evidence for this is discussed elsewhere in this book.

Matt 6:12, 14–15; 18:23–35

Matt 6:12, 14–15; 18:21–35 discuss conditionality in divine-human forgiveness explicitly using ἀφίημι to describe the divine-human interrelationships. Three items in 6:12, 14–15 are particularly relevant for our argument over the significance of interpersonal forgiveness in and around the Prayer. The first item is the phrase ὡς καὶ ἡμεῖς in verse 12 (with its effects in vv. 14–15 and beyond). The reading of this phrase in this passage is subject to much controversy. The conditional reading of it is to be preferred because the grammar of the text does demand it and the co-text of the passage supports it; this reading is decisively substantiated by the explanatory comment in 6:14–15 which immediately follows the Prayer and is primarily related to the petition in verse 12. Apparently implicit in verse 12, the conditional element becomes clearer in verses 14–15, where it is explicit and emphasized by being stated both positively and negatively. As Todd Pokrifka-Joe has noted, there is no sound exegetical reason to reject this straightforward reading of these verses.[6]

The aorist tense ἀφήκαμεν in verse 12 is the second element. This aorist (vs. the Lukan present ἀφίομεν) seems to have been used for ethical purposes. As Pokrifka-Joe has also noted, with the past tense ἀφήκαμεν in the second clause of verse 12, the petition would place significant responsibility on those praying to make sure they *have already forgiven* others if they desire to be forgiven by God.[7] Finally, we have an antithetical parallelism in verses 14–15, in which a positive assertion is followed by a negative one. In reality, verse 14 takes up the petition for forgiving debts in verse 12, whereas verse 15 considers what would happen to potential unforgiving disciples: "[N]either will your Father forgive your trespasses." (v. 15b)

Clearly, the use of the comparative phrase ὡς καὶ ἡμεῖς (v. 12), of the aorist ἀφήκαμεν (v. 12) and of an antithetical parallelism (vv. 14–15) in and around the Prayer is indeed not without significance. The use of them here surely serves to highlight the responsibility of the disciple toward their fellow humans. Matthew used these rhetorical devices for ethical motivation purposes, a motivation of course grounded in his theology: for him, it is the responsibility of the believer to forgive those who have wronged them (vv. 12b, 14–15). It is the responsibility of the believer to

---

6. Pokrifka-Joe, "Probing the Relationship between Divine and Human Forgiveness in Matthew," 166.

7. Ibid.

also seek forgiveness whether from God (v. 12a) or from fellow humans (5:23–26).

On the issue of the relationship between divine and human forgiveness in Matthew, Pokrifka-Joe has probably offered an acceptable solution. His conclusions provide an excellent connection between interpersonal forgiveness and mercy. He carefully studies this issue in the gospel and argues that in 6:12, 14–15 and 18:23–35, "human acts of forgiveness are both an essential expression of divine forgiveness *already* received and an essential condition of the *continued* and *ultimate reception* of that divine forgiveness."[8] He has identified three key moments in the story of divine-human forgiveness in the two key Matthean interpersonal forgiveness texts. These moments can be shown as follows:

Key moments and situation described thereto	6:12–15	18:23–35
Moment 1: The moment of God's gracious initiative	—	✓
Moment 2: The moment of human response	✓	✓
Moment 3: The moment of God's response to human response	✓	✓

According to this scheme, and as Pokrifka-Joe has it, while the concept of conditionality in Matt 18 describes the relationship of all the *three* moments to one another, the conditional statements in Matt 6 describes the relationship of the *last two* moments to each other; as such, the scope of the conditions in 6:14–15 do not include the first moment of unconditioned divine forgiveness.[9] This seems to make a lot of sense insofar as it provides a kind of framework within which suggestions such as "human mercy has the *purpose* of causing divine mercy"[10] would probably make sense. The statement above by Luz gives the impression that God's mercy given to us is the result of our mercy given to others. Stated in forgiveness language and to use Hagner's expression, "God's forgiveness of us is the result of our forgiveness of others."[11] When Luz' statement above is read against Pokrifka-Joe's scheme, it makes one realize that divine mercy/forgiveness here clearly does precede human mercy/forgiveness.

In the First Gospel, the concept of reciprocity and the link between mercy and forgiveness is also closely linked to reluctance in the *praxis* of

---

8. Ibid., 165–66; emphasis added.
9. Ibid., 168.
10. Luz (*Matthew*, 1:196), referring to *1 Clem.* 13.2 and Polycarp, *Phil.* 2.3.
11. Hagner, *Matthew*, 1:152.

them and punishment. For the first evangelist, refusing to show mercy to or to forgive others does lead to God's refusal to do the same to the unmerciful or unforgiving person. More than that, it calls punishment upon them. This is powerfully stated in the parable of the unmerciful debtor in 18:23–35 and implicitly in 6:15. Demands to be merciful (5:7), not to retaliate (5:21–23) and not to judge (7:1–2) are also implied in this reading.[12] As we shall see later in this work (ch. 4), the idea of accountability as related to mercy and forgiveness is rare in biblical Judaism. Sir 28:1–4 is the only very close early Jewish parallel. Only relevant verses are cited here in an attempt to support the point that is being made; the whole text can be found in chapter 4 where it is discussed.

> 2Remit your neighbour the wrong they have done (ἄφες ἀδίκημα τῷ πλησίον σου), and then your sins will be remitted when you pray (δεηθέντος σου αἱ ἁμαρτίαι σου λυθήσονται) . . . 4If one has no mercy towards another like themselves, can they then seek forgiveness for their own sin?

Because of the similarity between the Matthean material and the Sirach material, Sir 28:1–4 (esp. v. 4) has been proposed as a possible basis for the parable of the unmerciful debtor of 18:23–35. Reimer, for example, in his treatment of Sir 28, has made a connection between Sir 28:1–7 and other texts within Sirach. To repeat aspects of what was said above, Reimer has shown how in Sir 5:4–7; 17:25–32; 18:8–14, notions of death and judgment sharpen the consideration of divine forgiveness. He notes that in Sir 28:1–2, this combination of traditional Jewish concepts of death as punishment for sin, obedience to the commandments of the law and loyalty to the covenant produces the conclusion that divine judgment can be said to be controlled by human activity. Most particularly, Reimer suggests that Sir 28:4 is a possible basis for the parable of Matt 18:23–35.[13] As just suggested, the concept of reciprocity and the link between mercy and forgiveness, together with the link between reluctance in practising them and punishment can be discerned from 6:15 (cf. the idea of *"not being forgiven* by the heavenly Father").

---

12. Note that the ideas of retaliation and punishment are closely related in Greek thinking, as is clear in the word ἀντιτίνω; cf. Liddell and Scott, *A Greek-English Lexicon*, 164.

13. Reimer, "The Apocrypha and Biblical Theology," 277–79.

The concept of reciprocity found in 18:23–35 and 6:12 may allow one to suggest that 18:23–35 is the parabolic equivalent of 6:12.[14] Perhaps it is necessary to also add that, although 18:23–35 and 6:12 share between them the concept of reciprocity in forgiveness, they also have in common the notion of judgment on the potential unforgiving person—a fact which is not always highlighted in scholarship.

All in all, the distinctiveness of the Matthean teaching about the concept of reciprocity and the link between mercy and forgiveness is the outcome of reluctance in forgiving. In Matthew, the sense of accountability in showing mercy or in forgiving is stronger than in any other NT writings.

Warranting mention is also the fact that an interest in understanding motives underlying a decision to forgive has been observed recently in a number of fields including psychology, psychiatry and theology broadly conceived. Two categories of these motivations are in order. These are *other-orientated* reasons on the one hand, and *self-orientated* reasons on the other hand. As was shown earlier in this work (ch. 1), how forgiving is viewed by most of scholars in the fields of study noted above tends to give the impression that the *other-orientated* reasons are much more evident than the *self-orientated* reasons.[15] J. W. Younger, R. L. Piferi, R. L. Jobe, and K. A. Lawler, however, are an exception to this generalization. In an article by them published recently, they argue that primary motives for forgiveness are largely self-focused, rather than altruistic.[16] In the First Gospel, it is the opposite of scholars' views of the *other-orientated* motives for forgiving which is true. In it both features of forgiveness mentioned above seem to be present, with surely the self-focused feature being predominant. A sense of accountability clearly motivates the acts of showing mercy and forgiving, as is evidenced by 18:33 and 7:1–2, as well as 6:12b, 14–15 and 5:7 (by implication). In these texts, the ultimate goal of these acts is the merciful person's or the forgiver's relationship with their heavenly Father.

---

14. E.g., Davies and Allison (*Saint Matthew*, 1:610), among others.

15. Worthington, Berry, and Parrott, "Unforgiveness, Forgiveness, Religion, and Health," 107–38; Exline et al., "Forgiveness and Justice," 337–48.

16. Younger et al., "Dimensions of Forgiveness," 837–55.

THE EMPHASIS ON THE OFFENDED PERSON'S RESPONSIBILITY TO FORGIVE AND THE LINK WITH THE CONCEPT OF THE SPIRITUALLY MATURE AND IMMATURE CHRISTIANS

The emphasis on the responsibility of the offended person to forgive and the link with the concept of *spiritually mature* and *immature* Christians is another possible piece of evidence for the prominence of the interpersonal forgiveness theme in Matthew. This, however, is not quite as easily discernible, and therefore requires justification. In an attempt to show the validity of this proposal, the term μικροί ("little ones") and related terms will be first discussed; this will be followed by the issue of *spiritually mature* and *immature* disciples and the link between this and the emphasis on the offended person to forgive.

To begin with μικροί, the identity of the group to which this term refers has been intensely debated in Matthean studies. Related to this is the relationship between the μικροί of 18:6–14 (cp. 10:42 and ἐλάχιστος[17] in 25:40, 45) and the παιδία/παιδίον of 18:2–5, together with the ἀδελφοί of 18:15–35. The main question is the extent to which each of these terms related to the μαθηταί of 18:1, if such a link exists at all. Two major possibilities emerge. Firstly, there are many who argue that the μικροί of 18:6–14 are all ordinary Christians. This viewpoint, held by most scholars,[18] is mainly based on the use of this term elsewhere in the gospel where it probably applies to the disciples (e.g., 10:42; 25:40, 45). It is then deduced from this evidence that in the entire gospel, μικροί refers merely to followers of Jesus, without any sense of distinguishing their level of spirutal maturity. This is clearly a generalization; there is no convicing argument that μικροί should be understood solely this way. An alternative reading of μικροί is to understand the "little ones" of 18:6–14 as referring to a certain category of Christians, "vulnerable disciples."[19] Jeannine K. Brown, for example, has recently argued that power dynamics are assumed and addressed by 25:31–46, which contains the "little ones" language. These dynamics, she proposes, are evidenced (1) by the

---

17. This is a superlative for μικρός.

18. E.g., Hagner, *Matthew*, 2:744–45; Senior, *Matthew*, 283–84; France, *Matthew*, 964–65; Garland, *Reading Matthew*, 248; Carson, *Matthew*, 520; Turner, *Matthew*, 605–6, among others.

19. E.g., J. Brown, "Matthew's 'Least of These,'" 8 (Online: https://bethelnet.bethel.edu/.../ntts718-201153-spl1-s1-brown); Hultgren, *The Parables of Jesus*, 317.

ἐλάχιστος language in 25:40, 45, (2) by authority themes more broadly in Matthew's gospel and (3) by the power shift that emerges in the climactic moment of the judgment scene in Matt 25.[20] The interest of the present author is in the first evidence, to do with ἐλάχιστος. In an attempt to validate this claim, Brown begins her argument by making a connection between the μικροί of 18:6–14 and the ἐλάχιστος of 25:40, 45, stating that in Matt 25, the evangelist draws on ἐλάχιστος to indicate a group that is marginalized and vulnerable. She argues that by using this term in line with the previous usages of μικρός (10:32; 18:6–14), Matthew underlines the lack of status and the vulnerability of "the least of these" as opposed to the other groups in this scene (i.e., the king, the sheep and the goats). She then states that by using this distinctive term (the superlative ἐλάχιστος, rather than the comparative μικρός) the low status of this group is especially stressed in Matt 25.[21]

This proposal has some advantages concerning the discussion at hand. Firstly, it recognises possible echoes of μικροί elsewhere in the gospel (10:32; 25:40, 45), and takes it seriously. The possibility of a close link between ἐλάχιστος and μικρός in Matthew's thinking (as evidenced by the texts concerned) is linguistically founded. Additionally, the logic in Brown's argument in this respect is compelling. About a decade before Brown, an attempt for a possible link between these terms was made by John R. Donahue, who reasonably included the ὀλιγόπιστοι ("those of *little faith*") of 6:30; 8:26; 16:8; 14:31 (ὀλιγόπιστε); and 17:20 (ὀλιγοπιστίαν).[22] The second merit of Brown's proposal is the fact that it sheds some light on the identity of the μικροί of 18:6–14 by recognizing two distinct categories of people within the Matthean Christian community. Her argument, that Matthew's use of ἐλάχιστος in Matt 25 and μικροί in Matt 18 illuminates a status category, is a strong one; it has a linguistic groundwork.[23] Her conclusions seem to do justice to these texts

---

20. J. Brown, "Matthew's 'Least of These,'" 7.

21. J. Brown, "Matthew's 'Least of These,'" 8. Cf also BAGD, "ἐλάχιστος, κτλ.," 314; Osten-Sacken, "ἐλάχιστος, κτλ.," 1:426; Zerwick and Grosvenor, *A Grammatical Analysis of the Greek New Testament* 1:84; Mounce, Smith, and Pelt, *Mounce's Dictionary*, 397; Via Jr, "Matthew 25:31–46," 92. Each of them indicates that ἐλάχιστος, formed from ἐλαχύς, is used as a superlative for μικρός.

22. Donahue, *The Gospel in Parable*, 72.

23. Louw and Nida also understand these words as possible *status* terms (cf. *Greek-English Lexicon of the New Testament based on Semantic Domains*, 1:739–40).

and seem to be in line with the flow of thought in Matt 18.[24] The present author's viewpoint links up with what Brown has said about the μικροί of 18:6–14 that these "little ones" are a broader group within the church and are characterized by lowly status.[25]

A question can be raised of whether there is any potential relationship between the μικροί of 18:6–14 and the παιδία/παιδίον of 18:2–5: Does μικροί in verses 6–14 refer back to παιδίον/παιδία in verses 2–5 so that the "little ones" are those who have become lowly like a "child"? Such an identification is quite possible on linguistical grounds. There is a strong evidence from both Hebrew and Greek that "little one" can mean "child."[26] In fact, the term παιδίον is a diminutive of παῖς which means "little child."[27] However, one needs to be cautious, and therefore open to the possibility of an ambiguity in the use of the παιδίον/παιδία here by the evangelist. We probably have both a literal and non-literal use of παιδίον/παιδία in verses 2–5. The fact is this. Jesus calls a παιδίον ("child") whom he puts in the midst of the ἀδελφοί ("disciples," cf. v. 1); he then strongly urges them to become like παιδία ("children"), if they are to enter the kindgom of heaven. It is clear that in the first case (v. 2, cp. v. 4) παιδίον is used literally, for the child is physically standing right there in the midst of the disciples. In the second case (v. 3, cp. v. 5), we probably have a non-literal use of παιδία. A comparision has been introduced: "becoming like . . ." (v. 3), "humbling oneself like . . ." (v. 4) and "receiving one such . . ." (v. 5). Here the physical reality of this child standing in the midst of the disciples seems to be taken to another sphere. In all likelihood, it can then be suggested that where we have a non-literal use of παιδίον/παιδία (like in vv. 3, 5), there the "little children" are identical to the "little ones." In an attempt to exclude the possibility of an identification of μικροί with παιδία in the passages above, Luz wonders why a statement about leading the "little ones" astray appears at the beginning of the discourse on

---

24. This is shown elsewhere in the present piece of work (ch. 6).

25. J. Brown, "Matthew's 'Least of These,'" 8; so also Hultgren, *The Parables of Jesus*, 317.

26. Cf. Hoehler et al., *The Hebrew and Aramaic Lexicon of the OT*, 2:378; Gundry-Volf, "Child, Children," in *NIDB*, 1:588–590, esp. 1:588–89; Mounce, Smith, and Pelt, *Mounce's Dictionary*, 106; Jastrow, *A Dictionary of the Targumim*, 1:176; BAGD, "μικρός, κτλ.," 651; Michel, "μικρός, κτλ.," 4:650.

27. Oepke, "παῖς, παιδίον, παιδάριον, τέκνον, τεκνίον, βρέφος, κτλ.," 638; Mounce, Smith, and Pelt, *Mounce's Dictionary*, 106.

community.²⁸ A possible answer to this, I shall suggest, is that this statement appears there because its main purpose was to strongly warn those with a relatively high spiritual status (i.e., the *spiritually mature* members of the church) about how they were to behave vis-à-vis and relate to the weaker members (i.e., the spiritually immature members) of the church. This proposal may find support in Judaism, where the socially weak, the childish and immature could be designated as "little ones."²⁹ An understanding of the "little ones" of 18:6–14 (cp. "little children," esp. in vv. 3, 5) in their Matthean context as referring to all ordinary Christians in Matthew's church is open to debate.

Warranting mention is also the fact that the discourse in Matt 18 is addressed to μαθηταὶ ("disciples," v. 1). It is interesting to note that the character roles fulfilled by people who are addressed appear to change throughout this chapter, which further complicates our understanding. On the one hand, they are those who might lead the μικροί astray or be contemptuous of them (vv. 6, 10), or be themselves in danger of channeling temptation to them (vv. 7–9). On the other hand, they appear as candidates of the potential misbehavior of the others (vv. 6, 10, 14). In spite of this difficulty, it is not hard to see the prominence of the μικροί theme in chapter 18. Donahue has argued that the tone of the whole chapter 18 is set by the concern for the "little ones," whom in their Matthean context are to be understood as those whose "faith is weak" (cf. 6:30; 8:26; 14:31; 16:8; 17:20—those of "little faith"), or those "who need special care" (10:42; cf. 25:40, 45—the "least").³⁰ Robert H. Gundry, on his part, has divided Matt 18 in two main parts based on the concept of the "little ones": care for the "little ones" (18:1–14) and care for sinners (18:15–35).³¹

Turning to the last main point of this section, the issues discussed in Matt 18 and how they are discussed in said text may provide a window to discerning the composition of the community behind the gospel itself. It is possible to imagine that this community was composed of two categories of people, with asymmetrical level of spiritual maturity. This seems to be supported by two facts, the first of which being the use of the μικροί/παιδία languages which abound in the first half of Matt 18. Second are

---

28. Luz, *Matthew*, 2:432.

29. Cf. Michel, "μικρός, κτλ.," 4:648; 2 *Bar.* 48:19; this fact is also recognized by Luz, who then distances himself from it (*Matthew*, 2:121).

30. Donahue, *The Gospel in Parable*, 72.

31. Gundry, *Matthew*, 358. For various structure proposals, see Luz, *Matthew*, 2:422.

exhortations and demands that emerge in this chapter: to "become like children" (18:3), to "humble oneself like a child" (18:4), to "receive one such a child" (18:5), not to lead *one* of the "little ones" astray (18:6, 10), to go after the straying sheep (18:12–14), to be reconciled with an unrepentant brother or sister (18:15–17), to be merciful and forgiving (18:21–35). These two sets of evidence seem to strongly suggest two possible categories of Christians within Matthew's church. These demands altogether seem to be primarily—but not exclusively—addressed to *spiritually mature* members of the community. The *spiritually immature* members too are part of the furniture. As members of the church and citizens of the kingdom, they too, it has to be said, are meant to behave properly vis-à-vis the other members of the community (either the *spiritually mature* or the *spiritually immature*), as well as outsiders.

Concerning the responsibility in forgiving, a twofold forgiveness pattern is clear in Matthew's texts: the responsibility of the offender for seeking forgiveness and that of the offended person for granting forgiveness; in only one occurrence (5:23–25), it has to be asserted, the former is in view; in all the rest of the occurrences (seven), the latter is emphasized (6:12b; 6:14–15; 18:12–14, 15^{32}–17, 21, 33). In 6:12a, the obligation of the potential sinner for seeking forgiveness is also apparently in view. The members of Matthew's community are much more firmly reminded that it is the responsibility of the offended person to grant forgiveness to their offenders. This is evident, first, from 6:12b and the *protasis* in 6:14–15; second, from 18:12–14 where this responsibility is embodied in the initiative of the shepherd to go after the straying sheep; third, from 18:15–17 through the initiative of the offended person to go several times after their offender for an eventual reconciliation; and fourth, from 18:21 through Peter's proposal and from 18:33 through the lord's rebuke to his unmerciful debtor for their failure in showing mercy and granting forgiveness to his fellow slave. The fact that the First Gospel has given more space to the responsibility of the offended person in forgiving (7 *logia*) than to that of the offender (1 *logion*) strongly suggests that he is extremely concerned about the possibility of his community members' reluctance to forgive and to be reconciled with their fellow brethren. This seems to fit nicely the flow of thought in Matt 18 (and beyond) which is concerned with the

---

32. The textual problem that occurs in this verse is discussed latter in this chapter. The present author argues for the εἰς σὲ reading because this phrase is attested in all text families, ranging from the Majority text to other important codices and various traditions (cf. p. 51n54 below).

issue of the preservation of the community (a major concern for it[33]). In Matt 18, the members of this community are portrayed as children of the heavenly Father-King and, therefore, their behavior as children of such a father.

All in all, it is this category of people—which is referred to in this work as "*spiritually mature* Christians"—that were primarily urged to carry greater duties, among which are caring for the *spiritually immature* members, the "little ones," those of "little faith" who need special care, the "least." Among other things, the *spiritually mature* members were meant to be welcoming the *spiritually immature* members in the sense of caring for them (18:5), making every effort to lose none of them, whether by their own behavior (18:6–10) or by the behavior of the *spiritually immature* members (18:12–17). In spite of the possibility that the *spiritually immature* members would show weakness in their relationships with *spiritually mature* members (and this may result in the former departing from the community), as part of their responsibilities, the *spiritually mature* members were meant to take the initiative of going to this member at risk, at least three times, using different approaches (18:15–17) either to retain them in the community or to bring them back to it, just as a shepherd would do with the straying sheep (18:12–14). As Donahue has noted, the location of this parable in Matthew (immediately preceding the juridical approach to failure within the community) shows that, "however community discipline is to be applied, order within the community is to be measured against the claims of the weaker members for special care and assistance."[34] The initiative of going to one's own offender more than once, with the aim of winning him or her,[35] suggests that the injured person has understood his or her responsibility toward the other and has enacted the principle underlying the demand.

REINFORCING THE FORGIVENESS CONCEPT BY THE USE OF RELATED IDEAS

A reinforcement of the forgiveness concept by the use of related concepts is employed in Matthew to stress the motif of interpersonal forgiveness. This comprises the concepts of mercy (5:7), brotherly reconciliation

---

33. The discussion over this issue is provided in ch. 5.
34. Donahue, *The Gospel in Parable*, 73.
35. So also Peter's concern in Matt 18:21.

(5:23-26), non-retaliation (5:38-42), loving enemies (5:43-45), being perfect (5:48) and measure for measure (7:1-2). In the First Gospel, this related language is employed to describe either divine-human or interpersonal relationships. Following are examples in this respect.

Matt 5:7, 21-26

In this text, the interpersonal forgiveness motif is stated indirectly by means of the languages of mercy (v. 7) and of reconciliation with an ἀδελφός (vv. 21-26). In this description of interpersonal relationships, the onus is placed on the offender. The antithesis in this passage is above all concerned with judgment. It comprises two loosely related examples in the form of little parables (vv. 23-26), the parables which apparently serve to illustrate how anger can be overcome through acts of reconciliation. The overall argument of the first antithesis can be outlined as follows:

ὀργιζόμενος (being angry) with an ἀδελφός makes one liable to κρίσις (judgment).

ῥακά (insult) to an ἀδελφός makes one liable to the συνέδριον (council).

μωρέ (saying "fool") to an [ἀδελφός] makes one liable to the γέεννα (hell of fire).

So,

Never dare to offend an ἀδελφός.

In the case you have already offended them,

please resolve *immediately* the problem before it is late;

or you will be in trouble;

being reconciled (διαλλάσσομαι) is the suitable solution to this problem.

This outline shows that judgment is the central idea in 5:21-26. One of the main exegetical issues in this pericope is the understanding of the succession of the three related terms (κρίσις, συνέδριον and γέεννα) in verse 22, which are used to convey the notion of judgment. There is much uncertainty about the relationship between them. The question is whether there is an ascending scale of juridical processes, corresponding to an escalation in the abuse.

Scholars' views on this diverge. France, for example, finds an ascending scale of severity in the descriptions of the punishment in this verse. For him συνέδριον is a metaphor in which the human institution stands for the more ultimate divine judgment.[36] Daniel Marguerat, on the other hand, has rejected this interpretation:

> La gradation des instances judiciaires que l'on postule dans cette interprétation (cour locale—sanhédrin—tribunal divin) impose à κρίσις (22a) le sens de tribunal local, qu'il ne revêt pas dans la κοινή; comme en 21b, κρίσις désigne le jugement, la sanction frappant l'infraction à la Loi, où la rigueur humaine médiatise la réprobation divine. Le parallélisme formel et terminologique de 21c et 22a (ἔνοχος ἔσται τῇ κρίσει) confirme la similitude de sens de κρίσις dans ces deux versets.[37]

Marguerat rejects the idea of an ascending scale in juridical processes (i.e., local court • Sanhedrin [supreme court] • divine trial [ultimate court]) in 5:22 for two reasons. First, because of the use of κρίσις in the *koiné*, where this term never had the meaning of "local trial"; and second, because of the parallelism between verses 21c and 22a in which ἔνοχος (v. 21c) and κρίσις (v. 22) seem to refer to judgment in which human severity renders divine reprobation. This argument is a strong one and cannot simply be bypassed. The strengths inherent in this argument, and because of the lack of progression in the sin committed (as shall be discussed further later), I rely on this argument for rejecting the proposal of an ascending scale in juridical procedures in 5:22.

A possibility of an escalation of the abuse in 5:22 has also been suggested. M. D. Goulder is one of the proponents of this viewpoint.[38] In fact, the descriptions of the abuse as found in the text above (moving from anger—which is in mind—to speech—which can be regarded as an actionable utterance) may cause one to suggest such a proposal. But, this proposal vanishes before a serious semantic study of the two terms for the insult in 5:22 (i.e., ῥακά and μωρέ). Marguerat has stated this as follows:

> La thèse de la gradation des insultes ne résiste pas . . . à l'analyse. Les termes ῥακά et μωρέ retranscrivent deux insultes araméenes

---

36. France, *The Gospel of Matthew*, 200–201n81.

37. Marguerat, *Le jugement dans l'Évangile de Matthieu*, 155; cf. Guelich, *The Sermon on the Mount* (esp. the comment on 5:22, ibid., 44).

38. Goulder, *Midrash and Lection in Matthew*, 257–58.

courantes en Palestine, de valeur anodique, dont on retrouve la trace dans les échanges entre rabbins! . . . L'analyse sémantique ne conduit pas à déceler de l'un à l'autre une aggravation justifiant le renvoi du délinquant à une instance supérieur; elle constate à l'inverse la synonymie de ces deux insultes, relevant toutes deux du langage courant, quotidien.[39]

Marguerat's suggestion that the two insults in 5:22 are to be understood as synonyms is quite reasonable, and is most likely in line with the flow of thought in 5:21–26. Most significantly, this reconciliation motif is stated in a more threatening scenario which is stressed by using a rhetorical device (antithesis) and by using two short parables that highlight punishment. The question is how the two examples in this text relate to each other and conform to the main argument of the unit. What follows may provide a possible answer.

Verse 22 states that anger with an ἀδελφός makes one liable (ἔνοχος) to judgment; insulting an ἀδελφός makes one liable (ἔνοχος) to the council; saying "fool" to somebody makes one liable (ἔνοχος) to the hell of fire. For the Matthean Jesus, an offence, broadly conceived, leads to judgment "both on the earthly and the heavenly planes."[40] Thus the main teaching seems to be something like this: never dare to offend others; if you have already offended them, seek reconciliation as quickly as you can so that you may not incur judgment. In this way and in this context, reconciliation appears like a means of preventing potential judgment or easing awful potential penalties for the offences committed.

The *logion* in verses 23–24 conveys a message similar to the one in Mark 11:25. The only difference is that, while in the Markan text the onus is obviously placed on the offended person, in the Matthean text we are left with an ambiguity: it is not clear whether it is the offender or the offended person who is in view. This therefore leaves room for speculation. The conceptual structure of 5:23–26 has caused some scholars to believe that here the offender is in view.[41] Others, however, think that here the offended person is given a strong emphasis on his or her responsibility to forgive or to be reconciled, that is observed in the rest of the First Gospel (6:12, 14–15; 18:15–17, 21–35). Nolland is among those who have followed this line of thought. Commenting on 5:23–24, he writes:

39. Marguerat, *Le jugement dans l'Évangile de Matthieu*, 155–56.

40. Osborne, *Matthew*, 190.

41. E.g., Davies and Allison, *Saint Matthew* 1:517; Carter, *Matthew and the Margins*, 145; France, *The Gospel of Matthew*, 202–3n88, etc.

"Where vv. 21–22 have focused sharply on the activity of the offender, in vv. 23–25 the perspective of the one wronged comes into view. That is to say, the state of relationship resulting from the offence is now being considered from the angle of the one wronged."[42]

Although in the interpersonal forgiveness texts and related texts in the rest of the gospel the offended person is clearly indicated (e.g., 5:38–42, 43–47; 6:12a, 14–15; 7:1–2; 18:15–17, 21–35), nonetheless in 5:23–26 the scenario is different. Here the emphasis is most likely on the offender, as seems to be suggested by the conceptual structure of the text itself. As Davies and Allison have also suggested quite reasonably, because in 5:21–26 the imperative is directed toward the offender, it is not unreasonable to imagine that the imperative in 5:23–24 is most naturally to be read as similarly addressed to the offender.[43]

Matt 5:23–24 has an obvious parallel in *Did.* 14.2 in which the notion of reconciliation is linked with that of sacrifice: " . . . let no one who has a quarrel with a companion join you until they have been reconciled (διαλλαγῶσιν), so that your sacrifice may not be defiled."[44] The parallelism between these passages on reconciliation relating to sacrifice may suggest a literary dependency of the latter on the former, and confirms the importance of horizontal relationships in the early church. The scenario in 5:25–26 also supports the argument that right relationships demand decisive action. The parable reinforces here the ethical message that no bad relationships should remain unresolved. It is quite clear that the first evangelist and his first recipients felt that it was essential that community harmony precede worship (cp. 6:14–15; 18:15–17, 21–35). This would then be the positive equivalent to the anger and abuse condemned in verse 22 where anger is overcome through reconciliation. A similar note is sounded in Eph 4:26: "Do not let the sun go down on your anger."

Summarizing, two points need noting. First, on reconciliation (a forgiveness-related idea) the following pattern is obvious: seeking reconciliation with a fellow human is the initiative of the offender; it aims at avoiding the potential judgment, or at alleviating its potential dreadful penalties. As France has remarked, "the inclusion of 'I tell you truly' . . . alerts us to a more ultimate purpose than merely avoiding imprisonment; like the other parable of debt and imprisonment (18:23–35), it is

---

42. Nolland, *The Gospel of Matthew*, 232.
43. Davies and Allison, *Saint Matthew*, 1:517.
44. This translation is by Holmes, *The Apostolic Fathers*.

a pointer to the divine judgment on those whose earthly relationships do not conform to the values of the kingdom of heaven."[45] Second, it is possible to recognize a piece of Matthean redaction (i.e., Matthew relying on his own longer memory) that has been shaped to function at two levels. The second little parable in this unit clearly reflects the conflict situation that seems to have existed between Matthew's community and his adversaries; it thus serves "to issue a plea not to provoke legal hostilities," as Paul Foster has also suggested.[46] Furthermore, at an individual level, there is an express call to enact reconciliation with any potentially litigious fellow.[47] It can now be suggested that the purpose of this first antithesis is to effect reconciliation.

Matt 5:38–42

In this passage, the idea of interpersonal forgiveness is stated indirectly but stressed by using the language of non-retaliation (cf. the turning of the other cheek language, v. 39). The main concern in this text is how the ἀδελφός is to respond to a potential aggression, whether physical abuse or distraint of one's property or forced services: they are not to resist and not to retaliate. There is strong evidence that a slap in the face was regarded as an expression of hate and as an insult; the insult is even more important than the pain (Isa 50:6; Lam 3:30). The issue here is any violent confrontation that may happen in everyday life. The slap on the *right* (δεξιάν) cheek is probably Matthew's addition for rhetorical reasons to highlight the gravity of the insult (i.e., a strong insult); for, as Luz and others have remarked, the slap on the *right* cheek is not what would ordinarily happen, since one either must be left-handed or hit with the back of the hand.[48]

Marcel Gilbert explains the purpose of the OT *lex talionis* thus:

> [L]a loi du talion dans l'A.T. . . . a pour fonction d'affirmer la responsabilité personnelle des actes posées, l'égalité des personnes devant la loi et la juste proportion entre crime et la punition encourue.[49]

---

45. France, *The Gospel of Matthew*, 203–4.
46. Foster, *Community, Law and Mission in Matthew's Gospel*, 102.
47. Ibid.
48. Luz, *Matthew*, 1.272; so also Osborne, *Matthew*, 19.
49. Gilbert, "La Loi du talion," 73–82.

The purpose of the OT *lex talionis* was to limit revenge. It was introduced "pour réagir au système anarchique de la vengeance illimitée qui caractérise le régime de barbarie."[50] For Matthew, as can be discerned from the fifth antithetical formulation, the *lex talionis* is categorically to be rejected as a principle that can be operative in his community. Retaliation is thus renounced. The purpose of this fifth antithesis is, to be sure, to effect peacemaking. Just as the other Matthean antitheses, this antithesis too has an ethical function: it provides instruction for Matthew's community to a different standard of justice (cf. 5:39b-42).

Matt 5:43-48; 7:12

The language of loving enemies is used in 5:43-48 to describe both divine-human and interpersonal relationships, the divine-human relationship being in the background (i.e., in their relating to or dealing with one another, the disciples are to emulate how God deals with his people both righteous and unrighteous). There is a clear thematic link between this antithesis and the preceding one; both call upon its hearers to display a radical attitude toward adversaries and enemies, an attitude that does not respond either with retaliation or hatred. The call for longing for perfection in 5:48 needs noting. It has to do with the notion of *imitatio Dei/ Christi* in the First Gospel.[51] The reasons for this demand include, first of all, the disciples' new identity in Christ: they are the children of the heavenly Father. Second is their potential reward (v. 46); and third is the expectation of them to do more than others do (v. 47).

In 5:43-48, the *imitatio Dei* includes loving one's adversaries and enemies and being perfect. By loving their adversaries and enemies, the disciples of Jesus reflect the character of God, who shows his gracious love and mercy to both the righteous and unrighteous alike (v. 45b: "for he makes his sun rise on the evil and on the good, and sends rain on the righteous and on the unrighteous."). It is quite possible to imagine than this sixth antithesis is to effect love of enemies within and outside Matthew's community. An aspect of the precept of loving adversaries and enemies is alluded to in 7:12. In it we find the concept of reciprocity in

---

50. Dumais, *Le Sermon sur la Montagne*, 212.

51. For a more updated discussion on the notion of *imitatio Dei/Christi* in the Synoptics and beyond, see Allison, *Constructing Jesus*, 311, 320-22, 325, 349, 355-56, 358, 368, 375.

dealing with, and relating to, one another. Although this passage seems not to be linked with 7:7–11 which deals with human relationship with God, it is most likely in connection with 5:17 which introduces a major section of the discourse dealing with the disciples' relationships with others. As France has reasonably stated, while the whole of Matt 6 and 7:7–11 have focused on the relationship with God, the way we treat others is an even more prominent theme of the discourse as a whole—not only in the discussion of fulfilling the law and the prophets (5:17–48), but also of the beatitudes (5:3–10), the metaphors of salt and light (5:13–16), the requirement to forgive (6:14–15) and the strictures on unfair criticism (7:1–5).[52] The Lukan equivalent of the *logion* in Matt 7:12, occurs in the context of the loving enemies command, which in turn is part of a set of commands: doing good, forgiving, being merciful, non-retaliating and not judging others (Luke 6:27–38). Most interestingly, in Luke these demands are linked to the *imitatio Dei* motif: "But love your enemies, do good . . . Your reward will be great, and you will be children of the Most High; for he is kind to the ungrateful and the wicked. Be merciful, just as your Father is merciful." (Luke 6:35–36).

It is clear that, in the antithesis in Matt 5:43–48, the Christians' love and mercy are meant to be modeled on God's gracious love and mercy, a notion which was familiar in the Christian tradition of the first-century. Christians are called to love others, including their adversaries and enemies, as God loves the righteous as well as the unrighteous: they are called to be merciful as God is merciful, perfect as God is perfect.

Although important qualifications need to be made because God is God and humans are humans (cf. Matt 19:26), for Matthew, God's gracious love and mercy provide the paradigm for how his community was to understand its vocation as members of the kingdom: they are to imitate God the heavenly father and king. In the First Gospel, the concept of fictive kinship of Christians with God is embedded in the notions of the fatherhood of God and the *imitatio Dei/Christi*.[53] The "good seed" (καλὸν σπέρμα) of the parable of the weed and wheat in 13:24–30 is likened to "the children of the kingdom" (υἱοὶ τῆς βασιλείας [13:38]). In 7:21 we are told that it is the one who "does the will of the heavenly Father" (ὁ ποιῶν τὸ θέλημα τοῦ πατρός μου τοῦ ἐν τοῖς οὐρανοῖς) who will enter the kingdom. In 13:43 we are informed that the righteous (δίκαιοι) will shine like

---

52. France, *The Gospel of Matthew*, 282.
53. See the comments in note 51 above.

the sun in the kingdom of their Father. In 19:14 the kingdom of heaven (ἡ βασιλεία τῶν οὐρανῶν) belongs to those who are like the "little children" (παιδία) who have been given high priority to come to Jesus. Matt 25:34 contains a statement by Jesus to "those at his right hand," declaring them blessed by his Father and welcoming them to inherit the kingdom prepared for them from the foundation of the world. The evidence for the fatherhood of God and the ethical implications of this is provided in the last chapter of this work.

Matt 7:1–2

In this text the measure for measure language is used to convey and stress the idea of interpersonal forgiveness. The passage contains warnings addressed to the disciples, warnings which are given in the context of interpersonal relationships. It has no connection in thought with what immediately precedes. The literary structure of this text in Luke (6:37–42ff) indicates that they logically follow from 5:48, the point at which Matthew departed from his source to introduce the material gathered in Matt 6. Verse 2 is not simply a recommendation to be moderate in judgment on others; the meaning is that, if you condemn, you surely exclude yourself from God's forgiveness. The "measure" saying is also found in Mark 4:24b where it refers to the spirit in which a person receives teaching. A possible meaning of 7:1–2 is this: If you want to be mercifully dealt with, show mercy as well. This is parallel to the meaning suggested for the preceding clause in verse 1.

Matt 18:15–17, 33

A textual problem appears in Matt 18:15; it has to do with the reading of the phrase εἰς σὲ. The decision about which reading to take has significant exegetical consequences for the understanding of the second half of Matt 18 (for our part, verses 15–17 and 21–35 to do with reconciliation and forgiveness respectively). Two clear readings of this phrase are in order. First of all, εἰς σὲ is omitted in a few important witnesses (e.g., codices Sinaiticus and Vaticanus, as well as minuscules and Family 1). Second, the εἰς σὲ reading is attested in all text families, ranging from the Majority text to other important codices and various traditions.[54] The present

---

54. These codices include Codex Claromontanus, Codex of Paris, Codex of

author prefers the second option because the reading of this phrase is supported by the majority of all consistently cited witnesses of the first order. Metzger and the Committee that worked on the UBS/Nestle-Aland text also have a preference for this reading.[55] The implication of this is that, for this study, the offence in 18:15 (ἐὰν δὲ ἁμαρτήσῃ [εἰς σὲ]) is personal in nature. A possible connection can therefore be made between 18:15–17 (to do with *brotherly* reconciliation) and 18:21–35 (to do with *interpersonal* forgiveness).

In 18:15–17, the idea of interpersonal forgiveness is stated indirectly using the language of reconciliation with an ἀδελφός. This similar language is used in 5:23–24. There, however, the onus is placed upon the offender, whereas here it is placed upon the offended person, as was shown earlier in this chapter. In 18:33, the idea of interpersonal forgiveness is stated indirectly using ἐλεέω (2x), one of the key terms in the First Gospel. The term in its verbal form occurs eight times in Matthew (versus 3x in Mark and 4x in Luke); its adjectival form (ἐλεήμων) occurs once in the gospel (versus 0x in Mark and 0x Luke); as a noun, ἔλεος occurs three times in Matthew (versus 0x in Mark and 6x in Luke). Other instances of mercy may include Joseph's attitude in not wanting to put Mary to open shame (1:19) and an appeal that a husband is to show mercy to his wife by not divorcing her (5:31–32).

Summary

The use of these related ideas in describing divine-human and interpersonal relationships in the Matthean forgiveness and related texts just surveyed surely serves primarily for ethical purposes—although not to be divorced from Matthew's understanding of God's grace. How Matthew may have intended his community members to behave in response to God's generous providence, gracious love and forgiveness, expressions of his mercy toward his creation (cf. 5:15; 6:25–34), has been summarized quite accurately by Stiewe and Vouga:

> Sa volonté qui doit être faite sur la terre comme au ciel est que les disciples, les auditeurs de Jésus (Mt 5,1–2) et tous les peuples

---

Washington, DC, and Codex of St. Gall; miniscules comprise Family 13; the traditions include the entire Latin versions, together with Syriac, Middle Egyptian (Mesokemic), and several Bohainic versions. Cf. Nestle-Aland, *Novum Testamentum Graece*, 50.

55. Nestle-Aland, *Novum Testamentum Graece*, 50.

(Mt 28,18–20) cherchent sa justice en vivant de son esprit de *don* et de *gratuité*, de la bonté de *sa miséricorde* et de *la perfection de son amour*, en se comportant avec douceur, esprit de paix et *miséricorde* et en reconnaissant l'Autre comme personne indépendamment de ses qualités.[56]

STRATEGIC RHETORICAL POSITIONING OF INTERPERSONAL FORGIVENESS AND RELATED MATERIAL WITHIN MATTHEW'S TEXT

The centrality of the theme at hand is evidenced by the strategic rhetorical positioning of the interpersonal forgiveness texts and related texts in the gospel: they occur at significant stages in the gospel. Matthew's rewriting of a few of these texts also tends to support this proposal, although there is a debate about how Matthew's changes of his sources are to be accounted for.[57] Matthew's outline follows the outline of both Mark and Q, Matthew's main sources. Unlike them, it is especially characterized by five discourses, interleaved with six narratives, as shown below.

    1–4   [Narrative] Jesus introduced

Ministry of Jesus in Galilee

    5–7   [Discourse] Sermon on the Mount

    8–9   [Narrative] Jesus' miracles and diverse activities

    10   [Discourse] Jesus' ministry through words and deeds

    11–12 [Narrative] Israel's negative response

    13   [Discourse] Parables of Jesus

    14–17 [Narrative] Jesus' miracles and identity

    18   [Discourse] Community Discourse

Ministry of Jesus in Judea

    19–23 [Narrative] Prophecy about Jesus' passion and what will follow

    24–25 [Discourse] Judgment and salvation

---

56. Stiewe and Vouga, *Le Sermon sur la montagne*, 131; emphasis added.

57. Stanton has questioned the redaction critics' reading of Matthew's changes of his sources; for the whole of Stanton's argument, see Stanton, *A Gospel for a New People*, 36–41; so also Riches, *Matthew*, 26–28.

26–28   [Narrative]   Jesus' passion and resurrection

Of particular significance for our purposes are the first and fourth discourses; they contain the two relevant interpersonal forgiveness and related passages to be explored in this work. This outline shows clearly how strategically the materials in Matt 5–7 and Matt 18 are positioned in the gospel.

The Sermon on the Mount (Matt 5–7)

The Sermon is Jesus' basic instruction on the life of discipleship. It is the first of the five great blocks of teaching material, the blocks which are a most striking feature of the structure of Matthew.[58] It is striking to note that it is in the Sermon that the first eight interpersonal forgiveness and related texts occur, as the outline below shows.

5–7	Diverse teachings of Jesus on the Mount
5:1–2	Narrative introduction
5:3–12	Blessings
5:7	The mercy blessing
5:13–16	The identity of the Disciples: salt and light
5:17–48	Jesus and the Law
5:17–20	The basis of Jesus' teaching
5:21–26	Concerning brotherly reconciliation
5:27–30	Concerning adultery
5:31–32	Concerning divorce
5:33–37	Concerning oaths
5:38–42	Concerning retaliation
5:43–48	Concerning love for enemies and being perfect
6:1–18	Jesus and the cult
6:1–4	Concerning almsgiving
6:5–15	Concerning prayer
6:12, 14–15	Concerning interpersonal forgiveness
6:16–18	Concerning fasting
6:19—7:11	Jesus and social issues

58. See, e.g., Hill, *The Gospel of Matthew*, 108.

6:19–23	Concerning treasures
6:24–37	Concerning worry
7:1–5	Concerning judging others
7:6	Concerning the holy
7:7–11	Concerning asking/knocking
7:12–29	Warnings and narrative conclusion
7:12	Treating others as one wishes to be treated

This outline shows that, firstly, these texts altogether more or less form an *inclusio* about this first block of teaching material. Secondly, this teaching material block is placed at the beginning of Jesus' ministry in Galilee, immediately after Jesus first calls his disciples (4:18–22) before the miracles story material. These texts are surveyed individually below, the main purpose of the survey being to show current locations of them in their respective sections, units and subunits. Detailed discussion of each text is provided elsewhere in this work.

Matt 5:7

The first statement about the theme of interpersonal forgiveness in the First Gospel can be discerned from 5:7. In this text, this theme is stated indirectly by way of the reciprocal principle of "mercy for mercy." It is striking that, in Matthew, this theme occurs near the beginning of the Sermon; it is located in the Beatitudes section (5:3–12). In fact, Matthew has nine beatitudes,[59] whereas Luke has four. The last Matthean beatitude excluded, the other eight beatitudes comprise two groups of four, which agree with the number of words in each.[60] The second group (vv. 7–10), beginning with the mercy beatitude, clearly exalts more highly the actions of humans (i.e., living righteously). In 5:7, living righteously consists in showing mercy to others. This mercy blessing (v. 7) is also found in Luke's Sermon on the Plain—not in the Beatitudes *per se*, but at the end of the love for enemy section (6:36); and there too, there is the question of whether Luke 6:36 is linked with what precedes or with what

---

59. A consensus, however, is far from being reached as to whether there are nine or eight beatitudes.

60. Luz has provided the following statistics: twice 36 words with a few uncertainties in the text; cf. Luz, *Matthew*, 1:185n4.

follows.⁶¹ As to the first, the second and the fourth Matthean beatitudes, they appear in similar form in Luke 6:20-23, which may mean that they already formed part of Q.

This phenomenon raises the fundamental question of why the evangelist rewrote the command of Q Luke 6:36,⁶² disconnecting it from the love for enemies commandment (its possibly "original" setting in the beatitude form) and placed it in its present location among the beatitudes extolling more highly the *actions of humans*.⁶³ He probably did so for ethical purposes; he was most concerned with instructions for proper conduct of the members of his Christian community. As G. Strecker has stated, "here the eschatological promise [note ἐλεηθήσονται in future tense] is made exclusively and originally to an ethical attitude."⁶⁴ It is quite possible that Matthew reworked his sources to compose the substance of this first beatitude to present his views on the subject of mercy.

Matt 5:21-26

This text contains the first of the six Matthean antitheses.⁶⁵ In terms of source, it has been suggested that in the Q tradition common to Matthew and Luke, there was no antithetical formulation, although the substance of the fifth (5:38-42) and the sixth (5:43-48) antitheses may be attested for Q.⁶⁶ The first, the second and the fourth antitheses, it has to be noted, are attested only in Matthew; only verses 25-26 in the first antithesis unit have a synoptic parallel with the Q material (cf. Luke 12:57-59). It is therefore possible to imagine that the Matthean material which forms the first antithesis has come about through a combination of traditional material and redactional reworking,⁶⁷ which here serves to address the issue of reconciliation. Using this strategy, Matthew recommends reconciliation as a means of prevention or avoidance of potential judgment for offending an ἀδελφός. He does this by juxtaposing two loosely related ex-

---

61. For the arguments in support of the link of this verse with what precedes, see Nolland, *Luke* 1:300.

62. "Be merciful (οἰκτίρμονες), just as your Father is merciful (οἰκτίρμων)."

63. The synoptic problem will be discussed in ch. 5.

64. Strecker, *The Sermon on the Mount*, 38.

65. The other antitheses sections are 5:27-30 (on adultery); 5:31-32 (on divorce); 5:33-37 (on oaths); 5:38-42 (on retaliation); and 5:43-48 (on love of enemy).

66. E.g., Strecker, *The Sermon on the Mount*, 63.

67. Foster, *Community, Law and Mission in Matthew's Gospel*, 97.

amples in the form of little parables (vv. 23–26), which apparently serve to illustrate how anger can be overcome through acts of reconciliation.

Matt 5:38–42; 5:43–48

These two sets of verses altogether comprise the climactic fifth and sixth antitheses in the first section of the Sermon. In this climactic conclusion of the larger unit 5:21–48, Matthew's church members are given two moral precepts; these are precepts related to interpersonal forgiveness: rather than exerting the power of violence, these members are to be devoted to peacemaking through diplomacy (5:38–41) and through loving their potential adversaries and enemies (5:43–47). This would then be an evidence of them *being perfect* as their heavenly Father is (5:48).

The fifth antithesis in 5:38–42 portrays Jesus speaking against the law of retribution, legislated by the conditions described in the Pentateuch (Exod 21:24, Lev 24:20; Deut 19:21). The antithesis in 5:38–39a is probably Matthean redaction; to this he seems to have appended a few traditional sayings (cf. 5:39b–48, cp. Q Luke 6:29–30). As to 5:43–48, a comparison with Luke 6:27–28 clearly shows that Matthew has largely reworked his sources to compose the substance of which 5:43–48 is made: he most likely used Q (cp. Luke 6:28, 32–36), which he abbreviated and tightened to compose this last antithesis.[68] The placement of the saying in 5:38–48 in its current location in the gospel, and the nature of the various themes which are being dealt with in this passage (all of which are forgiveness-related subjects) do suggest something. Here, the combination of traditional materials and the reworking of them are quite clearly parts of Matthew's technique in composing his text which seeks to call upon the members to display a radical attitude toward their potential adversaries or enemies—an attitude that does not respond either with retaliation or hatred, but seeks peacemaking.

Matt 6:12, 14–15

Matt 6:12, 14–15 belongs to a literary unit 6:5–15 dealing with prayer, which in turn belongs to 6:1–18 which is concerned with Jesus and the Temple cult. Allison has shown how central the unit 6:5–15 is to the

---

68. For the detail with regard to this, see Luz, *Matthew*, 1:284.

Sermon.⁶⁹ In fact, the Prayer (6:9-13) plus 6:14-15 are more or less in the middle of the Sermon. On top of that, the position of this text in the Sermon (placed at about the centre of the Sermon) and its expansion beyond the Prayer (6:14-15 and beyond) seems to emphasize this. The forgiveness petition in verse 12, being the only petition of the Prayer to be expanded and stated emphatically (cf. vv. 14-15), also adds to the emphasis. These verses are quite clearly Matthew's interpretation of the Prayer, as is evident from their Markan parallel (11:25) in which the equivalent of verse 15 is missing in the more reliable Greek texts.⁷⁰ The fact that the substance of verse 15 is not recorded in Luke may suggest that this substance is Matthew's redaction, which serves a purpose: to emphasize the place of forgiving in interpersonal relationships.

Matt 7:1-2

The saying in 7:1-2 is an exhortation, which contains a prohibition against passing judgment on others at any time. It is stated by means of a general moral maxim: Μὴ κρίνετε, ἵνα μὴ κριθῆτε (v. 1). This first bit of the saying has a parallel in Luke 6:37, which suggests that it possibly came from Q. The reason for the maxim is given (γὰρ ... [v. 2a]), and is stated by means of a double sentence: ἐν ᾧ γὰρ κρίματι κρίνετε κριθήσεσθε, καὶ ἐν ᾧ μέτρῳ μετρεῖτε μετρηθήσεται ὑμῖν (v. 2). This second part seems to have come from Mark (4:24-25).

Two things require mention. First, Matthew has reworked his Q material by replacing the καὶ of καὶ οὐ μὴ κριθῆτε (Q Luke 6:37a) with the ἵνα of ἵνα μὴ κριθῆτε (Matt 7:1). He has also dropped the prohibition to condemn statement (Q Luke 6:37a) and the forgiveness statement (Q Luke 6:37b), moving it to Matt 6:14. Second, he has kept intact his Markan source. As one may realise, in this text, we have a combination of traditional material and Matthew's redaction by dropping materials he deemed irrelevant to the point he was trying to make in this text.

---

69. Allison ("Matthew: Structure, Biographical Impulse and the *Imitatio Christi*," 1203-21), among many others.

70. E.g., Codex Sinaiticus and Codex Vaticanus.

Matt 7:12

A comparison with the *logion* in Luke 6:31 suggests that the one in 7:12 originated from Q. Three things are notable. Firstly, this saying occurs in different contexts in Matthew and in Luke. In Luke it is located in the section dealing with love of enemies; in Matthew, however, it introduces a section which is concerned with putting in practice the word which it describes as the Law and the Prophets (i.e., God's revelation). Secondly, the Matthean phrasing stresses not only the quality of the action (ποιεῖτε αὐτοῖς, "do so"), as does Luke, but also the quantity of it, as is evident from the position of πάντα in the sentence ("*everything* [πάντα] that you wish people to do"). Thirdly, the second part of 7:12 ("for this is the law and the prophets") is absent in Luke, and probably did not belong to the primitive tradition. This is an indication of Matthean redaction. So in this text, we have a combination of traditional material and Matthew's redaction.

The Community Discourse (Matt 18)

As was the case with the Sermon in Matt 5–7, the Community Discourse in Matt 18 is strategically placed in the gospel. It occurs right at the end of Jesus' ministry in Galilee and the beginning of his ministry in Judea, between the second and third announcements of his passion and trial, thus setting up his ministry program in Jerusalem.

The idea of interpersonal forgiveness runs throughout Matt 18, which deals with the maintenance of relationships in the believing community.[71] To write it, the evangelist selected some materials of Jesus' *logia* in Mark and Q, materials to which he has given his own interpretation. This is clear as one compares them with the text in Mark and with their parallels in Luke. Five things are evident from a comparison with their Markan and Lukan counterparts. Firstly, the catchwords παιδία and μικροί occur both in Mark 9:36, 42 and Matt 18:2–6, 10, 14. At first, clearly Matthew follows the thread of Mark. However, while in Mark 9:34 the conversation about *who is the greatest* follows without the Temple tax episode, in Matthew, this episode is discussed before the conversation—the location and mention of the house of Mark 9:33 having been already included in Matt 17:24–25. This episode was surely so important

---

71. The nature and circumstances of this community are discussed in ch. 5.

to the evangelist that he chose it as an introduction to the Community Discourse. In addition, an ἀμὴν λέγω ὑμῖν saying is introduced, which is appropriate here (18:3); it does not appear in Mark until 10:15.

Secondly, the subsection 18:10–14 consists of a parable probably from Q (cf. Luke 15:3–7). To this, the evangelist supplies a new introduction (v. 10) and a new conclusion (v. 14). It is worth noting that the meaning of this parable is different in Matthew and Luke. Apart from the differences in the respective audiences[72] and in their concerns, in Luke the parable ends with a note of joy; whereas in Matthew, it ends with a warning. Thirdly, some expansions and special materials are apparent in the gospel. Matt 18:15–22 can be regarded as a Matthean expansion of Q (cf. Luke 17:3–4). What Matthew does here with his Q material is that he expands it with the likely purpose of achieving his agenda, which here consists in stressing the role of the offended person in reconciliation. Matt 18:15 is reminiscent of Luke 17:3, and Matt 18:21–22 of Luke 17:2. Fourthly, 18:23–35, it has to be stressed, is without parallel: the parable in 18:23–35 is exclusively Matthean.

It is worth noting that aspects of the problems of the Matthean community, as can be discerned from the teaching on the subjects of care for the little ones, brotherly reconciliation and interpersonal forgiveness, are brought up at this strategic location in the text. Furthermore, as was the case with some of the previous forgiveness and related materials in the Sermon, here too Matthew has reworked his sources to compose the substance of this block of teaching material.

PROPORTION OF INTERPERSONAL FORGIVENESS AND RELATED TEXTS WITHIN THE SERMON AND THE COMMUNITY DISCOURSE

Interpersonal forgiveness and related texts occupy a significant proportion in two of the five Matthean blocks of teaching. Firstly, the Sermon contains a large number of interpersonal forgiveness and related passages: 392 of the 1,990 words (roughly 20 percent) of the material in it are devoted to brotherly reconciliation (5:21–26), non-retaliation (5:38–42), loving enemies (5:43–47; 7:12), being perfect (5:48), forgiving (6:12, 14–15) and not judging others (7:1–2). This percentage is indeed not insignificant, especially in a discourse in which various subjects are

---

72. That is the scribes and the Pharisees in Luke against the disciples in Matthew.

discussed. On top of that, within the Sermon, the interpersonal forgiveness material altogether in and around the Prayer has the lion's share: 43 of the 91 words (around 47 percent) of this material is devoted to the issue of forgiving. That is surely a significant proportion in a single unit. Secondly, in the Community Discourse in Matt 18, about 60 percent of the material is devoted to the subjects of brotherly reconciliation (18:15–17) and forgiveness and mercy (18:21–35)[73]. This is a significant proportion in a single section.

The fact that Matthew has given so much space to the subject of interpersonal forgiveness and related subjects in these two blocks of teaching suggests that he was extremely concerned about the possibility of his Christian community members' being reluctant to forgive their fellow brothers and sisters. Thus, he expressly wanted to stress the kind of behavior which was appropriate to them as members of the kingdom.

CONCLUSIONS

Eleven Matthean texts have been considered in this survey. The analysis has shown that the theme of interpersonal forgiveness is central to the message in Matthew. This was made clear by a number of indications in the Matthean text itself. First is the concept of reciprocity and the link between mercy and forgiveness, together with the link between reluctance in the *praxis* of them and judgment (5:7; 6:12, 14–15; 18:32–35). Second is the emphasis on the responsibility of the offended person to forgive and the link with the idea of the *spiritually mature* and *immature* Christians (Matt 18). Third is a reinforcement of the forgiveness concept by the use of related ideas: the languages of reconciliation (5:24–25; 18:15–17), loving enemies (5:43–47; 7:12), non-retaliation (5:38–42), not judging others (7:1–2) and being perfect (5:48).

Fourth are the strategic rhetorical positioning of the interpersonal forgiveness texts and related texts. All these texts are grouped into two blocks of teaching material and occur at significant stages in the gospel narrative. In the Sermon, they occupy strategic rhetorical locations; this is quite evident from the locations in it of the first antithesis in 5:21–26, the fifth in 5:38–42 and the sixth in 5:43–48. Some of these materials are Matthew's reshaping of his sources. On the one hand, we have Matthew's special material (5:21–22; 5:27–28; 5:33–36; 5:38–39a; 6:15; 18:23–35).

---

73. For more detail, see the structure of Matt 18 provided in ch. 6.

On the other hand, Matthew has introduced diverse material and rearranged Mark's narrative and Q's *logia*, among other sources. He has included or omitted material (5:38–39a; 6:15; 7:12b; 7:1–2, cp. Q Luke 6:37b–38); he has located it at particular point in the gospel (5:7, cp. Q Luke 6:36; Matt 7:12, cp. Q Luke 6:31); he has juxtaposed it with what precedes and follows (5:39b–48, cp. Q Luke 6:29–30; Matt 18:10–14, cp Q Luke 15:3–7); he has added to or abbreviated a sentence, a pericope or a section (5:23–24; 6:14–15, cp. Mark 11:25; Matt 18:21–22, cp. Q Luke 17:3–4); he has used particular words and style (7:1–2, cp. Q Luke 6:37a). How do we account for all these changes? The best way is probably to think of them in terms of Matthew's own theological understanding and his keen desire to address the needs and situation of his Christian community. Also warranting mention is that the Community Discourse in Matt 18, which contains interpersonal forgiveness and related themes, occur at the end of Jesus' ministry in Galilee and the beginning of his ministry, trial and passion in Jerusalem.

3

The Rhetoric of Interpersonal Forgiveness in First-Century Secular Literature

THIS CHAPTER IS MAINLY an interaction with primary sources. It explores the meaning of discourse of interpersonal forgiveness in the first-century CE in representative writings of Dionysius and Seneca. The purpose of the present chapter is to understand the concepts of interpersonal forgiveness in these sources, and findings of it will then be compared with their counterpart in Matthew (chs. 5 and 6). In an attempt to draw a plausible meaning of the discourse about interpersonal forgiveness in these materials, due attention will be paid to the text, the co-text, the inter-texts and the context. By "text" here is meant the interpersonal forgiveness texts from Dionysius and Seneca; "co-text" refers to the body of the text surrounding and relating to these extracts; "inter-texts" refers to contemporary interpersonal forgiveness texts and texts related to this theme; by "context" is meant the socio-historical setting of the first-century CE world in which the writings of these authors emerged.

The reading of this literature should be done with the intention of describing the dynamics of human forgiveness, or divine forgiveness (or both where applicable), and of drawing a pattern to be compared with the one provided in Matthew. Tables will be employed to show the occurrences of the key Greek and their equivalent Latin terms for forgiveness and, where necessary, their cognates, as found in representative writings of Dionysius and Seneca. The present chapter consists of two main sections, examining the rhetoric of interpersonal forgiveness in these authors. A conclusion then presents a summary and includes a discussion of the implication of the findings for chapters 5 and 6.

THE RHETORIC OF INTERPERSONAL FORGIVENESS IN DIONYSIUS

Dionysius of Halicarnassus is a Greek critic and historian writing close to the first-century CE. It is generally believed that he was born around 60 BCE and died at the beginning of the Common Era. As Valérie Fromentin has pointed out, many aspects of Dionysius' life and personality are a matter of hypotheses: "[O]n ignore tout de sa jeunesse et de sa formation intellectuelle. On ne sait pas non plus dans quelles circonstances il vint à Rome, ni s'il retourna jamais dans sa patrie."[1] What is certain is that he lived and taught rhetoric in Rome. He is the author of *Roman Antiquities*, from which our interpersonal forgiveness passages are taken. This influential work exists in 20 books, and all have survived to some extent. While the first 10 books are complete and a good portion of book 11 is available, the last 9 books exist only as fragments.[2] Fortunately, all our interpersonal forgiveness texts from Dionysius come from the set of books which exist in full, thus requiring no reconstructions.

Roman Antiquities is in essence an apologetic piece of work. With it Dionysius mainly seeks to reconcile his Greek compatriots to the Romans, as the preface of book 1 (§§ 1–8) seems to suggest. From this preface it is possible to construe erroneous ideas and some sort of propaganda among Greek historians about the Romans' origins and the causes of their successes, as Fromentin has also noted.[3] Dionysius' overall study in this regard has reasonably been summarized by Fromentin:

> [L]es origines de Rome ne sont pas barbares mais grecques; Romulus et Rémus, les fondateurs ... de la cité—et, à travers eux, tous les Romains—ont pour ancêtres des colons grecs venus ... s'établir au Latium, sur le site de la future Rome, plusieurs années avant la fondation ... En effet, si les Romains sont des Grecs, les Grecs cessent du même coup d'être des vaincus,

---

1. Fromentin, *Denys d'Halicarnasse* 1.xiii.
2. Ibid., 1.xxiii.
3. Ibid., 1.xxxv.

puisqu'ils participent depuis l'origine à l'extraordinaire aventure de Rome. L'histoire romaine apparaît dès lors comme un chapitre, parmi les plus glorieux, de l'histoire grecque. Qui plus est, cette réconciliation des ennemis d'hier débouche sur une nouvelle conception de l'hellénisme, qui s'imposera à l'époque impériale: un hellénisme qui n'est plus affaire seulement de race mais aussi de culture et d'éthique . . .[4]

All this has significant implications for how the interpersonal forgiveness texts in Dionysius are to be read. The table below shows all the occurrences of the key words for forgiveness from *Roman Antiquities* in quotes that are relevant for this study.

Word	Occurrence
ἀφίημι	2
ἄφεσις	1
συγγινώσκω	3
συγγνώμη	1

In the passages in Dionysius to be studied, ἀφίημι and συγγινώσκω are used to communicate the idea of forgiveness. How they are used in these texts and whether they are the same need to be determined. To be sure, in the Dionysius texts surveyed, these verbs are employed with either an impersonal object (offences) or a personal object (people). The question is whether ἀφίημι or συγγινώσκω a *person* is different from ἀφίημι or συγγινώσκω an *offence*. There are two tendencies among scholars over this issue. While the first tendency seems not to differentiate between forgiving the person and forgiving the offence or penalty (or both),[5] the other sharply distinguishes between the two notions. F. Gerald Downing is among those who distinguish between the two notions. However, unlike those who distinguish between the two notions, based on the grammatical ground (i.e., the personal dative object with the verb), he claims this as the reading noted in the NT texts—a point which is often not noted in most contemporary English translations.[6]

It is possible to distinguish between forgiving the *person* and forgiving the *offence* for the offender. As we shall see, the distinction seems to be supported by a number of the Dionysius forgiveness texts, especially

---

4. For more detail see ibid., 1.xxxi, xxxiv.
5. E.g., Benn, "Forgiveness and Loyalty," 374, among many others.
6. Downing, *Making Sense in (and of) the First Christian Century*, 72–74.

where the offender is in the dative. In the examples in Dionysius to be surveyed below, ἀφίημι is used merely with impersonal object; the sense conveyed tends to be something like to "remit," or to "put away," or to "let go." Συγγινώσκω, on the other hand, is used with either personal object (persons) or impersonal object. In the first case, the meaning conveyed is most likely something like "bearing with"; whereas in the second case, it is something like to "tolerate."

Ant. Rom. 2.54.3; 2.55.4–6

> The third war Romulus engaged in was against the . . . city of Veii . . . in which the Romans were victorious, after killing many of the Veientes and taking more of them prisoners. Even their camp was taken . . . This was the third triumph that Romulus celebrated, and it was much more magnificent than either of the former. And when, not long afterwards, ambassadors arrived from the Veientes to seek an end to the war and to ask pardon for their offences (συγγνώμην τῶν ἁμαρτημάτων), Romulus imposed the following penalties upon them: to deliver up to the Romans the country adjacent to the Tiber . . ., and to abandon the salt-works near the mouth of the river, and also to bring fifty hostages as a pledge that they would attempt no uprising in the future. When the Veientes submitted to all these demands, he made a treaty with them for one hundred years and engraved the terms of it on pillars. He then dismissed without ransom all the prisoners who desired to return home; but those who preferred to remain in Rome . . . he made citizens, distributing them among the curiae and assigning to them allotments of land on this side of the Tiber.[7]

The assumption in this text is that the Veientes had wronged the Romans. They then seek the dismissal of their offences from, and reconciliation with, the Romans. The Romans impose penalties before the request is considered. The Veientes abide by the demands imposed upon them. As a result, the dismissal of the offences is granted, reconciliation takes place and peace is re-established between the Romans and the Veientes. A new point of departure begins, as is evidenced by the treaty concluded between the two parties.

---

7. Dionysius, *Ant. Rom.* 2.54.3; 2.55.4–6.

In the text cited above, the noun συγγνώμη is used to describe the content of the Veientes' request: συγγνώμη is said to be asked for ἁμαρτημάτων ("offences"); the emphasis seems to lie on the *offences*, rather than on the *authors* of them (i.e., the people). In this context of desperation, where the Veientes had failed to conquer the Romans in all their three attempts, asking forgiveness for the offences amounts to an appeal for dismissal of them. The ἁμαρτημάτων for which συγγνώμη is sought here has to do with the idea of violation of something, or an injustice. In this account, what the Veientes attempt to seek from the Romans is the dismissal of their offences for having conducted unfairly war against them; they seek that their guilt be distanced from them; they desperately seek a sort of relief.

Ant. Rom. 2.52.1–4

This text gives an account of a complex tension between the Lavinians and the Romans, a tension which saw Tatius murdered by the Lavinians and his body given honourable burial in Rome.

> This violence committed against the [Lavinian] ambassadors appeared to Romulus . . . as a terrible crime and one calling for speedy expiation since it had been in violation of a sacred law . . . [H]e himself, without further delay, caused those who had been guilty of the outrage to be seized and delivered up in chains to the ambassadors to be led away. But Tatius not only was angered at the indignity which he complained he had received from his colleague in delivering up of the men, but was also moved with compassion for those who were being led away . . .; and immediately, taking his soldiers with him, he went in haste to their assistance . . . [H]e took the prisoners from them. But not long afterwards, as some say, when he had gone with Romulus to Lavinium in order to perform a sacrifice which it was necessary for the kings to offer to the ancestral gods for the prosperity of the city, the friends and relations of the ambassadors who had been murdered, . . . slew him at the altar . . . But Licinius writes that he did not go with Romulus nor . . . on account of any sacrifices, but that he went alone, with the intention of persuading those who had received the injuries to forgive the authors of them (ἀφεῖναι τοῖς δεδρακόσι τὴν ὀργήν), and that when the people became angry because the men were not delivered up to them in accordance with the decision both of Romulus and the

Roman senate, and the relations of the slain men rushed upon him in great numbers, . . . and was stoned to death by them . . . His body was brought to Rome, where it was given honourable burial; and the city offers public libations to him every year.[8]

One of the two apparent versions of this story is Licinius' version. For my point of view, Licinius' version is the one of interest; Dionysius himself seems to have preferred this version of the story. According to Licinius, Tatius was murdered by the friends and relations of the Lavinians' ambassadors—to satisfy their injuries and anger—when he went alone to them to seek forgiveness on behalf of his fellow countrymen.

In the text above, ἀφίημι is used to describe what Tatius went to seek from the victims of the injuries caused by some of his countrymen. In it ἀφίημι is used to convey the idea of forgive. This verb emerges in the context of tension between two communities, a tension caused by a barbarous act of one community against the other. Here ἀφίημι has τὴν ὀργήν as direct object. The dynamic underlying ἀφίημι here, in the cotext of this passage to do with resentment by the offended party, seems to require that seeking forgiveness on behalf of the perpetrators be understood as something like to "put away." The Lavinians carried resentment because of the wrong done against them.[9] What was sought from them was that their anger against the guilty friends of Tatius be put away. Asking for forgiveness in this situation amounts to requesting what R. D. Enright and C. T. Coyle have described as "a merciful restraint from pursuing resentment or revenge."[10]

An aspect of honor is clear in the fact that Tatius' body is said to have been given honorable burial in Rome. A further illustration of honor can also be observed in the action of Romulus to revenge Tatius' murder. On this, Dionysius comments that Romulus brought to trial the Lavinians who had conspired against Tatius and had been delivered up by their own city.[11] In this text, the forgiveness sought has had a price to pay: it has cost life to the one seeking it on behalf of the injuring party; the forgiveness sought is denied, as the injured party retaliates.

---

8. Ibid., 2.52.1–4.
9. Ibid., 2.51.3.
10. Enright, and Coyle, "Researching the Process Model of Forgiveness within Psychological Interventions," 140.
11. Dionysius, *Ant. Rom.* 2.53.

Ant. Rom. 8.50.1–4

This passage is an account of a tension between Marcius and his Roman countrymen, a tension which has seen a third party being involved in mediation.

> ... [Y]ou carry your wild and mad resentment even to the point of enslaving them [countrymen] and razing their city; and you showed no regard even for the envoys sent to you by the senate, men of worth and your friends, who came to offer you a dismissal of the charges (τῶν ... ἐγκλημάτων ἄφεσιν) ..., nor yet for the priests whom the commonwealth sent at the last to you, old men holding before them the holy garlands of the gods; but these also you drove away ... For my part, I cannot commend these harsh and overbearing claims, which overstep the bounds of human nature, when I observe that a refuge for all men and the means of securing forgiveness for their offences (παραιτήσεις ὧν ἂν ἐξαμαρτάνωσι) one against another have been devised in the form of suppliant boughs and prayers, by which all anger is softened and instead of hating one's enemy one pities him; and when I observe also that those who act arrogantly and treat with insolence the prayers of suppliants all incur the indignation of the gods and in the end come to a miserable state. For the gods themselves, who in the first place instituted and delivered to us these customs, are disposed to forgive the offences of men (συγγνώμονες τοῖς ἀνθρωπίνοις εἰσὶν ἁμαρτήμασι) and are easily reconciled; and many have there been ere now who, though greatly sinning against them, have appeased their anger by prayers and sacrifices. Unless you think it fitting, Marcius, that the anger of the gods should be mortal, but that of men immortal! You will be doing, then, what is just and becoming both to yourself and to your country if you forgive her her offences (ἀφεὶς αὐτῇ ἐγκλήματα), seeing that she is repentant (μετανοούσῃ) and ready to be reconciled and to restore to you now everything that she took away from you before ...[12]

The overall setting of this narrative, as well as of the narrative which follows, is a tension between Marcius and the Romans. Marcius is a Roman aristocrat, one of the great legendary heroes and generals of Rome. He was forced to go into exile because he was charged with tyrannical conduct and opposing the distribution of grain to the starving Plebs. He

---

12. Ibid., 8.50.1–4.

then withdrew to his old enemies, the Volscians, who cheerfully welcomed him and he became their leader in a war against Rome.[13] In two devastating campaigns, Marcius captured a series of Latin cities and led his forces to the gates of Rome, where he was persuaded to turn back by his mother Veturia and his wife Volumnia—the extract above is Veturia's petition, part of her argument, in an attempt to persuade Marcius to come back to reason. In the end he was then killed by the Volscians for not having brought the war to a successful end as agreed.[14]

The situation in Dionysius regarding the subject of interpersonal forgiveness is as follows.[15] Marcius is at war against Rome, now his "enemies." With the military support from the Volscians, along with their allies, they begin war against Rome. With Marcius commanding the troops, they go from one victory to another, invading Roman cities and leaving behind them often chaos and desolation.[16] Being informed of the considerable destruction of the cities, considering the unending progress of the enemy, and given the urgency of the matter, the senate sends envoys to Marcius to negotiate with him for a possible cease-fire and reconciliation. Despite the status of the delegation and their previous relationship with Marcius, he shows no regard for them. He pursues his campaign, conquering other important cities, including Lavinium.[17] The enemies are now at the gates of Rome. In their desperation, the senate sends other envoys to Marcius that he once again drives away.[18]

Marcius' second refusal to put an end to the war and come to the negotiation table causes panic in the whole of Rome. The Roman authorities give up, the people lose hope; they are desperately just waiting to see the catastrophe—the fall of Rome. The paradox is that at this very moment as the men lose hope, the women stand up and go forward to face the challenge. Valeria[19] gathers the women together, along with their children.

---

13. Cornell, "Marcius Coriolanus, Gnaeus," 922.

14. Ibid.

15. Given here is only a summary of the story as related to the subject of forgiveness. It may be helpful to read the whole account in Dionysius, *Ant.* 8.

16. Cf. especially Veturia's words to Marcius in ibid., 8.50.1–2.

17. Lavinium is the first city built by the Trojans, who landed in Italy with Aeneas, and the one from which the Romans derive their origin (cf. ibid., 8.21.1; 8.22.4).

18. Ibid., 8.38.

19. Valeria was the sister of Publicola, one of the men who had freed Rome from the kings. She is described by Dionysius as "a matron distinguished in birth and rank... and capable of discreet judgment" (cf. ibid., 8.39.2).

She leads this crowd to Veturia[20] to request that she takes their appeal for mercy to Marcius and plead with him to stop the war. Then the proposal that the women along with their children led by Veturia to go to Marcius is brought to the senate for approval. After a serious evaluation of it, the senate gives its consent. Veturia, Valeria and the women, along with their children, go to the enemies' camp to take the plea for mercy.

In the extract above, two terms are used to convey the notion of forgiveness: ἀφίημι (and its cognate noun ἄφεσις) and συγγινώσκω; here both ἀφίημι and συγγινώσκω are connected with impersonal objects (ἐγκλημάτων, "charges" and ἁμαρτήμασι/ἐγκλήματα, "the offences"). The co-text of the passage, to do with desperation of Rome, seems to suggest that ἀφίημι and συγγινώσκω be understood as to remit. Rome is enduring the consequences of her offences against Marcius. Troubled by their guilt, Marcius' fellow countrymen seek forgiveness from Marcius, asking that their offences be remitted; so does Veturia's plea. In other words, the plea to Marcius seeks him to overcome wrongdoing with good by giving up his resentment and revenge.

This narrative brings about two features of forgiveness: divine forgiveness and interpersonal forgiveness. In both cases, ἀφίημι and συγγινώσκω are used to describe divine-human and interpersonal interrelationships; both the gods and humans are shown as the subjects of either ἀφίημι or συγγινώσκω: the gods are supernatural beings that are ever disposed to tolerate (συγγινώσκω) the offences of men; human beings, on the other hand, are to show the same disposition toward their fellow humans. In this text, from the point of view of the offended person, interpersonal forgiveness appears like something which *primarily* benefits them; forgiving is viewed as a means of avoiding incurring the indignation of the deities, who are said to have *in the first place* delivered to human beings the customs that consist of seeking forgiveness and reconciliation by means of prayers and sacrifices, among other things. What is relevant to this study is the imitation of deities. Reluctance to imitate them in forgiving clearly has potentially severe consequences on the unforgiving person. In this text, this piece of general truth is evident from Veturia's statement that "those who act arrogantly and treat with insolence the prayers of suppliants all incur the indignation of the gods and in the end come to a miserable state."[21]

---

20. Veturia, Volumnia and Marcius' children remained in Rome when Marcius went into exile.

21. Ibid., 8.50.1–4.

The above text from Dionysius links the theme of forgiveness to the notions of the imitation of deities, reconciliation and restitution. To begin with the imitation of deities, Marcius is reproved by Veturia for carrying a wild and mad resentment and for driving away the envoys sent to him by the senate. The purpose of the coming of these envoys to Marcius was to seek reconciliation with him for his countrymen's abuse of him in the past. In an attempt to persuade Marcius, Veturia uses an argument stressing the deities' disposition both to forgive men and to be easily reconciled. As to repentance, Veturia's argument is worth noting. It reminds Marcius of his countrymen's sincere repentance, their abasement and readiness both to be reconciled and to repair the damage caused. All this is evidenced by suppliant prayers and prayers aimed at appeasing Marcius' anger. A final comment is needed. The initiative of seeking forgiveness and reconciliation is taken by the injuring party. Interestingly, this seeking process involves suppliant prayers and sacrifices as a means of securing forgiveness and reconciliation.

Ant. Rom. 8.54.5; 8.57.1

The text quoted below is the last episode of the tension between Marcius and his countrymen, an episode which culminates in the cost of it to Marcius, his murder.

> Then Marcius in an assembly of the troops laid before those present the reasons why he intended to put an end to the war; and after earnestly beseeching the soldiers both to forgive him (συγγνῶναί τε αὐτῷ) and, when they returned home, to remember the benefits they had received from him and to strive with him to prevent his suffering any irreparable injury at the hands of the other citizens, and after saying many other things calculated to win their support, he ordered them to make ready to break camp the following night ... After the departure of the women from the camp Marcius roused his army about daybreak and led it away as through a friendly country; and when he came into the territory of the Volscians, he divided among the soldiers all the booty he had taken, without reserving the least thing for himself, and then dismissed them to their homes. The army ... which had shared in the battles with him, returning loaded with riches, was not displeased with the respite from war and felt well disposed toward him and thought he deserved to be forgiven (συγγνώμης τε ἄξιον ἡγεῖτο) for not having brought the war to a

successful end out of regard for the lamentations and entreaties of his mother.²²

According to this story, not in this text, Marcius is murdered by a faction of the young men from the Volscians with the complicity of Tullus Attius, jealous of Marcius' exploits. In the text above, συγγινώσκω is used to describe Marcius' plea to his allies. As with the previous episode, συγγινώσκω occurs in the context of interpersonal tension. Συγγινώσκω is used twice and is connected with the person—rather than with the offences. In the first case, συγγινώσκω is said to be sought by the author of the offences, namely, Marcius. Marcius' offence consists in not having brought the war to a successful end, according to the terms and conditions of the agreement between him and the Volscians. The co-text of the passage, to do with an attempt of persuading the offended party, seems to require the sense of bearing with for συγγινώσκω: Marcius requests his allies to bear with him for his failure to fulfil the terms and conditions of their agreement.

Conclusions

The findings from Dionysius on the subject of interpersonal forgiveness can be summarized as follows. Two verbs are used in the data surveyed for what can be referred to as forgive: ἀφίημι (and its cognate) and συγγινώσκω (and its cognate). Of these two verbs, συγγινώσκω alone is employed either with "offences," or "persons" object. When it is used with personal object, συγγινώσκω tends to mean something like "bearing with"²³; when it is used with impersonal object, the meaning conveyed is something like to "tolerate."²⁴ With regard to ἀφίημι, it is used merely with impersonal object, and the sense conveyed tends to be something like to "remit," or "put away," or "let go."²⁵

Further, the following can be identified in the Dionysius texts surveyed in this chapter. First, one party has wronged another.²⁶ Second, seeking the dismissal of the offences from, and reconciliation with, the

---

22. Ibid., 8.54.5; 8.57.1.
23. E.g., ibid., 8.54.5; 8.57.1.
24. Ibid., 8.50.1–4.
25. Ibid., 2.52.1–4; 8.50.1–4.
26. Ibid., 2.54.3; 2.54.4; 2.55.1; 2.55.4–6; 2.522; 8.54.5; 8.50.1–4; 8.57.1.

injured party is a moral obligation on the part of the injuring party.[27] Third, the seeking of forgiveness process involves suppliant prayers (i.e., repentance) and sacrifices as a means for securing forgiveness and reconciliation.[28] Fourth, a third party is involved in the forgiveness and reconciliation seeking process.[29] Fifth, the process of granting of forgiveness does or does not require a prior satisfaction of some penalties.[30] Sixth, the dismissal of the offences is granted, reconciliation takes place, peace is re-established between the two parties and a new point of departure is reached in the form of a treaty being concluded between the two parties.[31]

There are two exceptions. First, occasionally forgiveness is denied, and as a result of that, the death of the one acting on behalf of the offending party occurs.[32] Second, there is a case where seeking forgiveness and reconciliation does cost something to the forgiveness seeker or the one acting on their behalf.[33] More to the point, *Ant.* 8.54.5; 8.57.1 gives a clear account of forgiveness that is granted but only partially enjoyed, as the forgiven person is shortly murdered by some of the offended party's members. The *self-oriented* motivation of forgiveness occurs in Dionysius. In one example, forgiving appears like something which primarily benefits the forgiver, and it is linked to the imitation of deities: forgiving helps the forgiver avoid incurring the indignation of the deities who themselves are disposed to forgive humans and be reconciled with them.[34] Reluctance to forgive is likely to lead to potentially severe consequences upon the unforgiving person.

THE RHETORIC OF INTERPERSONAL FORGIVENESS IN SENECA

Seneca the Younger is our second example of a first-century CE secular writer to have discussed the issue of interpersonal forgiveness. He was almost everything: an orator, a writer, a poet, a philosopher and statesman.

---

27. Ibid., 2.54.3; 2.54.4; 2.55.4–6; 2.52.2; 8.54.5; 8.50.1–4; 8.57.1.
28. Ibid., 8.50.1–4.
29. Ibid.
30. Ibid., 2.54.3; 2.54.4; 2.55.4–6.
31. Ibid.
32. Ibid., 2.52.2.
33. Ibid.
34. Ibid., 8.50.1–4.

Born in Spain between 4 and 1 bce, he died in 65 CE. He was brought up and educated in Rome, where he studied grammar, rhetoric and philosophy. In 49 ce, he was made *praetor*, and then was appointed tutor to Nero, then 12 years old. With the emperor's accession to the throne in 54 ce, Seneca exchanged the role of tutor for that of political adviser. As an adviser, Seneca managed to guide Nero for several years, ensuring a period of good governance of the emperor.[35] *De clementia* from which our interpersonal forgiveness extracts are taken, was composed in the early years of Nero (around 55 and 56 ce) to whom it is dedicated. In it most of the descriptions of Seneca above are not hard to find. To be sure, it is Seneca as a writer, philosopher and statesman who, through this treatise, is providing moral and general guidance in practical politics to the young emperor Nero. The treatise clearly suggests the way in which Nero was encouraged to behave, as an emperor.

Seneca was an eclectic philosopher, largely in the Stoic tradition. *De ira* and *De clementia* are perhaps two of Seneca's four most interesting moral essays; for, as John M. Copper and J. F. Procopé have also written, "They provide an attractive insight into the social and moral outlook of a Stoic thinker at the centre of power in the Roman empire of the mid first century ad."[36] Interpersonal forgiveness texts from Seneca to be studied in the present work appear in *De clementia*. For the purposes of this investigation, it is worth noting that forgiveness is a recurrent theme in Seneca's *De clementia*. The historical and intellectual contexts of *De clementia* require mention because they are likely to help us in reading the interpersonal forgiveness texts in this treatise. *De clementia* seems to have been composed with a twofold intent. Copper and Procopé have reasonably suggested that the work was intended for the emperor Nero "to celebrate the start of his principate, to admonish on how to conduct it, and to stress the need for mercifulness in all his dealings."[37] On the other hand, the work "was intended to reassure the public about the character of the new regime and to show that Nero's adviser [Seneca] was by no means as harsh in his attitudes as Stoics were commonly thought to be."[38] This can easily be verified from the work itself. While the first intention

---

35. Reynolds, Griffin, and Fantham, "Annaeus Seneca (2), Lucius," *Oxford Classical Dictionary*, 96–98; "Seneca the Younger," *Oxford Dictionary of the Classical World*, 658–61; A. Dible, "Seneca," 88–105.

36. Copper and Procopé, *Seneca*, page number not provided in the book.

37. Ibid., 119.

38. Ibid., 119–20.

described above is evident from the preface of the treatise,[39] later in this piece of work it also becomes clear that Seneca is aware of the "bad reputation" the Stoic school might have had among some people for being too hard and unlikely to give good advice to princes and kings.[40] This seems to suggest an apologetic purpose, as one of possible motivations underlying this treatise. In spite of the fact that as a philosopher Seneca himself seems to have preached higher standards than can be realistically reached,[41] it is quite possible to learn something about interpersonal forgiveness from the principles and moral values he teaches.

What *De clementia* might have represented to its author (Seneca), its primary intended reader (Nero) and their contemporaries has been well documented. One thinks, for instance, of works by Bernard Mortureux and many others before him.[42] Mortureux, on his part, has concentrated on the vocabulary and composition of *De clementia*. Most relevant for my purposes is, first of all, the explanation he supplies to "inconsistencies" that can be observed in the way in which particular key terms sometimes appear to be used paradoxically in the *De clementia*'s first two books, *venia* ("forgiveness") being among them.[43] Second is Mortureux's explanation of the complex relationships between *clementia* and *venia*, *ignoscere* and *misericordia*. As we shall see later in this chapter, the explanation Mortureux offers probably constitutes significant information of how the Seneca interpersonal forgiveness texts are to be read.

De clementia is divided into three parts, a division which has been provided by Seneca himself[44]: the first part, on lenience, deals with relaxing one's animosity; the second part demonstrates the nature and disposition of mercy; the third part enquires how the mind may be led to mercy (i.e., how it may establish it firmly and by practice make it its own). This third part unfortunately never survived. François Préchac, however, has strongly argued that this last part of the treatise never got lost. Based on his study of the text of the *De clementia*, which culminated in a piece of work published in 1921, Préchac came up with something he claimed to be the "lost" bit of the third part of the treatise. The reconstruction of

39. Seneca, *De clementia* 1.1–9.

40. Seneca, *Clem.* 2.5.2.

41. Reynolds, Griffin, and Fantham, "Annaeus Seneca (2), Lucius," 96–98.

42. Mortureux, *Recherches sur le "De clementia de Sénèque"*; Grimal, *Conte-rendu de Sénèque*, 179–184.

43. Mortureux, *Recherches sur le "De clementia de Sénèque*," 75–83.

44. Seneca, *Clem.* 1.3.1.

this "lost" section can be found in his *Sénèque: De la clémence*.⁴⁵ What he has come up with has been far from convincing, and has thus remained unpopular. Interpersonal forgiveness texts from Seneca to be studied in the present work are taken from both the first two parts of the treatise. In them, the idea of forgiveness is conveyed by *venia* and *ignoscere*, terms which appear in connection with *clementia*.

According to Lewis and Short, *ignoscere* means literally to not wish to know, or to not search into, with special reference to a fault or crime.⁴⁶ This verb is broadly defined as to forgive, to excuse, to overlook and to make excuse to justify.⁴⁷ As for *venia*, Lewis and Short present its range of meanings as including "complaisance," "indulgence and kindness"; second is "obliging disposition or conduct," "mercy," "grace," "favor and forbearance" in view of any wrong that has been done; third is "remission."⁴⁸ This allows for the possibility that the notion of *venia* also consists of a feeling and an attitude; other examples of *venia* with the same range of senses are heavily attested elsewhere.⁴⁹ *Venia* is probably the most regular Latin noun for the concept of forgive, and *ignoscere* the common verb for it.⁵⁰

Seneca's view of what can be referred to as mercy is worth discussing at this point. Seneca argues that mercy is above all a virtue of rulers⁵¹; he illustrates this claim with an extended story about Augustus⁵² and rounds off by contrasting the life of a king with that of a tyrant.⁵³ Most importantly, as Copper and Procopé have also correctly seen, throughout the book the moral is "mercy enhances not only a ruler's honour, but his safety."⁵⁴

45. Préchac, *Sénèque*.
46. Lewis and Short, *A Latin Dictionary*, 1:882.
47. Ibid.
48. Ibid., 1:1968.
49. Following are the examples: Cicero, *Orationes Philippicae in M. Antonium* 8.11.32; *Oratio in Pisonem* 41.98; *De Partitione Oratoria* 37.131; Ovidius Naso, *Metamorphoses* 6.32; Titus Livius 37.45.7; Suetonius Tranquillus, *Domitianus* 9; Quintilianus, *Institutiones Oratoriae* 1.5.11; 10.1.72. Cf. Lewis and Scott, *A Latin Dictionary*, 1.1968.
50. See also Braund, *Seneca: De clementia*, 414.
51. Seneca, *Clem.* 1.3.2–8.
52. Ibid., 1.9–11.3.
53. Ibid., 1.11.4–13; cf. Copper and Procopé, *Seneca*, 121.
54. Cf. Copper and Procopé, *Seneca*, 124.

Word	Frequency
ignoscere	4
venia	7
clementia	4

This table summarizes the occurrences of the Latin terms that convey the notion of forgiveness in *De clementia* in which the verb *ignoscere* and the noun *venia* appear to be used interchangeably, as we shall see in this chapter.

Clem. 2.7.1

> "But why will he never grant pardon (*ignoscet*)?" Let us now also establish what pardon (*venia*) is, and then we shall realize that it should not be granted by the wise man. Pardon (*venia*) is the remission of a deserved punishment. The reasons why the wise man should not give this are explained at greater length by people who subscribe to this principle. My explanation, to put it briefly, as if in someone else's formulation, is: Pardon (*ignoscitur*) is granted to a person who ought to be punished. Yet the wise man does nothing that he should not do and omits nothing that he should do. Therefore he does not waive a punishment that he ought to exact.[55]

This extract provides an answer to a rhetorical question. Two terms are used in it for what can be understood as pardon or forgiveness[56]: *ignoscere* and *venia*.

Because Seneca appears to use *ignoscere* and *venia* interchangeably to mean something like "forgive" in the sense of remission of a deserved punishment, one might risk generalizing that these two terms were used interchangeably in Seneca's time to convey the same notion; but this needs to be verified. *Ignoscentia*, which does not appear in the selected quotes in Seneca, is another term for the idea of forgiveness. Lewis and Short note that this term is post-classical and very rare.[57] This would reasonably well explain why the term is lacking in *De clementia*. The question

---

55. Seneca, *Clem.* 2.7.1.

56. In this book, "pardon" and "forgiveness" are viewed as synonyms; so also Braund, *Seneca: De clementia*, 30n99.

57. Lewis and Short, *A Latin Dictionary*, 1:882.

for the purposes of this study is whether the actions denoted by *venia* or *ignoscere* can be extended to a fellow human.

Clem. 2.7.2–3

This passage is a continuation of the previous text which has dealt with the rhetorical question of the reason why the wise man should not grant pardon to his fellow human.

> ... In one case, he [the wise man] will simply deliver a verbal reprimand without inflicting a punishment, if he sees that the person's age makes them capable of reform. In another case, where the person is clearly labouring under the odium of his crime, he will tell him to go scot-free, because he was led astray, because he lapsed under the influence of wine. He will let his enemies go unharmed and sometimes even commend them, if they were incited to fight for honourable motives—out of loyalty or because of a treaty or for their liberty—to drive them to war. These are all actions not of pardon (*veniae*) but mercy (*clementia*). Mercy (*clementia*) has a freedom of decision. It forms its judgements not according to the letter of the law but according to what is right and good. And it is allowed to acquit or to set the damages in a case at any level it likes ... But to pardon (*ignoscere*) consists of not punishing a person whom you judge should be punished. Pardon (*venia*) is the remission of a penalty that is due. Clemency's (*clementia*) prime effect is that it pronounces that the people it lets off deserved exactly that. It (*venia*) is more complete and more than honourable.[58]

This text is quite rich semantically on the subject of interpersonal forgiveness. The question of whether or not *venia* or *ignoscere* can be granted to an offender is a crucial one for my purposes. A salient fact is that, in this passage (and elsewhere in *De clementia*), both *ignoscere* and *venia* are connected with *clementia*. Earlier we indicated the difficulty in explaining the complex relationships between *clementia*, *venia* and *ignoscere* in *De clementia*. Seneca strongly maintains, on ethical grounds, that what is represented by *venia* or *ignoscere* should not be granted to a fellow human. For him, granting it clashes with the ethics of a wise man. He stresses the fact that discipline ought to be applied to the guilty person and, therefore, punishment should be endured by them. There seems to

---

58. Seneca, *Clem.* 2.7.2–3.

be some confusion in the way in which Seneca understands the ideas of *venia* and *ignoscere*. Mortureux has also spotted this confusion:

> Lorsqu'il [Sénèque] s'efforce d'expliquer pourquoi il rejette le pardon (*venia*), il n'est pas loin de s'embrouiller dans d'inquiétantes subtilités, affirmant que le sage ne doit pas pardonner, mais doit agir comme s'il pardonnait, tout en ne pardonnant pas.[59]

Confusion in Seneca's reasoning on the notions above is also evident from a clear contradiction which can be observed in a number of places. In *Clem.* 2.7.4–5, for example, he argues that *venia* ought not to be granted.[60] He also states that it is not proper to "forgive" (*ignoscere*) as a general rule. To "forgive" (*ignoscere*) everyone, he maintains, is as much a cruelty as to pardon (*ignoscere*) none.[61] Yet elsewhere in *De clementia* more than once he urges that, in a more honorable way, a wise man could bestow upon his fellow human what they wish to obtain by "forgiveness" (*venia*).

A point of Seneca's confusion in his understanding of *clementia* and *venia*/*ignoscere* seems to be in the fact that he sees these terms as synonyms to the point of sometimes substituting *clementia* with either *venia* or *ignoscere*, or vice versa. Braund, however, speaks of this fact in terms of distinction rather than confusion:

> Seneca ... carefully distinguishes *clementia* from its apparent synonyms, or kindred terms ... *Clementia* is not the same as *misericordia* ... or *mansuetudo* ... or *moderatio* ... or *indulgentia* or *lenitas* or *comitas*. The actions denoted by *venia* ... and *parcere* ... and *ignoscere* ... are not a straight match either ...[62]

A synoptic table is presented on next page with the purpose of illustrating inconsistencies in Seneca's use of *clementia*, *venia* and *ignoscere*. It is quite possible to imagine that this contradiction in Seneca's reasoning was probably due to his Stoic background. Stoics appeared to be notorious for being pitiless. Why? The reason may be that in Stoic eyes, pity was a negative virtue, a kind of malady to avoid. In Seneca's own terms, pity "is no more than a sentimental compassion for the unfortunate, which comes from overestimating the significance of their misfortunes. It is

---

59. Mortureux, *Recherches sur le "De clementia de Sénèque,"* 78.
60. Seneca, *Clem.* 2.7.4–5.
61. Ibid., 1.2.
62. Braund, *Seneca: De clementia*, 188, 272 (cf. table on p. 81 below).

thus an emotional malady, no less than is anger or cruelty . . ."[63] According to Susanna M. Braund, in *De clem.* 2.7.1–3 Seneca is trying to show that criticism of hard-line Stoicism, stated at 2.5.2,[64] does not render the Stoic *sapiens* inhumane.[65] As she has noted, Seneca's argument here is probably feeble.[66] As we shall see below, it contains some confusion.

Clementia can probably be distinguished from *venia* and *ignoscere*. Lewis and Short have proposed that one sense of *clementia* be understood as "forbearance," or more correctly "forbearing conduct towards the errors and faults of others," "clemency," or "mercy."[67] *Clementia* with this meaning occurs elsewhere in secular literature in Latin.[68] So understood, *clementia* is likely a wider concept, which may enclose the idea of *venia*, or *ignoscere*. In her advice to Augustus, Livia suggests to her husband and emperor thus: "Now, find out how clemency (*clementia*) can turn out for you: pardon (*ignosce*) Lucius Cinna."[69] Another point of confusion in Seneca's reasoning on the issue of forgiveness can be found in *Clem.* 1.6.2–3 and 2.7.1 when read against each other. The synoptic table below of these texts may make this possible confusion clearer.

---

63. Seneca, *Clem.* 4.4–5–1.

64. "I realize that among the ill-informed the Stoic school has a negative reputation for being excessively harsh and least likely to give good advice to emperors and kings. It is criticized for saying that the wise man does not show pity or forgiveness (*quod sapientem negat misereri, negat ignoscere*)" (Braund's translation).

65. Braund, *Seneca: De clementia*, 414.

66. Ibid., 415.

67. Lewis and Short, *A Latin Dictionary*, 1:352.

68. E.g., Cicero, *De Inventione rhetorica* 2.54.164; *De officiis* 1.25.88; *Actio in verrem* 2.5.44.115; *Oratio pro rege deiotaro* 15.43; *Oratio pro ligario* 3.10; *Epistulae ad Atticum* 14.19.2; Ovidius Naso, *Metamorphoses* 8.57; Quintilianus, *Institutiones oratoriae* 9.2.28, etc. Cf. Lewis and Short, *A Latin Dictionary*, 1:352.

69. Cf. Seneca, *Clem.* 1.9.6.

Clem. 1.6.2-3	Clem. 2.7.1
... And is anyone more reluctant to grant pardon (*veniam*), I wonder, than a person who has cause to seek it all too often? We have all made mistakes, some of us serious ones, some of us more trivial ones, some on purpose, some by chance impulse or carried away by the wickedness of other people. Some of us have not stood firm enough by our good intentions and have lost our guiltlessness unwillingly and while trying to hold on to it. And it is not only that we have done wrong, but we shall continue to do wrong to the very end of our lives.	"... [W]hy will he never grant pardon (*ignoscet*)?" Let us now also establish what pardon (*venia*) is, and then we shall realize that it should not be granted by the wise man. Pardon (*venia*) is the remission of a deserved punishment ... My explanation, to put it briefly, as if in someone else's formulation, is: Pardon (*ignoscitur*) is granted to a person who ought to be punished. Yet the wise man does nothing that he should not do and omits nothing that he should do. Therefore he does not waive a punishment that he ought to exact.

As one may notice from this comparison, while in *Clem*. 1.6.2–3 Seneca advises his readers not to be reluctant in granting forgiveness (*venia*) to their potential offenders, in *Clem*. 2.7.1, he strongly argues that forgiveness (*ignoscere/venia*) ought not to be granted the offender. This seems to be confusing. It is not without reasoning that Mortureux has described what is going on here in the Seneca passage as "inconsistencies" because of the paradoxical use of the same word in the same piece of work.[70]

The text in the first colon belongs within *Clem*. 1.5–6, a section which describes potential benefits one may gain in practising clemency. One of the motives underlying forgiving is clearly stated: humanness. The implication of this would be that withholding forgiveness to one fellow human is unthinkable, for as human beings, we sometimes also find ourselves in the position of the offender. In this situation, forgiveness most likely looks *primarily* egocentric.

Clem. 1.9.3–7

The passage of *Clem*. 1.9.1–7, 11–12, which contains the text to be surveyed below, belongs to section 9 which is concerned with Cinna's trial, stressing Augustus's approach in an attempt to handle the matter; this was set as an example for Nero to mirror as far as the virtue of forgiveness is concerned. The entire episode of Cinna's trial is made of three

---

70. Mortureux, *Recherches sur le "De clementia de Sénèque,"* 75–83.

main parts: the first part (*Clem.* 1.9.1–5) describes Augustus wondering about which attitude to adopt; the second (*Clem.* 1.9.6) is concerned with Livia's piece of advice to Augustus; and the third (*Clem.* 1.9.7–12) is about what Mortureux has described as "faux dialogue où l'interlocuteur reste muet"[71] because Cinna was not allowed to respond to the charges against him. The episode has reasonably been described as "le récit d'une action judiciaire transformée en action politique."[72] This can be derived from the vocabulary of the text which uses a juridical language throughout.[73]

The background of the story contained in *Clem.* 1.9.1–7, 11–12 is as follows. Augustus is in his forties and is staying in Gaul. The information is brought to him that Lucius Cinna was concocting a plot against him: he was told where, when and how Cinna meant to attack him. Augustus then resolves to inflict revenge upon Cinna and summons a council of his friends. The extract below describes Augustus' feelings on receiving the news, and the action he wished to undertake in this regard.

> ... He [Augustus] spent a disturbed night reflecting that it was a young man of noble birth, otherwise unblemished ... that was to be condemned, and that though he had dictated the proscription edict to Mark Antony ..., he was now unable to kill a single individual. He groaned repeatedly and kept coming out with conflicting exclamations: "So what should I do? Let my assassin walk free while I am full of anxiety? So shall he not pay the penalty? ... What's the point of your staying alive, if your death benefits so many people? When will the reprisals end? Or the bloodshed? For noble young men I am the obvious target for them to sharpen their sword-points. Life is not worth living if so much has to be destroyed so that I can survive." Finally his wife Livia interrupted him and said: "Will you take a woman's advice? Do as the doctors do. When the usual remedies have no effect, they try the opposite. Harshness has done you no good so far. After Salvidienus there was Lepidus, after Lepidus there was Murena, after Murena there was Caepio, after Caepio there was Egnatius, not to mention the others whose great audacity is shameful. Now, find out how clemency (*clementia*) can turn out for you: pardon (*ignosce*) Lucius Cinna. He has been detected— he cannot now do you any harm, but he can enhance your reputation." Augustus was delighted that he had found a supporter

---

71. Ibid., 25.
72. Ibid., 26.
73. For the list of this language, see ibid.

for himself. He promptly thanked his wife, but immediately gave the order to cancel the message to the friends who he had called to conference and summoned Cinna on his own...[74]

The resentment felt by Augustus for the failed conspiracy by Cinna to murder him and his attempt to retaliate are clear underlying factors in the text above. In this context, to do with resentment with an eventual revenge, Livia's request for forgiveness on behalf of Cinna is most likely best understood as an appeal for goodwill from Augustus. Given the fact that this plea seeks merciful restraint from pursuing revenge, *ignoscere* probably means forgive in the sense of bearing with.

It is worth noting that a third party's intervention on behalf of the offender not only manages to move away the offended person's anger, but also spares the offender's life. As was the case with one of the Dionysius accounts (where the third party intervening on behalf of the offender was somebody on the side of the offender[75]), here this third party is somebody on the side of the offended person; and in both cases the lives of the offenders (and their associates) are spared. The difference between the two accounts is striking: while in this Dionysius text the third party's intervention is on request, here in the Seneca text this intervention comes from the third party's own initiative. Both cases seem to suggest the possibility of a common understanding of the demand for seeking forgiveness on behalf of the guilty person. In this narrative, *clementia* is put side by side with *ignoscere*; the two terms are put in Livia's mouth. Here *clementia* appears to be a broader concept than *ignoscere/venia*. The idea of forgiveness is connected with that of honor: forgiveness is said to be for the sake of Augustus' reputation.[76] One of the obvious outcomes of granting forgiveness in this account is a new departure, a departure for both Augustus and Cinna, formerly offended person and offender respectively, and life goes on.

---

74. Seneca, *Clem.* 1.9.3–7.

75. Dionysius, *Ant. Rom.* 8.50.1–4.

76. The honor or reputation language here can be taken as another piece of evidence in support of the reading of honor as one of the core values in Mediterranean societies of the time.

Clem. 1.9.11–12

This text is the last episode of the tension between Augustus and Cinna. It constitutes an indication that Augustus took into account the piece of advice his wife Livia gave him—advice consisting in showing clemency to Cinna for the sake of Augustus' own reputation.

> "For a second time I give you your life, Cinna—the first time it was as an enemy and now it is as a conspirator and assassin. From this day let friendship begin between us. Let us compete with each other to see which of us acts in better faith—I, in granting you your life, or you, in owing it to me." Later on, he conferred the consulship on him unsolicited, complaining of his not venturing to stand for office. He found Cinna most devoted and most loyal . . . He was not the target of any more plots.[77]

Neither *ignoscere* nor *venia* appear in this text. But the idea of forgiveness is evident from the expression "granting life to somebody." Here what can be referred to as forgiveness seems to carry its paradoxical sense of something like "letting go," or what R. D. Enright has aptly described as "the foregoing of resentment or revenge when the wrongdoer's actions deserve it and giving the gifts of mercy, generosity and love when the wrongdoer does not deserve them . . . [T]he overcoming of wrongdoing with good."[78] In fact, Cinna did deserve death; he is granted life instead through Augustus' tolerance and generosity.

In this text, self-orientated reasons clearly underlie Augustus' patience and act of generosity in tolerating Cinna's deviant behavior: Augustus forgave Cinna to save his own reputation—not as a way of avoiding incurring the indignation of the deities as in Dionysius.[79] More to the point, the text above relates the notion of forgiveness to the ideas of friendship and safety. As a result of this act of generosity, strong friendship and a new relationship between the then enemies begins. It is easy here to see the idea of turning one's enemy to some profitable use, an idea which Plutarch has developed in two arguments in his *How to Profit by One's Enemies*.[80]

---

77. Seneca, *Clem.* 1.9.11–12.

78. Enright, "Forgiveness." Online: http://www.forgiveness-institute.org/html/about_forgiveness.htm.

79. Dionysius, *Ant. Rom.* 8.50.1–4.

80. Plutarch, *Moralia: How to Profit by One's Enemies* 91a–b; 91.10f–92a.

Conclusions

What the synopsis of the Senecan texts has provided can be summed up as follows. It is quite possible to imagine that for Seneca and his first readers, *ignoscere* and *venia* meant something like "forgive" in the sense of remission, or letting off, or forbearance, or mercy. Also, in Seneca forgiving seems to be a means of saving one's own reputation and of securing one's own safety and security through friendship.[81] The following emerges from the Seneca texts surveyed in this chapter. The forgiveness sought is granted as honorable practice from the offended person's point of view.[82] This granting of forgiveness is *essentially* stirred by the disposition of the deities to forgive humans, as well as by the worthlessness of humankind—all humans are sinners and are forgiveness seekers.[83] Also, the *self-oriented* motivations of forgiveness seem to be present in Seneca's thinking. As was the case with Dionysius, in Seneca, forgiving appears to be something which primarily benefits the forgiver.[84] However, while in Dionysius forgiving is meant to avoid incurring the indignation of the deities, who themselves are willing to forgive humans and be reconciled with them, in Seneca the forgiver's reputation is part of the reasons for forgiving. Besides, in Seneca the granting of forgiveness is variable; it is dependent on the circumstances and the character of the offender(s).[85] Hardly ever is a third party involved in the process of seeking forgiveness; intervention on behalf of the offender manages to move away the offended person's anger, and also spares the offender's life.[86] A similar scenario can be observed in one Dionysius example where the third party intervening on behalf of the offender was somebody on the side of the offender.[87] Rarely is an attempt by the injured person to retaliate observed in the Senecan text.[88] Thirdly, the outcome of forgiving brings a kind of harmony to the relationships between the two parties.[89]

---

81. Seneca, *Clem.* 1.9.1–7; 1.9.11–12; so also Plutarch, *Moralia*, 91a–b; 91.10f–92a.
82. Seneca, *Clem.* 1.6.3–4; 1.9.1–7; 1.9.11; 2.7.1–2; 2.7.2–3; 2.7.3–4.
83. Ibid., 1.6.3–4.
84. Ibid., 1.9.11.
85. Ibid., 2.7.3–4.
86. Ibid., 1.9.1–7.
87. Dionysius, *Ant. Rom.* 8.50.1–4.
88. Seneca, *Clem.* 1.9.1–7.
89. Ibid., 1.9.11.

CONCLUSIONS

A survey of the representative writings of Dionysius and Seneca has shown that forgiveness was a recurrent theme outside Jewish and Christian religions in the Graeco-Roman world. In addition to the use of the concept itself, four Greek terms (ἀφίημι, ἄφεσις, συγγινώσκω, and συγγνώμη) and their two Latin counter-parts (*ignoscere* and *venia*) were mainly used in the rhetoric of forgiveness in Dionysius and Seneca respectively. With all probability, what can be understood as "forgive" most likely had the following three ranges of meanings in the material from these two authors: the first range includes causing something to undergo separation (remission, or removal, or putting away, or letting off something); the second range includes a feeling (forbearance, or tolerance); and the third range includes abandonment or giving up (letting go, or forgetting about). Although it is not certain to produce a unifying forgiveness pattern from the Dionysius and Seneca selected extracts surveyed, the following forgiveness pattern tends to be invariable throughout .

Dionysius Data	Seneca Data
[1] A wrong is committed. [2] The offender, or the one acting on their behalf, seeks forgiveness. [3] The offended person grants forgiveness as: • an honorable practice, stemming from both awareness of humans' inclination to evil and God's (or the deities') forgiving disposition; • a way of avoiding incurring the indignation of the deities who themselves are disposed to forgive humans and be reconciled with them.	[1] A wrong is committed. [2] The offender, or the one acting on their behalf, seeks forgiveness. [3] The offended person grants forgiveness as: • an honorable practice, stemming from both awareness of humans' inclination to evil and God's (or the deities') forgiving disposition; • for the sake of their own honour.

As this table shows, both in Dionysius and in Seneca seeking forgiveness is the initiative of the offender. This feature seems to stress the offending person's desperation for seeking forgiveness. On the other hand, forgiving looks like an appropriate moral act toward the offender: forgiving is an appropriate moral act, stemming from the deities' disposition to forgive humans, as well as the humans' inclination to evil. The question remains whether the same scenario can be found in Matthew's texts. One of the main tasks of chapters 5 and 6 would be to verify this. It is worth noting that in Dionysius and in Seneca, the demand for satisfaction, or the obligation for reparation, as a prerequisite or a corroboration of the offer of forgiveness, is variable: it is dependent upon the kind of person the offended person is. This demand may be useful in understanding why reparation (or penalty) does not emerge in Matthew as a prerequisite (or as corroboration) for granting forgiveness. Besides, neither of the two authors above is concerned with what will happen to the unforgiving person.

4

The Rhetoric of Interpersonal Forgiveness in Jewish Literature in Greek

The present chapter explores the rhetoric of forgiveness in Jewish literature in Greek as represented by the LXX, and the writings of Philo and Josephus. The theme of interpersonal forgiveness is discussed in these materials. The notion of forgiveness is stated quite directly in these passages with the use of various terms that denote interpersonal interrelationships, these terms being ἀφίημι/ἄφεσις, συγγινώσκω/συγγνώμη, αἴρω, δέχομαι, λύω, and προσδέχομαι. (Some of the texts to be surveyed in this chapter, although not specifically on interpersonal forgiveness, are brought into the work because they are likely to contribute to the understanding of the nature of forgiveness and the character of God, the forgiver *per excellence* to be emulated in the *praxis* of forgiveness.) In an attempt to draw a plausible meaning of what can be understood as forgiveness from these data, due attention will once more be paid to the text, the co-text, the inter-texts, and the context. These materials will be read with the aim of discerning their understanding of the dynamic of human forgiveness and of drawing out a possible pattern of forgiveness to be compared with its pattern in Matthew.

Tables will be used to show the occurrences of the terms for forgiveness, and where crucial their cognates, as found in the literature above. This chapter is structured around three sections, examining the rhetoric of forgiveness in the LXX, Philo, and Josephus respectively. A conclusion then is drawn from the entire chapter, presenting a summary for the findings to be taken up in chapters 5 and 6.

THE RHETORIC OF INTERPERSONAL FORGIVENESS IN THE LXX

Interpersonal forgiveness is one of the themes discussed in the LXX. For its expression of the concept, the LXX uses five terms in the rhetoric of interpersonal forgiveness: αἴρω, ἀφίημι, δέχομαι, λύω, and προσδέχομαι. Of these terms, ἀφίημι is the most used term in the LXX's focused interpersonal forgiveness texts, being deployed three times in them. The table below shows all the relevant occurrences of these verbs in the LXX forgiveness texts surveyed for the purpose of this study.

Word	Occurrence
αἴρω	2
ἀφίημι	3
δέχομαι	1
λύω	1
προσδέχομαι	1

It is interesting to observe the absence in the LXX of συγγινώσκω, the other key term for forgiveness in Jewish literature in Greek. The reason underlying its absence in the LXX remains a question. Following are the key LXX texts for the purposes of this study. They are Gen 50:15–21; Exod 10:16–20; 1 Sam 15; 1 Sam 25; 1 Macc 13:36–40; and Sir 28:1–7. In them the Greek terms used for forgiveness appear in a range of senses.

Gen 50:15–21

This text is the last episode of a family relationship tension between Joseph and his brothers.

> 15When they realized that their father was dead, the brothers of Joseph said, "What if Joseph still hate us and pays us back for all the evil that we did to him!" 16So they approached Joseph, saying, "Your father gave this instruction before he died, 17'Say to Joseph: I implore you, please let go the crime of your

brothers and the wrong they did in harming you.' (ἄφες αὐτοῖς τὴν ἀδικίαν καὶ τὴν ἁμαρτίαν αὐτῶν) Now, please accept graciously the crime of the servants of the God of your father." (δέξαι τὴν ἀδικίαν τῶν θεραπόντων τοῦ θεοῦ τοῦ πατρός σου) Joseph wept when they spoke to him. 18Then his brothers also wept and fell down before him and said, "Behold, we are here as your slaves." 19Joseph said to them, "Do not be afraid! Am I in the place of God? 20Even though you intended to do harm to me, God intended it for good, in order to preserve a numerous people, as he is doing today. 21So have no fear; I myself will provide for you and your little ones." And he comforted them, speaking kindly to them.

Ἀφίημι is used in this narrative in the context of family relationship conflict. This verb is used with a pair of accusatives of direct object (τὴν ἀδικίαν καὶ τὴν ἁμαρτίαν). It is for the crime (τὴν ἀδικίαν) and the wrong done (τὴν ἁμαρτίαν) that ἀφίημι is sought.

Ἀφίημι is used in the LXX to translate fifteen Hebrew verbs, and ἄφεσις thirteen Hebrew words.[1] The range of the meanings of ἀφίημι in the LXX and its cognate noun includes to "let go," "leave," "leave alone" (2 Sam 16:11), "give up," "leave behind" (2 Sam 15:16; 20:3), "allow" (2 Sam 16:11), "leave over something" (Ps 17:14), "release" (Deut 15:2), "spare" (Gen 18:26), "bear" (Gen 4:13), and "forgive."[2] Interestingly, ἀφίημι is used sparsely of forgiving. The verb with this sense occurs only eighteen times in the LXX: in the Pentateuch (Gen 50:17; Exod 32:32; Lev 4:20; 5:10, 13; Num 14:19; 15:25, 26, 28), in Wisdom literature (Pss 25:11; 32:1, 5; 85:2), in the Prophets (Isa 22:14; 33:24; 55:7), and in deuterocanonical literature (1 Macc 13:37; Sir 28:2). These instances may seem abundant; yet, it is also true that they are still minor compared to all the occurrences of ἀφίημι in the LXX with other senses. On this Vorländer, for example, argues that where ἀφίημι occurs, it usually renders three Hebrew verbs נשא or סלח and כפר.[3] Why the LXX translates three different Hebrew verbs by a single Greek word ἀφίημι is unclear. Regarding ἄφεσις, which does not occur in Gen 50:15–21, it appears more than fifty times elsewhere in the LXX.[4]

---

1. Cf. Hatch and Redpath, eds., *A Concordance to the Septuagint and the Other Greek Versions of the Old Testament*, 183.

2. Ibid.; see also Vorländer, "Forgiveness," 1:698.

3. Vorländer, "Forgiveness," 1:698.

4. See the statistics in Hatch and Redpath, eds. *A Concordance to the Septuagint and the Other Greek Versions of the Old Testament*, 183–84.

To return to the rhetoric of forgiveness in Gen 50:15–21, this text appears in the broader context of family relational tension, a tension which is finally resolved. This tension had been between Joseph and his brothers; their relationship had been damaged because of his brothers' unfair treatment of him in the past. In actual fact, Joseph was ready to be reconciled with them, as is clear from his deeds and words recorded in Gen 45. They never asked for forgiveness, and so, "their feelings of guilt had continued to haunt them."[5] Now with their father Jacob dead, they are anxious that their past treatment of Joseph will come back to trouble them. To use Wenham's words, "they are gripped by fear that all Joseph had done [Gen 45] was motivated by affection for Jacob, not out of real love for them."[6] They decide to plead for forgiveness. They are so worried that they put some words into their recently deceased father's mouth, reporting his instruction that Joseph forgive them.

As Reimer has correctly noted, the reader does not have certain knowledge about the truth of this claim, but one is hesitant to accept it at face value.[7] In any case, interestingly, the aim of the appeal is to seek forgiveness. In Gen 50:15–21, two terms are used to describe the object of this appeal: ἀφίημι and δέχομαι. The semantic range of meanings of δέχομαι includes to "take," "accept graciously," "understand," "receive," and "welcome."[8] The meaning of "accept graciously" for δέχομαι seems to fit best the co-text of Gen 50:17, to do with alleged hatred by Joseph. In this situation, ἀφίημι is best understood as something like to "let go," and δέχομαι as to "accept graciously" the offences. Following their crime against Joseph, his brothers implore that their offences *be let go*, that he foregoes his potential resentment and any potential intent to accept graciously the situation. They are, thus, appealing for his mercy to tolerate and to overcome their wrongdoing with good. In this text, the offending party is actively involved in the forgiveness-seeking process. The idea that seeking forgiveness is part of the offender's responsibilities[9] abounds in Judaism.[10]

---

5. Wenham, *Genesis*, 489.

6. Ibid.

7. Reimer, "Stories of Forgiveness," 369; see also Sternberg, *The Poetics of Biblical Narrative*, 379.

8. Liddell and Scott, *A Greek-English Lexicon*, 382.

9. The term "responsibility" with regard to interpersonal forgiveness passages surveyed in this work means that no onus is placed on the offended person.

10. E.g., in LXX (in Exod 10:16–20, Pharaoh seeks forgiveness; in 1 Sam 25:26–28, Abigail (a third party) does so on behalf of her husband Nabal), in rabbinic literature

Exod 10:16–17

> 16Pharaoh hurriedly summoned Moses and Aaron and said, "I have sinned against the Lord your God and against you. 17Please receive favorably my sin (προσδέξασθε οὖν μου τὴν ἁμαρτίαν) once more, and pray to the Lord your God that he may take away from me this deadly thing."

In this text the author of Exodus puts προσδέχομαι in Pharaoh's mouth to convey the idea of forgive: Pharaoh is said to seek forgiveness for his ἁμαρτίαν (sin). The range of meanings of προσδέχομαι includes to "receive favorably," "accept and admit" an argument.[11] The co-text of verse 17, to do with desperation, seems to require that προσδέχομαι be understood to mean something like "forgive" in the sense of receiving favorably the sin. Pharaoh does admit that he has wronged not only Moses, but most importantly Moses' God Yahweh himself. His request to Moses implores favor from the God of Moses and Aaron. What this wrong consists of can be found in Exod 10:10–11. John I. Durham has commented thus: "Pharaoh's angry suspicion of Moses' motives and his peremptory ejection of Moses from his presence."[12] This account links the idea of forgiveness with that of repentance. Pharaoh does acknowledge his sin both against God and God's servants (Moses and Aaron). He seeks his sin to be received favorably, imploring Moses and Aaron to plead with God on his behalf.

1 Sam 15:24–25

This text offers a tragic story. The text runs as follows:

> 24Then Saul said to Samuel, "I have sinned; for I have transgressed the commandment of the Lord and your words, because I feared the people and obeyed their voice. 25Now I beg you, take away my sin (ἆρον τὸ ἁμάρτημά μου) and return with me, so that I may worship the Lord."

(*m. Yoma* 8.9; *y. Yoma* 45c, a person seeking forgiveness from the one offended against is said to bring others into the picture if their own private attempts at appeasement are unsuccessful; *b. Yoma* 86b–87a), etc.

11. Liddell and Scott, *A Greek-English Lexicon*, 1505.
12. Durham, *Exodus*, 137.

The Rhetoric of Interpersonal Forgiveness in Jewish Literature in Greek

The setting of the story is as follows. Yahweh gives instructions to Saul through Samuel to completely erase the Amalekites. This is all but done. Saul, however, spares Agag, the Amalekite King (vv. 9, 20); the people on their part spare the best of the livestock (vv. 9, 15, 21). In this way, Yahweh's instructions are rejected (v. 23) in the sense that they are not followed carefully. As a result of this, Saul is also rejected by Yahweh. When Samuel takes the opportunity to explain this to Saul, Saul protests (vv. 15–23). But Samuel's message finally gets through. It is then that Saul repents (vv. 24–25). But is there still chance for him? No; it is too late (vv. 26, 28–29, 35).

Αἴρω is used in this story to convey the idea of what can be understood as forgive. The range of senses of αἴρω includes to "lift," "take up and bear," "remove," "take away," and "put an end to."[13] The co-text of verse 25, to do with fear for the consequences of the transgression, seems to require that αἴρω be understood to mean something like to "take away" something from the offender. Saul has offended the Lord, and he is rejected by him. What he implores is possibly the removal of his sin.

Interestingly, αἴρω appears in the context of divine-human and interpersonal relationships. Saul realizes that, because of his sin, he has lost fellowship both with God and with Samuel (God's representative). He thinks that the only solution to his trouble is to seek forgiveness through Samuel. Forgiveness in this circumstance quite likely involves an attitude (or lack of it) on the part of the offended person. As far as Saul is concerned, it was too late for him, despite his insistence and the apparent reason behind this (vv. 25, 30, 31). Commenting on this, Reimer writes, "Now this may be simply Saul's code for joining in with the people in the victory feast, but in any case it does not alter the result. He is rejected as king; he will die in shame; his son will not succeed him."[14] Samuel can do nothing on behalf of Saul, for Yahweh has decided (v. 29).

1 Sam 25:26–28

This text gives an account of a tension between David and Nabal, a tension which involves a third party, Abigail.

> 26Now then, my lord, as the Lord lives and as your soul lives, since the Lord has restrained you from bloodguilt and from

---

13. Liddell and Scott, *A Greek-English Lexicon*, 27.
14. Reimer, "Stories of Forgiveness," 374.

> taking vengeance with your own hand, now let your enemies and those who seek to do evil to my lord be like Nabal. 27And now let this present that your maidservant has brought to my lord be given to the young men who follow my lord. 28Please take away the trespass of your maidservant (ἆρον τὸ ἀνόμημα τῆς δούλης σου); for the Lord will certainly make my lord a sure house, because my lord is fighting the battles of the Lord; and evil shall not be found in you so long as you live.

Abigail is in effect trying to obtain forgiveness for Nabal's action, but her *words* as cited and translated above only ask for forgiveness for her own action. She is, however, implicitly accepting that she is (unwilling and unwitting) involved in her husband's act. As it stands in our text, the narrated *action* by Abigail seeks to avert vengeance; the *words* Abigail uses seem to refer only to her own action. The setting of the account is this: David is desperately in need of food for his hungry band of four hundred men. He sends some of his men to Nabal to seek food. Nabal's reply to David's request is negative; from David's perspective, it is an insult. Abigail (Nabal's wife), having been informed of her husband's hostility toward David, takes the risk of trying to solve the matter herself. Verses 26–28 are a description of the tactics she employed: she sends ahead gifts, abases herself at David's feet and speaks of her servanthood with firmness, asking him to let go her trespass.

This strategy in effect seeks forgiveness for Nabal's behavior. With her wisdom, Abigail manages to prevent David from what J. P. Fokkelman describes as "acting on his destructive impulse."[15] It prevents David from something which could have discredited him, namely, "guilt from shedding blood—no matter how justified it might seem to be in this case."[16] But, as Ralph W. Klein has also noticed, "the real protector of the future king's integrity is Yahweh himself"[17]—not Abigail as such. Here, as in some of the previous examples, the common verb ἀφίημι is not used in the rhetoric of forgiveness. It has given place to αἴρω. In this narrative, the seeking of forgiveness is said to be for τὸ ἀνόμημα (the trespass). As to the meaning of αἴρω, the context of the story seems to suggest that here this verb be understood to mean something like taking away the wrong done. Therefore, in this circumstance, asking that Abigail's trespass be forgiven is appealing for David's mercy that an end be put to her wrong.

---

15. Fokkelman, *Narrative Art and Poetry in the Books of Samuel*, 2:473.
16. Klein, *1 Samuel*, 250.
17. Ibid.

The following observation emerges from the text under scrutiny. One person has wronged another; a punitive action against the offender is about to take place; a third party intervenes on behalf of the offender (and ironically on her own behalf) in the forgiveness seeking process; the initiative of intervening is that of the third party, who uses gifts in an attempt to secure forgiveness; forgiveness is granted and looks like a gift which spares the life of the offender: David does not kill Nabal, but God does shortly after. As with the Pharaoh-Moses/Aaron account (Exod 10:16–17) and the Saul-Samuel account (1 Sam 15:24–25), here also the third party's role in the forgiveness seeking process is massive. The difference, however, is that in the former this role is played on the request of the offender; whereas in the latter, the third party's role is her initiative.

1 Macc 13:36–40

This text gives an account of a tension between the Jews and the Seleucids.

> 36King Demetrius to Simon, the high priest and friend of kings, and to the elders and nation of the Jews, greetings! 37We have received the gold crown and the palm branch that you sent, and we are ready to make a general peace with you and to write to our officials to grant you release from tribute (ἀφιέναι ὑμῖν τὰ ἀφέματα). 38All the grants that we have made to you remain valid, and let the strongholds that you have built be your possession. 39We cancel any errors and offenses committed (ἀφίεμεν ἀγνοήματα καὶ τὰ ἁμαρτήματα) to this day, and cancel the crown tax that you owe; whatever other tax has been collected in Jerusalem shall be collected no longer. 40If any of you are qualified to be enrolled in our bodyguard, let them be enrolled; let there be peace between us.

The setting of this narrative is the conflict between the Jews (represented by Simon and the Jewish troops) and the Seleucids (represented by Trypho and the Seleucid troops). The young king Antiochus of Syria has just been killed by Trypho. As a result of this, Trypho becomes the king in the place of Antiochus. Simon, supporting the king Demetrius against Trypho, sends envoys to Demetrius with the plea for the relief from tributes and certain types of taxes. The relief is granted Israel. In this narrative, ἀφίημι is used twice: in the first case, τὰ ἀφέματα are said to be released from; in the second case, ἀγνοήματα (errors made in ignorance) and ἁμαρτήματα (offences) are said to be cancelled. In both cases, the focus is clearly on that which is been released from and cancelled, rather than on authors of the wrong. The co-text of the sentence, as shown above, seems to call for the sense of *release* for ἀφίημι in the first case, and for that of *cancel* in the second case. From the point of view of King Demetrius, the offer of release from tribute, following the Jews' presents in an attempt to secure reconciliation and peace, can be understood as an expression of goodwill. This is indicative of the fact that Demetrius has given up his resentment when the Jews' actions of the past deserve it, and has given the gifts of mercy and generosity when the Jews do not deserve them, so to speak.

The following forgiveness pattern is evident from this story. One party has wronged another; the offending party does seek forgiveness as part of their duty (they plead for mercy and forgiveness); and gifts accompany the forgiveness seeking process. The last feature of the pattern is similar to the one found in the David-Abigail/Nabal account in 1 Sam 25:26–28 (cp. the Jacob-Esau account in Gen 32–33) in which gifts are a part of the strategy for seeking forgiveness. Further, the dynamic in the story quoted above is like the one in the Pharaoh-Moses/Aaron account insofar as a third party is involved in the forgiveness seeking process. However, it should be highlighted that in the Pharaoh-Moses/Aaron account, the initiative in seeking forgiveness is taken by the author of the offence themselves (Pharaoh); whereas in the David-Abigail/Nabal story, this initiative is taken by a third party (Abigail).

Sir 28:1–7

This text uses ἀφίημι and λύω to convey the idea of forgiving. Verses 1–4 are most relevant for the purposes of this study; it reads as follows:

> 1The vengeful person will face the Lord's vengeance, for he keeps an exacting account of their sins. 2Remit your neighbor the wrong they have done (ἄφες ἀδίκημα τῷ πλησίον[18] σου), and then your sins will be remitted when you pray (δεηθέντος σου αἱ ἁμαρτίαι σου λυθήσονται). 3Does anyone harbor anger against another and expect healing from the Lord? 4If one has no mercy towards another like themselves, can they then seek

---

18. Note grammatical oddity of τῷ πλησίον; thanks to Dr Peter Oakes and Prof. George Brooke for having brought to the attention of the present author that this word is used widely in its adverbial (accusative) form as an indeclinable noun.

forgiveness for their own sin? (καὶ περὶ τῶν ἁμαρτιῶν αὐτοῦ δεῖται;)

The co-text of this passage, 27:30–28:11, addresses various related issues. It is part of a larger literary unit 27:22–28:26 in which we have a series of poems on various topics: first is malice (27:22–27); second are anger and vengeance (27:28–28:1); third is forgiveness (28:2–7); fourth is quarrelling (28:8–11); and fifth, lastly, evils of the tongue (28:12–16; 28:17–26). As to the poem in 28:2–7, it addresses the duty of forgiving and not holding grudges, as P. W. Skehan has also noted.[19] Two verbs are used in the passage cited above to convey the idea of forgiveness: ἀφίημι and λύω. As noted earlier, this is the sole explicit LXX text in which forgiving is shown as a condition for both seeking and receiving God's forgiveness. In this text, πλησίος (the person, neighbour) and ἀδίκημα or ἁμαρτίαι (sin(s) are direct objects of the verbs. As to λύω, its range of meanings includes to "loose," "untie," "set free," "release," and "deliver."[20] The co-text of Sir 28:2, to do with God's vengeance hanging over the vengeful and unforgiving person, demands that both ἀφίημι and λύω be understood to mean something like to "forgive" in the sense of remit.

The concept of reciprocity and the link between mercy and forgiveness is plain in Sir 28:1–7. The petitioner forgiving others is clearly linked with the Lord forgiving them. Stated rhetorically, it is unthinkable that the unmerciful person can dare to seek God's forgiveness and expect to receive it; for, as Reimer has clearly stated, "Those who lack mercy obstruct forgiveness from God when they seek it."[21] As J. L. Crenshaw has also observed, verses 2–5 insist that anyone who desires forgiveness from the Lord must first exercise that compassion toward their fellow human beings, including their enemies.[22] And this desire for God's forgiveness is here interestingly set in the context of prayer.

Aspects of the teaching about forgiveness contained in Sir 28:1–7 (esp. 2–4) are similar to its teaching in Matthew (6:12, 14–15; 18:32–35), in Mark (11:25), in Luke (11:4) and in James (2:13). Significantly, as just observed, both in Sir 28 and in Matt 6:12, 14–15, the idea of conditionality in divine-human forgiveness emerges in the context of prayer. This phenomenon can also be observed both in Mark 11:25 and in Luke 11:2–4,

---

19. Skehan and Di Lella, *The Wisdom of Ben Sira*, 362.
20. Liddell and Scott, *A Greek-English Lexicon*, 1068–69.
21. Reimer, "The Apocrypha and Biblical Theology," 276–77.
22. Crenshaw, "The Book of Sirach," 5:772.

in which the forgiveness motif emerges in the same setting. Further, in LXX Exod 10:16–17, for example, we read that after Pharaoh had sinned against God and God's servants (Moses and Aaron), he acknowledged his sin and implored that this sin be removed from him. His request to Moses and Aaron to plead with God on his behalf anticipates the fact that Moses and Aaron will present his plea to their God in prayer. The connection between forgiveness and prayer thus has an obvious Jewish foundation. In Sir 28:1–7, disgrace, anger, and wrath are associated with unforgiving people. The stress of God's vengeance is on those who eventually fail to forgive their fellow humans. It is this same stress which quite obviously underlies the teaching in Matt 18:23–35, as we shall see in chapter 6.

Conclusions

A survey of the LXX material above has shown that interpersonal forgiveness is discussed in the LXX. In addition to the use of the concept itself, this theme is expressed in five Greek terms: αἴρω, ἀφίημι, δέχομαι, λύω, and προσδέχομαι. Taken together the results suggest that the LXX readers of the first-century CE probably understood these terms to mean something like forgiveness in the following range of meanings. First is the sense of causing something to undergo separation or removal (e.g., 1 Sam 15:25 where αἴρω is best understood as "take away," 1 Macc 13:37 where ἀφίημι can be translated "release"). Second is abandonment or leaving something (e.g., Gen 50:17 where ἀφίημι seems to mean "leave behind," or "let go," 1 Sam 25:28 where αἴρω can be understood to mean "cancel," 1 Macc 13:38 where ἀφίημι can be understood as "remit," and Sir 28:2 where ἀφίημι can be translated "remit"). Third is the sense of acceptance (e.g., Exod 10:17 where προσδέχομαι can be understood as "receive favourably"). It is quite clear that in all the LXX examples surveyed, the impersonal object of the verbs, which are used to convey the idea of forgiving, is in view.

The following typical forgiveness pattern from the LXX texts surveyed in this chapter is apparent and constant. Firstly, one party having wronged another, as well as the seriousness of the injury, are the underlying factors (Gen 50:15–21; Exod 10:16–20; 1 Sam 15:24–25; 25:26–28; 1 Macc 13:36–40). Secondly, fear for potential retaliation or a punitive action motivates the seeking of forgiveness by the offender themselves or by a third party acting on their behalf. In Gen 50:15–21, for example, we read

The Rhetoric of Interpersonal Forgiveness in Jewish Literature in Greek 99

that the suspicion and fear of Joseph's brothers for reprisals continued even after the death of their father (cp. Exod 10:16–20; 1 Sam 15:24–25; 25:26–28; 1 Macc 13:36–40). Thirdly, seeking forgiveness appears as part of the responsibility of the offender, or of the third party acting on their behalf. In Gen 50:15–21, for example, having acknowledged their faults, Joseph's brothers abase themselves and come to Joseph, claiming that before he died, Jacob had left specific instruction about the necessity for Joseph to forgive them (cp. Exod 10:16–20; 1 Sam 15:24–25; 25:26–28; 1 Macc 13:36–40, the offenders plead for mercy). Acknowledging one's faults and pleading for mercy does clearly highlight the offender's responsibility for seeking forgiveness.

Fourthly, a third party may be involved in the forgiveness seeking process (Exod 10:16–20; 1 Sam 15:24–25; 25:26–28). The third party's role in this process is massive, as is evident from the Pharaoh-Moses/Aaron account in Exod 10:16–17 and from that of Saul-Samuel in 1 Sam 15:24–25. The difference, however, is that while in the former this role is played on the offender's request in the latter Abigail's role is her personal initiative. The involvement of a third party in the forgiveness seeking process in the LXX texts studied in this work can also be observed in the texts on interpersonal forgiveness in Dionysius[23] and in Seneca[24] surveyed in chapter 3 of this book. This seems to stress the third party's role in the forgiveness seeking process whether in religious and secular circles. Fifthly, the granting of forgiveness looks like an act of generosity from the perspective of the offended person; forgiveness is granted unconditionally (Gen 50:15–21; Exod 10:16–20; 1 Sam 25:26–28 [1 Macc 13:36–40 is probably an exception]). Forgiveness is a gift which spares the life of the offender; in 1 Sam 25:26–28, for example, David does not kill Nabal at all, but God does shortly after (cf. also the Pharaoh-Moses/Aaron account in Exod 10:16–20). Sixthly, when forgiveness is granted, the danger is driven away for the offender, and the fullness of life is restored for them (Exod 10:16–20). The granting of forgiveness ends the circle of hostility between the opponent parties (1 Macc 13:36–40). This dynamic can be observed in the David-Abigail/Nabal account in 1 Sam 25:26–28 and in that of Jacob-Esau in Gen 32–33.

A few particularities in the LXX passages surveyed with regard to interpersonal forgiveness which seem not to fit the forgiveness pattern

---

23. Dionysius, *Ant. Rom.* 8.50.5.
24. Seneca, *Clem.* 1.9.1–7.

just described need noting. First, gifts seldom accompany the seeking of forgiveness (1 Sam 25:26–28). Second, a penalty is not often imposed as satisfaction for the offence of the past (1 Macc 13:36–40). Third, forgiveness is rarely denied; but when it is, heavy consequences on the offender are observed—the denial of forgiveness does cost the offender his life (1 Sam 15:24–25). It is quite striking that in the Saul-Samuel account in 1 Sam 15:24–25, forgiveness is denied despite the offender's attitude and approach in his attempt to seeking forgiveness and despite the offended person being God. Fourth, and more importantly, forgiving appears as an act which is demanded of the offended person in Sir 28:1-4. In this text, forgiving is demanded, stemming from the inevitability of humans' inclination to evil, therefore, their constant need to secure forgiveness for themselves. This feature is observed nowhere else in the LXX. Sir 28:1-4 may thus be helpful for our understanding of the two key Matthean interpersonal forgiveness texts, and precisely Matthew's focus on the offended person's obligation toward the person who has sinned against them (6:12, 14–15; 18:15–17, 21–35). In Sir 28:1-7, however, nothing quite definite is said of what will happen to the potential unforgiving person: in verse 1 we read that the actively vengeful will face God's vengeance; this vengeful person can be understood to refer to anybody who fails to forgive their fellow humans. In Matthew, what will happen to them is clearly stated: they will be punished. It is punishment which is the main concern in 18:23–35, as we shall see later (ch. 6). The question remains whether Sir 28:1-4 can be regarded as the basis for the parable in Matt 18:23–35, as is sometimes suggested.[25]

It comes therefore as something of a surprise that teaching about conditionality in divine-human forgiveness is nonexistent in the Hebrew Bible, and it is also rare in the LXX. Does this mean that this teaching is absent in Jewish thought at all? The examination of the interpersonal forgiveness theme in Philo and in Josephus may provide a partial answer.

THE RHETORIC OF INTERPERSONAL FORGIVENESS IN PHILO

There are sound reasons behind the choice of Philo of Alexandria. First, he is one of the two last great Jewish writers in Greek in antiquity whose

---

25. E.g., Reimer has suggested that Sir 28:4 as a possible basis for the parable of Matt 18:23–35 (cf. Reimer, "The Apocrypha and Biblical Theology," 277–79).

The Rhetoric of Interpersonal Forgiveness in Jewish Literature in Greek 101

work has survived, the other being Josephus. Second, he is a contemporary of the author of the first canonical gospel. Third, the interpersonal forgiveness motif abounds in his writings. Fourth, as J. K. Aitken has also written, he interpreted and expounded the Greek Bible, reading it in terms of Greek (and especially Stoic) philosophy.[26]

Philo is a first-century CE Hellenistic Jewish biblical exegete, philosopher, and thinker. Although the exact dates of his birth and death are unknown, it is generally admitted that he was born between 20–15 BCE and died around 50 CE. Bringing together Jewish tradition and Greek philosophy is recognized as one of his legacies: Philo seems to have been deeply loyal to the Jewish scriptures, religion, and people, as well as thoroughly familiar with Greek philosophy, learning, and culture.[27] A prominent and wealthy member of the Jewish community, he was an apologist for Judaism in a rich Hellenistic culture. His aim was to interpret a non-rabbinic Judaism in terms of Platonic philosophy. Although he was a Jew, Philo's writings plainly show that he received a Greek education and that he possessed a command of Greek language, literary style, and philosophy. He appears to have reflected more firsthand knowledge of Hellenistic culture in general and Greek philosophy in particular than any other known Hellenistic Jewish writer. He is also considered by many scholars as a forerunner of early Christian thought.[28]

Most of Philo's works are commentaries on the Greek Pentateuch, whose authority he seems to have considered equal to the Hebrew original. Philo retells biblical narratives and discusses laws. Both retelling these narratives and discussing laws by Philo seem to suggest he may have assumed that his readers had little or no knowledge of Jewish Scripture or practice.[29] The selected forgiveness extracts below are his retelling of the biblical narratives. These texts are taken from two pieces of his work: first is *On the Special Laws*, and second *On Rewards and Punishments*. Both pieces of works were chosen because the theme of interpersonal forgiveness is discussed in them. In them three terms are used for the notion of forgiveness, namely, συγγνώμη, παραίτησις, and ἀμνηστία. It

---

26. Aitken, "Jewish Tradition and Culture," 89; see also Goodman, "Philo Judaeus," 675–76; Roberts, "Philon (2), 'Philo,'" 563.

27. Birnbaum, "Philo of Alexandria," 512.

28. Browning, "Philo"; see also Borgen, "Philo of Alexandria," 97–154; "Philo of Alexandria," 233–82.

29. Birnbaum, "Philo of Alexandria," 512.

is interesting to note that only συγγνώμη is prominent in the Philonic texts surveyed.

Word	Occurrence
συγγνώμη	4
παραίτησις	2
ἀμνηστία	1

Laws 1.67

This text is Philo's re-writing of Deut 12:5–7, 11–14, 17–18. It reads as follows:

> There is also the temple made by hands; for it was right that no check should be given to the forwardness of those who pay their tribute to piety and desire by means of sacrifices either to give thanks for the blessings that befall them or to ask for forgiveness and pardon for their sins (ἁμαρτάνωσι συγγνώμην καὶ παραίτησιν αἰτεῖσθαι). But he [Moses] provided that there should not be temples built either in many places or many in the same place, for he judged that since God is one, there should be also only one temple.[30]

Both συγγνώμη and παραίτησις are used in this passage to convey the idea of forgiveness. It is worth mentioning that παραίτησις is rare in Philo and beyond.[31] It occurs only once more in Philo (cf. *Laws* 2.196). The range of its meanings includes supplication, entreaty, excuse, apology, pardon, dismissal, intercession, and begging off.[32] The co-text of the sentence, to do with intercession seeking blessings, seems to require that συγγνώμη be understood as something like "forbearance," and παραίτησις as "pardon." This idea of forgiveness arises in a cultic context and is linked with piety, forwardness, payment of the tribute, blessings, and gratitude. The point seems to be this: there is no obstacle for those desiring piety. The sacrifices aim at giving thanks for the blessings received, or imploring συγγνώμην ἁμαρτάνωσι ("forgiveness of sins"). In

---

30. Philo, *Laws* 1.67. Note that the rendering of συγγνώμη and παραίτησις is the present author's alteration.

31. See also statistics in Liddell and Scott, *A Greek-English Lexicon*, 1311.

32. Ibid.

The Rhetoric of Interpersonal Forgiveness in Jewish Literature in Greek

this situation, the worshipper's request for the forgiveness of their sins can be understood as an appeal for tolerance of their sins.

Laws 1.235–36

> These and similar regulations for involuntary offences are followed by his [Moses'] ordinances for such as are voluntary. "If ... a man lies about a partnership or a deposit or a robbery or as to finding the lost property of someone else, and, being suspected and put upon his oath, swears to the falsehood—if then after having apparently escaped conviction by his accusers he becomes convinced inwardly by his conscience, ... reproaches himself for his disavowals and perjuries, makes a plain confession of the wrong he has committed and asks for pardon (τὸ πραχθὲν ἀδίκημα συγγνώμην αἰτῆται)—then the lawgiver orders that forgiveness (ἀμνηστίαν) be extended to such a person on condition that he verifies his repentance not by a mere promise but by his actions, by restoring the deposit or the property which he has seized or found or in any way usurped from his neighbour, and further has paid an additional fifth as a solatium for the offence..."[33]

In this text, συγγνώμη and ἀμνηστία are employed to convey the notion of forgiveness. Warranting mention is that ἀμνηστία is rare in Philo and beyond.[34] This term is attested only three times in the whole LXX (cf. Sap 14:26; Sir 11:25; 3 Macc 3:21 in the form ἀμνησικακίαν). It means something like "forgetfulness."[35]

In the Philonic passage above, both συγγνώμη and ἀμνηστία emerge in the context of human relationship where it is said of it to be expected of the offended person. This noun is used in a discourse regarding regulations for both involuntary and voluntary offences. From the co-text of the sentence, it is reasonable to think of συγγνώμην to mean something like "forbearance." Seeking forgiveness out of prompting by one's conscience can be understood as imploring tolerance and patience from the offended person; it appeals to the offended person's mercy and generosity. On the other hand, granting or extending forgiveness in this context can be understood as something like bearing with the repentant

---

33. Philo, *Laws* 1.235–36.
34. See statistics in Liddell and Scott, *A Greek-English Lexicon*, 84.
35. Ibid.

offender; forgiving in this situation looks like an expression of overcoming wrongdoing with good, a kind of contribution to the betterment of the sinner, as R. D. Enright would say.[36]

The text under examination links the idea of forgiveness with the notions of offences, conscience, confession, repentance, and restitution. The point that Philo seems to make is probably that, generally as humans, offending our fellow humans is inevitable. We offend one another either voluntarily or involuntarily. Whichever the case, in this text, talking from the offended person's perspective, the disposition to forgive the offender appears as an appropriate moral act, a response to a moral wrong. Forgiving looks like a response to a moral wrong. On the other hand, for this act of generosity to take place, some prerequisites are to be fulfilled. Following are the pre-conditions which involve two parties. The offender should make plain confession of their wrong deeds and implore forgiveness. The confession and the pleading for forgiveness should be sincere; the one seeking forgiveness should be really convinced inwardly by their conscience: they must reproach themselves for their disavowals and perjuries. On the other hand, some requirements are necessary before the injured person offers forgiveness: there must be a change in thinking and behavior on the side of the injuring person, there must be evidence of readiness for restitution from the injuring person, and the obligation for the injuring person to pay an additional fifth for the offence. It is then that forgiveness could be extended to the offender. This is true of involuntary and voluntary offences.

Laws 2.196

> Because the holy-day is entirely devoted to prayers and supplications, and men from morn to eve employ their leisure in nothing else but offering petitions of humble entreaty in which they seek earnestly to propitiate God and ask for remission of their sins (παραίτησιν ἁμαρτημάτων), voluntary and involuntary, and entertain bright hopes looking not to their own merits but to the gracious nature of Him Who sets pardon (συγγνώμην) before chastisement.[37]

---

36. Enright, "Forgiveness." Online: http://www.forgiveness-institute.org/html/about_forgiveness.htm.

37. Philo, *Laws* 2.196.

In this text, παραίτησις and συγγνώμη are used to convey the notion of forgiveness. They appear in divine-human relationship in the context of prayers and supplications. The connection between forgiveness and prayer can also observed in Matt 6:9–15 (cp. Mark 11:25–26; Luke 11:2–4). According to the passage just cited, on a specific chosen day, worshippers are to humbly offer petitions in which they seek God's favor. This favor essentially seeks to turn away God's anger and ask for forgiveness for the sins of the offenders, whether voluntary or involuntary. The co-text of sentence, to do with intercession seeking propitiation, seems to require that παραίτησις be understood as something like "pardon," and συγγνώμη as "tolerance," or "leniency," or "merciful restraint." To be sure, aspects of God's ability (to remit sins) and his character and will (to set forgiveness before chastisement) are here in view: humans offend the Creator either voluntarily or involuntarily; there is hopefully an efficient remedy for this human failing; συγγνώμη is said to be set in the first place for them. Most important for our purposes is the relationship between forgiveness and chastisement: God sets tolerance, expression of his mercy, *before* chastisement. From this example, one may risk generalizing that for Philo, God punishes people only after they have failed to acknowledge the grace he freely offers to them; or when they are insensible to his offer of lenity, then he moves on to punishment.

Punishments 166–67

> Three intercessors they have to plead for their reconciliation with the Father. One is the clemency and kindness of Him to whom they appeal, who ever prefers forgiveness (συγγνώμην) to punishment. The second is the holiness of the founders of the race because with souls released from their bodies they show forth in that naked simplicity their devotion to their Ruler and cease not to make supplications for their sons and daughters, supplications not made in vain, because the Father grants to them the privilege that their prayers should be heard. The third is one which more than anything else moves the loving kindness of the other two to come forward so readily, and that is the reformation working in those who are being brought to make a covenant of peace, those who after much toil have been able to

pass from the pathless wild to the road which has no other goal but to find favour with God, as sons may with their father.[38]

As was with the previous text, here the noun συγγνώμη occurs in divine-human relationship in a context of prayer. This noun is used for what can be referred to as forgiveness in the sense of "tolerance," or "leniency." The connection between forgiveness and prayer also appears in Matt 6:9–15 (cp. Mark 11:25–26; Luke 11:2–4).

In the example above, the notion of forgiveness is linked with the idea of the fatherhood and kingship of God, as well as the notions of mercy, kindness, holiness, reconciliation, peace, and punishment. God is described as both father and ruler (king). A similar connection is found in the First Gospel in which God is depicted as a tender, kind, loving, and forgiving king and father. A more detailed discussion of this is provided elsewhere in this work (chs. 5 & 7). In the Philonic text above, the relationship between this father and king, and the worshippers appears to have been broken because of the worshippers' sins. They therefore plead for reconciliation for a possible restoration and enjoyment of peace from him. Because of his holiness, God punishes sins as sin is against his nature; yet, even so, he is so gentle that he ever prefers magnanimity (συγγνώμη) to punishment.

This example shows clearly that, for Philo, offences break relationships, and reconciliation is necessary from the point of view of the offender; they are the one to take the initiative of seeking reconciliation. This reconciliation sought is potentially to materialize given the character of the victim. On the other hand, the offender is expected to change their thinking and behavior, and plead for reconciliation by means of forgiveness. Most significant, for Philo, reconciliation has a personal goal: rather than merely seeking to propitiate the victim, reconciliation also seeks the reformation of the offender and peace with themselves.

Conclusions

The findings on the subject of forgiveness from Philo can now be summed up. The rhetoric of forgiveness in Philo is carried out through συγγνώμη, παραίτησις, and ἀμνηστία. In the Philonic passages surveyed, συγγνώμη means something like "forbearance,"[39] or "leniency," or "tolerance," or

---

38. Philo, *Punishments* 166–67.
39. E.g., Philo, *Laws* 1.235–36; 1.67; *Punishments* 166–67.

The Rhetoric of Interpersonal Forgiveness in Jewish Literature in Greek

"magnanimity"[40]; παραίτησις probably means something like "pardon,"[41] and ἀμνηστία something like "forgetfulness."[42]

The following typical forgiveness pattern seems constant throughout. First, one party having wronged another is the underlying factor.[43] Second, forgiveness is sought by the offender as part of their responsibility.[44] Third, the seeking of forgiveness by the offender is motivated by and grounded in their victim's character and will: the readiness of the victim to forgive.[45] A similar theme can be found in the Matthean Prayer in which the petitioner is clearly on firm ground when they ask God to forgive their debts, a request which is grounded in and motivated by the character and will of God (6:1–8). Fourth, forgiveness is granted and looks like honorable practice toward the offender; however, it seems not to be compulsory from the perspective of the offended person, for they can choose to grant or deny it. Fifth, a penalty is sometimes imposed on and reparation demanded of the offender as prerequisite(s) of forgiveness[46]; in which case, ironically, fulfilling these demands makes forgiving look like an offender's right.

THE RHETORIC OF INTERPERSONAL FORGIVENESS IN JOSEPHUS

Flavius Josephus was a Jewish priest, politician, soldier, and historian. Born in 37 CE to an aristocratic and priestly family in Jerusalem, he died in 100 CE. His writings provide valuable information for our understanding both of biblical history and the political history of Roman Palestine in the first-century CE. Josephus was raised not in the Diaspora, but in Jerusalem, where he received an excellent education, and was well acquainted with Jewish traditions, customs and religious practices. He went on a diplomatic mission to Rome and successfully pleaded for the release of some fellow priests who had been sent there to be judged by Nero. On his return to Jerusalem, he found a revolt against Rome already

---

40. E.g., Philo, *Punishments* 166–67.
41. E.g., Philo, *Laws* 1.67; 2.196.
42. E.g., ibid., 1.235–36.
43. Ibid., 1.67; 1.235–36; 2.196; *Punishments* 166–67.
44. Ibid.
45. Philo, *Laws* 2.196; *Punishments* 166–67.
46. Philo, *Laws* 1.235–36; *Punishments* 166–67.

underway. He tried to oppose it, being convinced of its ineffectiveness and fearing the consequences for his nation. Being unable to contain the revolt, he unwillingly joined it and operated as a commander in Galilee. He was defeated and surrendered himself to the Romans. He ended up being made a Roman citizen and spent the rest of his life in Rome, where he devoted himself to writing historical books on Jewish issues.[47] *Jewish War* and *Jewish Antiquities* are among these books.

Five out of seven interpersonal forgiveness texts from Josephus to be studied in this work are taken from *Jewish War*, from units and sections 5.114, 261, 361, 541; 6.94, 365 in which Josephus is trying to persuade the Jewish rebels to give up the fight before it is too late. Only two of them are taken from *Jewish Antiquities*, which covers the entire history of the Jewish people from the creation of the world until the outbreak of war in 66 CE.

Josephus' use of ἀφίημι and συγγινώσκω (and its cognate noun συγγνώμη) probably reflects Hellenistic Jewish understanding of the notion of forgiveness. The selected narratives below use two terms to convey the idea of forgiving. Some other Greek terms for ideas related to forgiveness were also taken into account. The table below shows all the relevant occurrences of these terms in these forgiveness narratives.

Word	Occurrence
ἀφίημι	1
συγγινώσκω	1
συγγνώμη	2

Ant. 6.92–93

The account in text is Josephus' own version of the story in 1 Sam 12:18–25.

> ... God gave such great signals by thunder and lightning, ... as attested the truth of all that the prophet [Samuel] had said, insomuch that they were amazed and terrified, and confessed they had sinned, and had fallen into that sin through ignorance; and besought the prophet, as one that was tender and gentle father,

---

47. Spilsbury, "Josephus, Flavius," *NIDB*, 3:403–4, esp. 403. So also Rajak, *Josephus*, 1, 11; Smallwood and Rajak, "Josephus (Flavius Iosephus)," *Oxford Classical Dictionary*, 798–99, esp. 798.

to render God so merciful as to forgive ... their sin (ἀφεῖναι τὴν ἁμαρτίαν), which they had added to those other offenses whereby they had affronted him and transgressed against him. So he promised them that he would beseech God, and persuade him to forgive them ... their sins (συγγνῶναι περὶ τουτων αὐτοῖς). However, he advised them to be righteous and good, and to be good, and ever to remember the miseries that had befallen them on account of their departure from virtue; as also to remember the strange signs God had shown them, and the body of laws that Moses had given them, if they had any desire of being preserved and made happy with their king.[48]

Two verbs are used in the retelling of the story to convey the idea of forgive: ἀφίημι and συγγινώσκω, the latter being used with a pair of objects. In this account, ἀφίημι is connected with τὴν ἁμαρτίαν (sin) where it is used to describe divine-human relation. The co-text of the sentence, to do with confession of sin, seems to require that ἀφίημι be understood as forgive in the sense of remit. An offence had been committed, and then confessed. An appeal seeking the offended party's mercy and generosity has been made by the offending party. This appeal is about ἀφεῖναι τὴν ἁμαρτίαν. In this context, the forgiveness of sins implored by the Jews can be understood as a request for their sins to be remitted.

In this text, the idea of forgiveness is linked with the notion the fatherhood and kingship of God as well as the notions of ignorance, repentance, salvation, and felicity. Repentance can be discerned from one of its components: confession of sins. The Jews, terrified by Yahweh's displeasure, confess their sins. This confession has to do not only with their current insolence and transgressions; it also involves previous offences, or violations. They therefore plead for Yahweh's mercy, so that he might forgive them. One of the reasons why they think there might be room for them to be granted forgiveness concerns their sin as being out of ignorance. The notion of mediation is linked with that of fatherhood. The concepts of the fatherhood and kingship of God may seem suggested by this text. Israel implores Samuel, whom they consider an affectionate father, to plead for Yahweh's forgiveness on their behalf. This raises the question here of how the Jews relate to Yahweh: Is he also a father or a king, or both? Though it is true that elsewhere God is held to be the Hebrews' father and king (the linked themes of fatherhood and kingship are

48. Josephus, *Ant.* 6.92–93.

for instance found in Philo),⁴⁹ here it is plausible only that God is seen as a king. This claim seems to be supported by the context of the narrative: Israel's demand for a king. 1 Sam 8:6b–7 also adds to the point: "Samuel prayed to the Lord, and the Lord said to Samuel, 'Listen to the voice of the people in all that they say to you; for they have not rejected you, but they have rejected me from being king over them.'" God's kingship is also a recurrent theme is Matthew, as was noted earlier in this chapter and will be discussed at great length later (chs. 5 & 7).

It becomes then clear that for Josephus, Yahweh, from whom forgiveness is expected, is a king. Most significant is the role that Samuel is playing here. As a loving father, Samuel also plays the role of an intermediary figure: he is a mediator between God and the people. Because their sins have distanced them from the king God, the Jews take the initiative of seeking Yahweh's forgiveness through Samuel. Samuel assures the people to plead for Yahweh's forgiveness for them. On the other hand, he warns them that if they were to desire Yahweh's ongoing salvation and felicity, they must be righteous and good, and ever people who can remember the consequences of sins.

War 6.104–7

This text provides an example of συγγνώμη, in Josephus, for the idea of forgiveness in the sense of leniency, or tolerance, or magnanimity. Warning John, Josephus writes:

> ... [W]hen the king of Babylon made war against him [Jeconiah], did, of his own accord, go out of the city before it was taken, and did undergo a voluntary captivity with his family, that the sanctuary might not be delivered up to the enemy, and that he might not see the house of God set on fire; on which account he is celebrated among all the Jews, in their sacred memorials, and his memory is become immortal, and will be conveyed fresh down to our posterity through all ages. This, John, is an excellent example in such a time of danger; and I dare venture to promise that the Romans shall still forgive you (συγγνώμην ἐγγυῶμαι). And take notice, that I, who make this exhortation to you, am one of your own nation; I who am a Jew do make this

---

49. Philo, *Punishments*, 166–67.

The Rhetoric of Interpersonal Forgiveness in Jewish Literature in Greek   111

> promise to you. And it will become you to consider who I am that give you this counsel . . .[50]

This passage uses the noun συγγνώμη to describe what is potentially to be a warrant to John and his countrymen. The co-text of the sentence, to do with persuasion for repentance, seems to suggest that συγγνώμη be understood to mean something like "forgiveness" in the sense of forbearance. The situation is that the Jews had been defeated by the Romans. Led by a certain John, they plan to attack the Romans, as a way of retaliating. Josephus, himself a Jew, warns them to give up their plans. He anticipates that attacking the Romans would surely result in chaos for the Jews and their country. He thus warns his countrymen to surrender, promising to secure συγγνώμη for them from the Romans. Far from being a subject for humiliation for Jews, their refraining would mean salvation of the nation, and would spare many lives, just as was the case with king Jeconiah, who chose to surrender (a sort of repentance, or the change of mind), the result of which was the salvation of Judah. In this state of affairs, warranting forgiveness is probably best understood as securing merciful refrain, or tolerance.

Ant. 9.214

This account is Josephus retelling the story of the prophet Jonah. This extract is a summary of Jon 3:1–4.

> . . . [O]n his prayer to God, he obtained pardon for his sins (συγγνώμην αὐτῷ παρασχεῖν τῶν ἡμαρτημένων), and went to the city Nineveh, where he stood so as to be heard; and preached, that in a very little time they should lose the dominion of Asia; and when he had published this, he returned. Now, I have given this account about him, as I found it written . . .[51]

This text uses συγγνώμη for what can be referred to as forgiveness. In it, this noun is connected with τῶν ἡμαρτημένων (sins). The co-text of the sentence, to do with culpability, seems to require that συγγνώμη be understood to mean something like "forbearance." The prophet has disobeyed God; this disobedience has stirred God's anger which resulted

---

50. Josephus, *War* 6.103–7. This translation has been improved by the present author by replacing "thee" and "thine" in the last three sentences by "you" and "your" respectively.

51. Josephus, *Ant.* 9.214.

in punishing him. He then prays and asks for συγγνώμην αὐτῷ τῶν ἡμαρτημένων. In this context, asking God's forgiveness for the prophet's sins probably amounts to an appeal for God's mercy to bear with him by remitting his sins. The prophet, to be sure, desperately needs God's "forbearance" so that he might use him again more effectively for this new mission that is being laid upon his shoulders. Although the content of his prayer is not revealed, the context seems to require that such prayer be both that of deliverance and of repentance.[52]

War 5.376–78

Four texts are discussed under this heading because they are closely related; the first three are concerned with the issue of retaliation, and the last with that of repentance. The backdrop is as follows. The Jews are ready to make war against the Romans. Josephus stands against such hazardous action. To him, his fellow Jews should not engage in war against the Romans, as a way of retaliation. Rather, they must rely on God, who never failed to avenge them if they were wronged. The first passage, thus, reads:

> ... "O miserable creatures! Are you so unmindful of those that used to assist you, that you will fight by your weapons and by your hands against the Romans? When did we ever conquer any other nation by such means? And when was it that God, who is the Creator of the Jewish people, did not avenge them when they had been injured? Will you not turn again, and look back, and consider whence it is that you fight with such violence, and how great Supporter you have profanely abused? Will not you recall ... the prodigious things done for your forefathers and this holy place, and how great enemies of yours were by him subdued under you? I even tremble myself in declaring the works of God before your ears, that are unworthy to hear them; however, hearken to me, that you may be informed how you fight, not only against the Romans but against God himself.[53]

In this extract, the Jews are warned to give up their plan of making war against the Romans, as a revenging action, on account of God's faithfulness in avenging the Jews if they were wronged. As an evidence of

---

52. On the subject of *repentance*, the editors of the Loeb write, "Joseph's brief summary of the book of Jonah omits the chief message of the story, the need of repentance." (cf. ibid., 9.214)

53. Josephus, *War* 5.376–78.

The Rhetoric of Interpersonal Forgiveness in Jewish Literature in Greek 113

God's faithfulness in this regard, Josephus points to their fathers' superhuman exploits in days of old. Now the second passage follows.

> In old times there was one Necao, king of Egypt, who was also called Pharaoh; he came with a prodigious army of soldiers, and seized queen Sarah, the mother of our nation. What did Abraham our progenitor then do? Did he defend himself from this injurious person by war, although he had three hundred and eighteen captains under him, and an immense army under each of them? Indeed, he deemed them to be no number at all without God's assistance, and only spread out his hands towards this holy place, which you have now polluted, and reckoned upon him as upon his invincible supporter, instead of his own army. Was not our queen sent back, without any defilement to her husband, the very next evening?—While the king of Egypt fled away, adoring this place which you have defiled by shedding thereon the blood of your countrymen; and he also trembled at those visions which he saw in the nightseason, and bestowed both silver and gold on the Hebrews, as on a people beloved of God.[54]

This account speaks of Abraham's response toward Pharaoh Nechaos' evil action of carrying off Sarah, his wife. It is striking that Abraham did not dare to take revenge on the ravisher. He could have done so given both the number and quality of the people he had in possession; but he chose not to. He rather left the matter with God, relying on his sovereign power and ability and faithfulness to avenge. This leads us straight to the third text.

> ... [W]hen Antiochus, who was called Epiphanes, lay before this city, and had been guilty of many indignities against God, and our forefathers met him in arms, they then were slain in the battle, this city was plundered by our enemies, and our sanctuary made desolate for three years and six months ...[55]

This text illustrates pertinently a possible effect on the retaliator, in some cases, of a revenging action. It probably also illustrates the ultimate goal of vengeance: it benefits almost nothing good to the retaliator; rather it essentially seeks to satisfy one's anger. What happened to the Jews when they sought revenge against Antiochus Epiphanes and the Syrians is indeed to the point; the Jews were humiliated: they were killed in great

---

54. Ibid., 5.379–81.
55. Ibid., 5.394.

number, their city plundered and their sanctuary lay deserted for almost three and a half years. The fourth text, lastly, may now be considered.

> However, there is a place left for your preservation, if you be willing to accept of it, and God is easily reconciled to those that confess their faults, and repent of them. O hardhearted wretches as you are, cast away all your arms, and take pity of your country already going to ruin; return from your wicked ways, and have regard to the excellency of that city which you are going to betray, and to that excellent temple with the donations of so many countries in it.[56]

This text is concerned with the issue of repentance in the sense of a radical change of mind and behavior. Here repentance is clearly understood as a way to reconciliation; God is said to be easily reconciled to those who confess and repent. On the other hand, repentance may bring salvation; it may spare many lives from peril. All taken together, the four examples above form a piece of evidence for the relationship between the notions of repentance and those of vengeance, salvation, and reconciliation.

Conclusions

The findings on the subject of forgiveness from Josephus can be summed up as follows. In Josephus, two terms are used to convey his idea of forgiveness: ἀφίημι and συγγινώσκω (and its cognate noun συγγνώμη). With all probability, it can be suggested that for Josephus and his first readers, ἀφίημι probably meant forgiveness in the sense of causing something to undergo separation: remit[57]; συγγινώσκω, on the other hand seems to have meant an attitude and feeling: bearing with, or tolerating, merciful restraint.[58] Where the impersonal object of ἀφίημι is envisaged,[59] the intended meaning tends to be remitting the offences; whereas, where the personal object of συγγινώσκω is in view,[60] the intended meaning is likely bearing with, or showing mercy, or being tolerant.

---

56. Ibid., 5.415–16.
57. E.g., Josephus, *Ant.* 6.92–93.
58. E.g., ibid., 6.92–93; 6.103–7; 9.214.
59. E.g., ibid., 6.92–93.
60. E.g., Josephus, *War* 6.103–7; *Ant.* 9.214.

The Rhetoric of Interpersonal Forgiveness in Jewish Literature in Greek 115

Moreover, following is a fourfold forgiveness pattern from the Josephan texts surveyed in this chapter. First, one party having wronged another is clearly the underlying factor.[61] Second, seeking revenge is a clear reaction on the part of the offended person[62]; but the advice to the offended party appears to prevent this potential revenging action to take place.[63] As a result of the advice being taken into account, the lives of many are spared.[64] Third, forgiveness is sought by the offender and seems to be their responsibility.[65] Fourth, forgiving appears as an appropriate moral act toward the offender.

However, a third party is involved in the process of seeking forgiveness, and that is on the request of the offending party.[66] Besides, demands are sometimes imposed for receiving ongoing salvation and felicity, they consisting in the promise of future righteousness and goodness, and commitment to remember the consequences of sins.[67] The fact should also be noted that in the Josephan texts surveyed there is a clear relationship between the idea of forgiveness and the notions of repentance, vengeance, salvation, and reconciliation.[68]

CONCLUSIONS

This chapter has given an account of the interpersonal forgiveness rhetoric in Jewish literature in Greek (LXX, Philo, and Josephus). In addition to the use of the concept itself, eight terms were used in Jewish literature in Greek to convey the idea of forgiveness: ἀφίημι/ἄφεσις, συγγινώσκω/συγγνώμη, δέχομαι, προσδέχομαι, αἴρω, λύω, παραίτησις, and ἀμνηστία. It was argued that in these Jewish texts, what can be referred to as forgiveness meant something like "remission," or "removal," or "release"; "acceptance"; "forbearance," or "tolerance"; and "leaving something behind" (whether a matter or a situation), or "letting go," or "cancelling." Further, the forgiveness pattern in the table below which has emerged from the Jewish literature in Greek surveyed was identified in this chapter.

61. Josephus, *Ant.* 6.92–93; 9.214; *War* 5.376–78; 6.103–7.
62. Josephus, *War* 5.376–78; 6.103–7.
63. Ibid., 5.376–78; 6.103–107.
64. Ibid., 5.376–78.
65. Josephus, *Ant.* 6.92–93; 9.214.
66. Ibid., 6.92–93.
67. Josephus, *Ant.* 6.92–93.
68. E.g., Josephus, *War* 5.376–78; 5.394.

LXX	Philo	Josephus
[1] A wrong is committed	[1] A wrong is committed	[1] A wrong is committed
[2] Fear for potential retaliation or a punitive action motivates the seeking of forgiveness by the offender (or by a third party acting on their behalf)	[2] Forgiveness is sought as part of the responsibility of the offender	[2] Revenge is sought by the offended person
[3] Forgiveness is sought as part of the responsibility of the offender, or of the third party acting on their behalf	[3] Asking for forgiveness is motivated by the character and will of the victims, and is grounded in it	[3] Forgiveness is sought as part of the offender's responsibility
[4] Forgiveness is granted *unconditionally* and looks like an act of generosity from the offended person's point of view	[4] Forgiveness is granted as an honorable practice towards the offender	
[5] Forgiveness is granted, the danger for the offender is driven away.	[5] Penalty is (sometimes) imposed on, and reparation demanded of, the injuring person as a prerequisite of forgiveness.	

The question to be asked is whether this pattern, or aspects of it, can be found in Matthew; this will be verified throughout chapters 5 and 6. The study of the rhetoric of forgiveness in Jewish data in Greek has also shown that, in these texts, nothing is said of what will happen to the potential unforgiving person. This trend may provide a clue which may help to shed some light on our understanding of the distinctiveness of Matthew's strong emphasis on the responsibility of the offended person in the act of forgiving.

5

The Rhetoric of Interpersonal Forgiveness in Matt 6:9–15

IN 6:12, 14–15, ASPECTS of the gospel's emphasis on interpersonal forgiveness can be observed. This emphasis is made clear, first, through the concept of reciprocity and the link of this with forgiveness, together with the link between reluctance in the exercise of forgiveness and judgment; second, through the responsibility of the offended person in forgiving; third, through the strategic rhetorical position of the forgiveness petition within the Prayer, as well as the position of the Prayer within the Sermon; and fourth, through the proportion of text the interpersonal forgiveness passages occupy in and around the Prayer.

In exploring this text, due attention will be paid to these features, for they provide evidence for how seriously Matthew stresses interpersonal forgiveness. These features will be pointed out and highlighted as the study develops. Moreover, as the exegesis develops, reference will be made to the parallels of 6:12, 14–15 in the LXX data surveyed in this work (ch. 4). In an attempt to draw a plausible interpretation of the discourse about forgiveness in 6:12, 14–15, due attention will, as previously, be paid to the text, the co-text, the inter-texts, and the context. The reading of this text will be done with the purpose of explaining the meaning of ἀφίημι and describing the dynamics of both divine and human forgiveness. The chapter is structured around seven main sections discussing (1) the Synoptic Problem; (2) the circumstances of Matthew's community; (3) the structure of Matthew; (4) the structure of Matt 6:9–15; (5) the textual problem of 6:9–15; (6) 6:9–15 within its co-text, including an analysis of 6:12, 14–15; and (7) a summary of the findings.

THE SYNOPTIC PROBLEM

Scholarship has long been aware of the Synoptic Problem; it is almost as old as Christianity itself, as E. B. Powery has explained.[1] The definition of the Synoptic Problem and the solutions that have been proposed can be grouped in five main categories: first, the Augustinian theory; second, the Griesbach hypothesis; third, the two-source theory; fourth, the four-source theory; and fifth, the Farrer hypothesis.[2] The two-source theory is the most dominant solution to the Synoptic Problem. The L/M hypothesis[3] recently proposed by Francis Watson, as an alternative for the two-source theory, has received a reasoned response by C. M. Tuckett. Concluding his response to Watson, Tuckett writes: "The Q hypothesis as part of the 2ST is a hypothesis . . . It is probably not an exact replica of historical reality . . .; but overall, and at significant points, it seems to provide a better hypothesis . . ."[4]

The two-source theory is assumed in the present study because it is a majority opinion. What this means to this study is that the substance of the interpersonal forgiveness and related material in Matthew were drawn from two main sources (Mark and Q). That is, Matthew used Mark as a source in composing his book; he also drew on Q as another source to which Mark had no access. According to this theory, Matt 6:9–13 is derived from Q, Matt 6:14–15 from Mark 11:25[–26] and Matt 18:21–22 from Q, whereas Matt 18:23–35 is Matthew's special material.

---

1. Powery, "Synoptic Problem," *NIDB*, 5:429–34, esp. 5:429.

2. For a more updated survey of the subject, see Kloppenborg, *Q, the Earliest Gospel*.

3. F. Watson, "Q as Hypothesis: A Study in Methodology," 397–415.

4. Tuckett, "The Q Hypothesis: A Good Hypothesis?" A paper presented on the 30th Annual Conference of British New Testament Conference, in Bangor, UK, 2–4 Sep. 2010.

MATT 18:1-14 AND ISSUES FACING THE MATTHEAN COMMUNITY

The main purpose of this section is to explore possible concerns of Matthew's Christian community and to find out how this relates to the theme of interpersonal forgiveness. A significant increase of interest in the relationship between the Matthean community and formative Judaism has been observed.[5] At the heart of the debate are the following questions: What explanation can we give to the Jewish world view of the evangelist and his group? How do we account for his vigorous criticism of the scribes and Pharisees, a fact which is clear in the gospel? Is it reasonable to think that the Jewishness of Matthew and his community places them within Judaism, or does his harsh polemic against "the scribes and Pharisees mean that this once Jewish group has now broken with its parent religion?"[6]

A broadly based consensus among Matthean scholars on this issue is that the Matthean community was originally a group of Jewish Christians that has come into conflict with other Jewish groups at this very point in the wake of the destruction of the Temple in 70 CE. However, scholars do not speak with one voice as to the precise relationship between the Matthean community and Judaism. While some argue that Matthew's group still defined itself within Judaism in spite of its dispute with other Jews,[7] others hold that it was no longer within the orbit of Judaism, but was forging a new identity independently from the Jewish faith.[8] What makes it almost impossible to reach an agreement on this issue, as David C. Sim has also pointed out, is the fact that scholars from both sides of the fence use the same evidence but with different emphasis and perspective.[9] The latter view (i.e., Matthew's group being forging a new identity independently from the Jewish faith) is most likely. My interest here is in

---

5. See, for example, Stanton, *A Gospel for a New People*; Saldarini, *Matthew's Christian-Jewish Community*; Overmann, *Matthew's Gospel and Formative Judaism*; Sim, *The Gospel of Matthew and Christian Judaism*; Repschinski, *The Controversy Stories in the Gospel of Matthew*; Aarde, "Jesus' Mission to All" (Online: www.sbl-site.org/assets/pdfs/aarde_jesus.pdf).

6. Sim, "The Social Setting of the Matthean Community," 269–70.

7. Key defenders of this view include Kilpatrick, Bornkamm, Overman, Saldarini, Harrington, Davies, Allison, and Sim, among others.

8. Scholars who hold this view include Stanton, Moule, Przybylski, Luz, and Hagner, among others.

9. Sim, "The Social Setting of the Matthean Community," 269–70ff.

inquiring about the life and concerns of this group in its struggle to forge a new identity separated from the Jewish faith; that is, the development of the moral and religious consciousness of this community in that period.

External Relationships

There is no concluding consensus concerning the location of the First Gospel geographically. The majority of scholars argue that it comes from Antioch of Syria—the city in which the followers of Jesus for the first time were called "Christians" (Acts 11:26)—for the Christian community living there. Three reasons in support of this proposal have been suggested. Firstly, Antioch was the capital of the Roman Province of Syria; it was probably the third largest city of the Roman Empire behind Rome itself and Alexandria.[10] Consequently, a large city like Antioch would make possible the rapid distribution of the gospel that occurred.[11] Secondly, Jews settled there. Thirdly, and importantly, "the Gospel is mentioned by Ignatius of Antioch shortly after the turn of the century."[12] This majority consensus, however, has been challenged in recent years. W. R. Schoedel, for example, is less certain that the first evangelist necessarily points to Antioch as its place of origin. For him, the theological traditions alive in Antioch in the time of Ignatius were so diverse and transcend the horizons of the First Gospel significantly.[13] However, there are no compelling reasons to reject the traditional view.

R. Stark has given a comprehensive picture of what the city and its life might have looked like in NT times:

> Any accurate picture of Antioch in New Testament times must depict a city filled with misery, danger, fear, despair, and hatred. Antioch was a city where the average family lived a squalid life in filthy and cramped quarters, where at least half of the children died at birth or during infancy, and where most of the children who lived lost at least one parent before reaching maturity. The city was filled with hatred and fear rooted in intense ethnic antagonisms and exacerbated by a constant stream of strangers. This city was so lacking in stable networks of attachments that petty incidents could prompt mob violence. Crime flourished

---

10. Downey, *A History of Antioch in Syria from Seleucus to the Arab Conquest*.
11. Riches, *Matthew*, 52.
12. Ibid.
13. Schoedel, "Ignatius and the Gospel of Matthew," 154.

and the streets were dangerous at night. And, perhaps above all, Antioch was repeatedly smashed by cataclysmic catastrophes. A resident could expect literally to be homeless from time to time, providing that he or she was among the survivors.[14]

Surely, it is among such socioeconomic, political and physical realities that the Matthean community was born.

The main clue to the social situation of Matthew's community seems to lie with conflict. As Jack D. Kingsbury has observed, Matthew's plot focuses on conflict; the evangelist seems to be engaged in some sort of polemic.[15] Scholars commonly argue that this conflict is between the Jesus group and some other groups within Judaism.[16] In fact, debate on the social situation of this community tends to focus on the relation of Matthew's community to Judaism.[17] *A church in transition* is perhaps a good way of broadly describing what has been suggested as the circumstances of this Christian community.[18] It has been observed that the Matthean community has probably been involved in an intense relationship with the surrounding dominant Jewish community.[19] A few internal pieces of evidence tend to support this claim. For example, as Boring has suggested, the gospel contains texts that seem to hint that Matthew's Christian community was still subject to the disciplinary measures of the synagogue authorities (10:17–23; 23:2), and perhaps still kept the Sabbath (24:20).[20] On the other hand, five times Matthew uses the phrase "their synagogue" (4:23; 9:35; 10:17; 12:9; 13:54) and "your synagogue" once (23:34) clearly to underline distance between Jesus and the synagogue community.[21] Warren Carter points out that several of these pas-

14. Stark, "Urban Chaos and Crisis," 160–61.

15. Kingsbury, "The Plot of Matthew's Story," 45–59.

16. E.g., Meeks, *The Moral World of the First Christians*, 137; Harrington, *God's People in Christ*, 97; Senior, *What Are They Saying about Matthew?*, 6–10; Segal, "Matthew's Jewish Voice," 35–37; White, "Crisis Management and Boundary Maintenance," 240; Duling and Perrin, *The New Testament*, 335; Aarde, "Jesus' Mission to All," 8–9 (Online: www.sbl-site.org/assets/pdfs/aarde_jesus.pdf).

17. Balch's edited collection of the twelve essays (with the exception of the essay by Gundry) devoted to *Social History of the Matthean Community* is a good illustration of this.

18. Cf. Meier, "Matthew, Gospel of," in *Anchor Bible Dictionary*, 4:622–40, esp. 4:625.

19. Boring, "The Gospel of Matthew," 42.

20. Ibid.

21. Carter, *Matthew and the Margins*, 31.

sages emphasize hostility between the synagogue and Jesus' disciples. In 10:17, for example, Jesus warns disciples that they will be flogged in *their* synagogues; in 13:54–58, *their* synagogue rejects Jesus; and in 6:2, 5 and 23:6, the behavior of "the hypocrites in the [not 'your'] synagogues" is condemned and contrasted with that of "you" in Christian groups.[22]

What has been said seems to reasonably relate with issues which Matthew is trying to address in his gospel. This can be derived from the demands and exhortations for being merciful (5:7; 9:13; 12:7; 18:23–35), for seeking and granting forgiveness (6:12, 14–15; 18:21–35) and reconciliation (5:23–24; 18:15–17), for loving one's enemies (5:44–47), for not retaliating (5:38–42), and for being perfect (5:48). The first evangelist seems to have both offered these as both part of conflict resolution strategies and strategy for survival in a hostile environment.

Internal Relationships

While an interest in the external relationships of Matthew's Christian community is important, perhaps an interest in the interior relationships of this community is more helpful and relevant for understanding various demands and exhortations across the gospel. Although the relation of Matthew's community to Judaism appears as one of the main issues in Matthew, issues of the relationship within this community were also pressing. As R. H. Gundry has noted, the more troublesome sociological problem of the Matthean community does not have to do with the relation of a Christian Judaism to the rest of Judaism, but with relations inside Matthew's community.[23] Now the main task is to determine what the route of this troublesome sociological problem is, and to discover Matthew's resolution.

What then are the most important possible issues in Matthew's community? False teaching, leadership, lawlessness, division, and scandal[24] and moral laxity[25] have been proposed as possible issues in this believing community. The last two proposals are attractive because they seem to fit quite nicely into Matthew's flow of thought in Matt 18, in

---

22. Ibid.

23. Gundry, "A Responsive Evaluation of the Social History of the Matthean Community in Roman Syria," 66.

24. Cf. Thompson, *Matthew's Advice to a Divided Community*, 258–64.

25. Mohrlang, *Matthew and Paul*, 128.

which the concern for church cohesion can be found. However, preservation of the community seems to be the likeliest, as suggested in chapter 2. A possible connection of the notion of preservation of the community to the theme of interpersonal forgiveness in the gospel and the concept of *spiritually mature* and *immature* Christians in Matt 18 tend to support this claim. Preservation of the community is clearly a major concern in Matt 18; it fits nicely Carter's description below of this community: a minority community, a community recently separated from a synagogue, a community in transition trying to build a new identity and lifestyle, and an alternative community on the cultural margins of society.[26] A strong emphasis on this can be discerned from a set of emphatic teachings in the Matthean section above, a section prefaced by a powerful teaching on humility. These teachings include becoming like and humbling oneself like παιδίον/παιδία, receiving one such παιδίον, caring for the μικροί, prohibition for losing *one* of the μικροί, avoidance of scandal, *brotherly* reconciliation and *interpersonal* forgiveness. Four of these teachings are worth discussing in detail.

First is the "little ones." This is quite clear through the μικροί language which dominates 18:6–14.[27] The centrality of this concept in Matt 18 has been recognized in scholarship. As was noted in chapter 2, the μικροί language has been taken as a basis for structuring Matt 18. For Robert H. Gundry, for example, this chapter is structured around two main parts: care for the little ones (18:1–14) and care for sinners (18:15–35).[28] Likewise, John R. Donahue thinks that the tone of the whole chapter 18 is set by the concern for the "little ones" whom he understands as those whose "faith is weak" (6:30; 8:26; 14:31; 16:8; 17:20—those of "little faith"), or those "who need special care" (10:42; cf. 25:40, 45—the "least").[29]

We suggested that this probably makes a lot of sense if we acknowledge that the instruction in Matt 18 is directed to a category of people within Matthew's Christian community with some level of spiritual

---

26. Carter, *Matthew*, 66–91.

27. A discussion over aspects of the significance of the μικροί/παιδία theme in Matt 18 can be found in ch. 2 of this work.

28. Gundry, *Matthew*, 358. For various structure proposals, see Luz, *Matthew*, 2:422.

29. Donahue, *The Gospel in Parable*, 72. For a recent development of the identity of the μικροί in Matthew, see Koskenniemi, "Forgotten Guardians and Matthew 18:10," 120–21.

maturity, for the sake of church cohesion. In verse 6, there is a strong warning that *one* of the little ones (ἕνα τῶν μικρῶν τούτων) should not be scandalized. In verse 10, "*one* of the little ones" (ἑνὸς τῶν μικρῶν τούτων) should not be despised. The parable of the lost sheep in verses 13–14 (Matthew's reworking of his Q material [cp. Q Luke 15:3–7]) is a strong warning to those who despise "*one* of the little ones." This parable serves to illustrate God's judgment awaiting anybody who will despise "*one* of the little ones." The parable points back to the point already made in verse 6 about the nature of the judgment awaiting people who scandalize "*one* of the little ones." The moral of the parable in 18:14 (vs. its moral in Luke 15:3–7) emphasizes the will of God toward "*one* of the little ones": "So it is not the will of your Father in heaven that one of these little ones should be lost." As Bornkamm has noted, in this context, this parable does not serve primarily for the proclamation of divine grace toward the lost; rather, it serves to impress upon the congregation their duty to care for the straying,[30] that is, the "little one(s)."

Second is humility (18:1–5). Using the παιδίον/παιδία language, the evangelist seems to strongly urge the members of his community about the appropriate behavior that is expected of them as members of the church and citizens of the kingdom. The disciples' concern itself (v. 1) presupposes that every believer in Christ is God's son or daughter, and therefore belongs to the family of the kingdom (cf. repetition of ἡ βασιλεία τῶν οὐρανῶν in 18:1, 3, 4; cp. v. 23). This wider family finds its fuller expression in the Church (cf. ἡ ἐκκλησία in 16:18 and 18:17 [2x]), the smaller family. Presumably, this community is composed of members with asymmetrical level of spiritual maturity, some being more *spiritually mature* than others. To live harmoniously as brothers and sisters of the same family and citizens of the heavenly kingdom, *spiritually mature* members are to become like "little children" and humble themselves like a "child" (v. 4). In their relationships, the *spiritually mature* members are to remind themselves of their responsibility to accept the *spiritually weaker* members in the name of Jesus in the sense of caring for them (v. 5). Apparently, the *mature* brothers and sisters are people who must have undergone a radical change in their lives (18:3). This would be visible in their relating to and dealing with one another, particularly with the *spiritually weaker* members.

---

30. Bornkamm, "The Authority to 'Bind' and 'Loose' in the Church in Matthew's Gospel," 106.

Third is avoidance of scandal (18:6–10). In addition to humility, negatively stated, the *mature* members should avoid being themselves a scandal and causing downfall to the *spiritually immature* members. Because the community is composed of members with asymmetrical levels of spiritual maturity, and given the fact that scandal is a potential threat to the unity of the congregation, all the more must the *spiritually mature* members avoid being a scandal and causing scandal to the *spiritually immature* members; rather, they are to do whatever they can to avoid losing even a single member. On the one hand, they are to be careful with their own behavior not to despise "*one* of the little ones" in any way (18:10a); on the other hand, if "*one* of these little ones" has begun to stray from the rest of the community because of their own behavior (18:12–17), as part of their responsibilities the *mature* members are the ones to take the initiative of going to this fellow ἀδελφός in danger, just like the shepherd had to leave the ninety-nine sheep to go in search of the straying one (18:13–14). As A. Plummer has stated, this sheep of verses 13–14, has strayed *foolishly* and *willingly*; yet, it still needs to be recovered and restored to the flock.[31] The way in which the shepherd deals with his straying sheep, Matthew strongly urges, is the way in which the *mature* members ought to deal with their erring brother or sister.

Fourth is reconciliation (18:15–17). Although a member may display his or her weakness in offending another, the *mature* member is bidden to go to the offender at least three times, using different approaches (vv. 15–17) either to retain the offender in the group (if they have not yet left) or to bring them back to it (if they have already left, cf. 18:12–14). This initiative of going to one's injurer more than once, with the aim of winning them, clearly suggests that the offended person has undergone radical change (cf. 18:1), marked by humility and having well understood their responsibility toward fellow church members. Teaching about *brotherly* reconciliation appears elsewhere in the First Gospel (5:21–26) and can be linked with the teaching about other issues related to interpersonal forgiveness, such as non-retaliation (5:38–42), loving enemies (5:43–47; 7:12), and being perfect (5:48).[32]

---

31. Plummer, *An Exegetical Commentary on the Gospel according to St. Matthew*, 252.

32. These issues and texts related to them are surveyed in ch. 2.

Conclusion

It can now be strongly suggested that preservation of the community is a major concern in Matt 18 and in the whole gospel. This is made clear by emphatic teachings on being and humbling oneself like "little children," caring for the "little ones," prohibition for losing *one* of the "little ones," avoidance of scandal, and *brotherly* reconciliation (Matt 18:1–17), together with the demands for being merciful (5:7; 9:13; 12:7; 18:23–35) and forgiving (6:14–15; 18:21–35), loving one another including one's enemies (5:44–47), not retaliating (5:38–42), and being perfect (5:48). The two key Matthean forgiveness texts (6:12, 14–15; 18:21–35) are to be read against this background. For the sake of church cohesion, wisdom in handling the straying ἀδελφός was required. One way of implementing such wisdom was for the *spiritually mature* members to show readiness in forgiving their offenders (6:14–15), to forgive them *limitlessly* (18:21–22). This would be a clear evidence of their understanding of their new identity in Christ and would legitimate their longing for the kingdom (cf. 18:1). Otherwise, they do not fit or will not fit at all in the kingdom (18:35; 6:15). This strong emphasis on interpersonal forgiveness in the Community Discourse (Matt 18), as well as earlier in the Sermon (Matt 5–7), is best understood as having been given *primarily* to a group that was struggling with animosity within the group. The demands for being perfect, being merciful, being reconciled and being forgiving, as well as loving one's enemies and not retaliating seem to support the proposal that the preservation of the community was a significant issue in Matthew's community. Matthew, therefore, most likely regarded readiness to forgive as a means by which the members of his community were to preserve union and harmony.

THE STRUCTURE OF MATTHEW'S GOSPEL

This section is concerned with the structure of Matthew with the purpose of determining its major units and sub-units, and to find out how this structure may help in the interpretation of 6:12, 14–15 and 18:21–35 and texts related to them.

The literary structure of Matthew is one of the main concerns that have arisen within recent studies of the gospel. Scholars interested in Matthew, and who have studied thoroughly its structure, have recognized unanimously the difficulty in discerning the structure.[33] Two factors underlie this difficulty. The first factor has to do with the gospel itself. It has been observed that what makes Matthew's overall structure complex is the interlocking literary structures found in the gospel; these take account of summary statements, cross-references, numerical patterns, repeated formulas and even geographical patterns.[34] Donald A. Hagner, for instance, has observed that Matthew contains an exceedingly large variety of structural elements; and so, there is apparently too much to comprehend under any single analysis.[35] Luz has identified three basic aspects of the phenomenon. The first aspect is Matthean highly formulaic language, which is apparent from numerous repeated expressions or individual words. The second aspect is the fact that beginning with chapter 12, Matthew follows closely the outline of Mark. The third aspect is Matthew's possible lack of interest in delimitations.[36] The second factor, which is about approaches to the gospel interpretation, can be found in Bauer's suggestion. Bauer suggests that to a large extent, the differences which are observed among scholars regarding Matthew's structure can be traced to differences of method, especially to various emphases in the application of redaction criticism to the text. He observes that those scholars who focus upon the process of redaction (i.e., changes or additions Matthew has made to received tradition) tend to view the structure of the gospel differently from those who stress the product of redaction (i.e., the final composition of the work).[37]

Despite the difficulties inherent in understanding the structure of Matthew, various structural proposals have been suggested over the centuries. The most prominent include the Pentateuchal, the chiastic, the tripartite and the geographical-chronological models. It is beyond the scope of this study to discuss each of them; scholars have done this thoroughly.[38] One has to bear in mind that though very useful, any proposed solution over the structure of Matthew is not final. As R. T. France

33. D. Bauer, *The Structure of Matthew's Gospel*, 7; see also Hagner, *Matthew*, 1:l.
34. M. Brown, "Matthew," *NIDB*, 3:839.
35. Hagner, *Matthew*, 1:li
36. Luz, *Matthew*, 1:4.
37. D. Bauer, *The Structure of Matthew's Gospel*, 135.
38. Scholars who have studied this issue thoroughly include: D. Bauer, *The Structure of Matthew's Gospel*; France, *Matthew*; Allison, "Matthew: Structure," 1203–21; Weren, "The Macrostructure of Matthew's Gospel," 171–200; Neirynck, *Evangelica*, 3–36.

reminds us, given that the text of Matthew is not provided with markers to draw attention to a comprehensive outline of sections within which the author intended it to be read, any proposed outline of the gospel is thus imposed by the interpreter. It is therefore open to discussion as to whether it truly represents the intended shape of the narrative.[39]

The Pentateuchal model, also known as Bacon's theory, is the best-known and most influential theory about Matthew's arrangement of his material; it is still popular today.[40] Many are the followers of Bacon's model, although they disagree in details either with Bacon himself or among themselves. Recent and contemporary defenders of this model include G. D. Kilpatrick, Pierre Benoit, R. H. Fuller, E. Lohse, S. Neill, and W. D. Davies. The Pentateuchal model is based on the five discourses that Matthew seems to have emphasized with an almost identical concluding formula: Matt 5–7; 10; 13; 18; 24–25. Bacon prefaced each of them with a narrative section so that the entire gospel consists of the five books (Matt 3–7; 8–10; 11:1—13:52; 13:53—18:35; 19–25), the introduction (Matt 1–2) and the conclusion (Matt 26–28).[41] A critical assessment of Bacon's thesis can be found in Luz.[42] Bacon's model is to be preferred because it is probably more sensitive to the text than other models. It suggests a reasonable structure which is based on, and takes quite seriously, one of important literary features (i.e., concluding discourse formula). As for this study, it is likely to help the reader to see clearly how strategically the interpersonal forgiveness and related texts are located in their respective teaching blocks in Matthew.[43]

As was noted earlier, the first seven of eight interpersonal forgiveness and related texts occur in the Sermon, each occupying a strategic rhetorical position, as was shown in chapter 2. This block of teaching material is placed at the beginning of Jesus' ministry in Galilee, and immediately after Jesus first calls his disciples (4:18–22). Matt 5:7 occurs near the beginning of the Sermon; it is located in the Beatitudes section (5:3–12). Matt 5:21–26 contains the first of the six antitheses, whereas 5:38–42 and 5:38–48 altogether comprise the climactic fifth and sixth antitheses in the first section of the Sermon. Matt 6:12, 14–15 belongs to the literary unit

39. France, *The Gospel of Matthew*, 2.

40. Neirynck, *Evangelica*, 15; see also Luz, *Matthew*, 1:3n6.

41. Bacon, "The Five Books of Matthew against the Jews," 56–66.

42. Luz, *Matthew*, 1:3.

43. A proposed detailed structure of the Matthean first discourse can be found in ch. 2 of this work.

6:5–15 about prayer, which in turn belongs to 6:1–18 which is concerned with Jesus and the Temple cult. The unit 6:5–15 is almost at centre of the Sermon, the Prayer (6:9–13) + 6:14–15 being more or less in the middle of the Sermon. Furthermore, interpersonal forgiveness and related texts altogether occupy a large proportion in the Sermon: about 392 of the 1,990 words of the material in it are devoted to interpersonal forgiveness and related subjects; this is not insignificant at all, especially in a block of teaching about various subjects. All this speaks volumes in favor of the centrality of the theme of interpersonal forgiveness in the Sermon.

THE STRUCTURE OF MATT 6:9-15

Two literary devices have proven helpful in determining the boundaries of 6:9–15 so as to see it as a unit. On the one hand we have οὖν (6:9); this device functions here possibly as an opening discourse marker. On the other hand, the end of the discourse in verse 15 is obvious: the temporal *deixis* marker ὅταν in 6:16 seems to clearly introduce another idea. Having that, the structure itself of 6:9–15 can now be proposed; the exegesis of 6:12, 14–15 will take into account the proposed heading for these verses in the structure below.

Introductory statement	(v. 9a)
Content of the prayer	(vv. 9b–15)
Address	*(v. 9b)*
Concerns for God	*(vv. 9c–10)*
Fatherhood of God	
Holiness of God	
Sovereign kingship of God	
Concerns for the needs of disciples	*(vv. 11–15)*
Need for food	(v. 11)
Need for forgiveness	(v. 12)
Need for deliverance and guidance	(v. 13)
Need for forgiveness expanded	(vv. 14–15)

TEXT-CRITICAL ISSUES IN MATT 6:12, 15

Textual problems occur in 6:12, 15. There are three major readings of verse 12b; some manuscripts have the aorist ἀφήκαμεν,[44] but others have the present ἀφίομεν[45] or ἀφίεμεν.[46] I prefer ἀφήκαμεν because the aorist reading is attested in some of the more important earliest Greek manuscripts, namely, codices Sinaiticus (א) and Vaticanus (B).[47] The second textual problem is in verse 15. There are two major readings of the first half of the verse. Some manuscripts have ἀνθρώποις[48] and some others read ἀνθρώποις τὰ παραπτώματα αὐτῶν.[49] The present author prefers ἀνθρώποις because this is the reading of at least one of the important Greek NT manuscripts: Codex Sinaiticus. Bruce Metzger and the committee also decided in favor of this shorter reading, based on internal evidence.[50]

---

44. This is the reading of the original hand of Codex Sinaiticus, as well as of B, Z and Family 1. Two early versions (Stuttgart edn of the Vulgate and Philoxenian Syriac version) translate this form of the verb; see Aland, ed., *Synopsis Quattuor Evangeliorum*, 86.

45. This is the reading of uncial codices D, L, W, Δ and Θ, as well as of a few other minuscules and possibly a Coptic manuscript; see Aland, *Synopsis Quattuor Evangeliorum*, 86.

46 This reading is supported by the first corrector of Codex Sinaiticus, as well as by Family 13. This is also the reading supported by the Majority text, by a *Didache* manuscript and possibly by a Coptic manuscript; see Aland, *Synopsis Quattuor Evangeliorum*, 86.

47 There is a good discussion on this problem in Metzger, *A Textual Commentary on the Greek New Testament*,

48. This is the reading of two uncial codices א and D, as well as of a few other minuscules and Family 1. A few early versions have translated the word; they include Vulgate, Peshitta (Pusey/Gwilliam, Gwilliam/Pinkerton/Kilgour), Middle Egyptian Coptic (Schenke), Bohairic Coptic (Horner). This reading is also attested in Augustine; see Aland et al., eds., *The Greek New Testament*, 19.

49. This is the reading of Codex Vaticanus, as well as of Codex of Paris, Codex of Washington DC, Codex of St. Gall, Codex of Tbilisi, and Codex of Münster/Westf. It is also supported by a few minuscules, including Family 1, by Byzantine witnesses and by a few Lectionaries; a number of early versions have also translated the phrase; these include Vulgate, Cyriac translations (Curetonian, Pusey/Gwilliam, Gwilliam/Pinkerton/Kilgour, White, and Lewis/Gibson), Coptic translations (Sahidic, Bohairic, and Middle Egyptian), Armenian, Ethiopic, Georgian, and Slavonic translations. The reading is also supported by Basil the Great.

50. Cf. Metzger, *Textual Commentary*, 14.

READING MATT 6:9-15 WITHIN ITS CO-TEXT

Matt 6:9–15 is located within a larger literary unit of 6:1–18, generally regarded as a discourse about righteousness, which in turn is located within the broader discourse in Matt 5–7. Matt 6:9–15 is a model prayer which is given in a context of a contrast: while the first contrast is with hypocrites (how, where and why they pray, 6:5–6), the second is with the Gentiles whose prayers are verbose and largely meaningless (6:7–8); then comes a model prayer (6:9–13), followed by a comment on forgiveness (6:14–15); this prayer is that of the righteous, as opposed to the unrighteous. Matt 6:9–15 fits in nicely within 6:1–18 and the broader discourse in Matt 5–7.

It is increasingly appreciated in our day that the study of any text involves considering a synopsis of any texts parallel to it, where applicable. In my case, in a synoptic table given below is Matthew's version of the Prayer and its counterpart in Luke.

Matt 6:9-15	Luke 11:2-4
9 Οὕτως οὖν προσεύχεσθε ὑμεῖς·	2 εἶπεν δὲ αὐτοῖς, Ὅταν προσεύχησθε, λέγετε,
Πάτερ ἡμῶν ὁ ἐν τοῖς οὐρανοῖς· ἁγιασθήτω τὸ ὄνομά σου·	Πάτερ, ἁγιασθήτω τὸ ὄνομά σου·
10 ἐλθέτω ἡ βασιλεία σου· γενηθήτω τὸ θέλημά σου, ὡς ἐν οὐρανῷ καὶ ἐπὶ γῆς.	ἐλθέτω ἡ βασιλεία σου
11 Τὸν ἄρτον ἡμῶν τὸν ἐπιούσιον δὸς ἡμῖν σήμερον·	3 τὸν ἄρτον ἡμῶν τὸν ἐπιούσιον δίδου ἡμῖν τὸ καθ' ἡμέραν·
12 καὶ ἄφες ἡμῖν τὰ ὀφειλήματα ἡμῶν, ὡς καὶ ἡμεῖς ἀφήκαμεν τοῖς ὀφειλέταις ἡμῶν·	4 καὶ ἄφες ἡμῖν τὰς ἁμαρτίας ἡμῶν, καὶ γὰρ αὐτοὶ ἀφίομεν παντὶ ὀφείλοντι ἡμῖν· καὶ μὴ εἰσενέγκῃς ἡμᾶς εἰς πειρασμόν.[B]
13 καὶ μὴ εἰσενέγκῃς ἡμᾶς εἰς πειρασμόν, ἀλλὰ ῥῦσαι ἡμᾶς ἀπὸ τοῦ πονηροῦ. 14 Ἐὰν γὰρ ἀφῆτε τοῖς ἀνθρώποις τὰ παραπτώματα αὐτῶν, ἀφήσει καὶ ὑμῖν ὁ πατὴρ ὑμῶν ὁ οὐράνιος· 15 ἐὰν δὲ μὴ ἀφῆτε τοῖς ἀνθρώποις, οὐδὲ ὁ πατὴρ ὑμῶν ἀφήσει τὰ παραπτώματα ὑμῶν.[A]	

[A]. Aland, The Greek New Testament, 18–19.
[B]. Ibid., 247–48.

From this table, it is easy to see that the material in the two gospels has similarities and differences, both in form and probably also in content. In terms of form, obviously, the wording of the Matthean version of the Prayer is more than double its Lukan version (91 words in Matthew against 44 words in Luke). This phenomenon has raised questions of source criticism. Two main hypotheses have been proposed. One hypothesis holds that Matthew is the "original" version; which means Luke abbreviated the Matthean material and adapted it. This hypothesis finds favor in the minority of scholars.[51] The other hypothesis suggests that Luke is the "original" version, which means Luke 11:2-4 is independent of Matt 6:9-13. This hypothesis is favored by the majority of scholars. To be sure, a proposal one suggests is determined by the solution one also has to the issue of the Synoptic Problem. The adherents of the two-source theory, for example, would logically say that Luke is probably closer to the "original."

Matt 6:9-15 represents the first evangelist's interpretation of the teaching of Jesus on the subject of prayer. How he has organized his material around this subject in this pericope is striking: he has the prayer in six petitions of almost equal length (vv. 9-13) and expands the fifth one (v. 12) rhetorically in two verses (14-15). With the help of personal *deixis* (σύ and ἐγώ in plural form), it is not hard to see that the first three petitions (6:9-10, where σύ occurs 3x in the expressions τὸ ὄνομά σου, ἡ βασιλεία σου, τὸ θέλημά σου) focus on God; whereas the following three (6:11-13, where ἐγώ occurs 4x respectively in forms of ἡμῶν [6x], ἡμῖν [4x], ἡμεῖς [2x] and ἡμᾶς [2x]) concentrate on the concerns of the disciples. As indicated in chapter 1, the exegesis of our first Matthean key interpersonal forgiveness pericope focuses on 6:12, 14-15 for two main reasons. First, because in it the idea of interpersonal forgiveness is stated quite explicitly by using the common verb ἀφίημι to describe interpersonal interrelationships; second, incorporated in it are the four strands of evidence that have been suggested in support of the argument for the prominence of the interpersonal forgiveness theme in Matthew. Having indicated that, the exegesis proper of 6:12, 14-15 may now be undertaken.

EXEGESIS OF MATT 6:12, 14-15

These passages can be outlined as follows:

---

51. E.g., Griesbach hypothesis holders.

6:12   Need for forgiveness: request for forgiveness and the basis of it

6:14–15 Need for forgiveness (expanded): the principle underlying God's forgiveness

Before embarking on the exegesis proper, two things need noting. First, the exegesis of this passage will not simply follow this outline because of the overlap between verses 12 and 14–15. So, the discussion of an issue in verse 12 would surely require that pieces of evidence from verses 14–15 (or beyond) be incorporated; the same can be said of verses 14–15. But the outline will remain in the background. Second, as was stated earlier (chs. 1 & 2), my main argument is that the interpersonal forgiveness theme is central to the message in Matthew. This is clear from the structure of the gospel itself and from four indications which altogether offer a distinctive pattern. Because almost all the four features of this pattern are incorporated in 6:12, 14–15, one of the main tasks of this section in exploring this text is to show how this pattern fits in this forgiveness text. Due attention will be paid to these features; they will be pointed out and stressed as the study of the text develops. In this chapter, we shall also seek to understand the nature of interpersonal forgiveness in 6:12, 14–15.

Four most important exegetical issues relating to the subject of interpersonal forgiveness can be identified in 6:12, 14–15. First is the meaning of the phrase ἀφίημι τοῖς ὀφειλέταις in verse 12 (so also ἀφίημι τὰ παραπτώματα in verses 14–15); second is the reading of ὡς καὶ ἡμεῖς in verse 12; third is the referent of the particle γὰρ in verse 14; fourth, lastly, is the scope of forgiveness in verses 14–15.

The Meaning of ἀφίημι τοῖς ὀφειλέταις (v. 12)

The meaning of the phrase ἀφίημι τοῖς ὀφειλέταις in verse 12 is one of the main exegetical issues in this text. The question is what the notion of debt behind ὀφειλέταις and that of trespass behind παραπτώματα (in the phrase ἀφίημι τὰ παραπτώματα in vv. 14–15) consist of, and the implications of this.

Rhetorical devices are used in verses 12, 14–15 in teaching on the subject of interpersonal forgiveness, repetition being just one of the more obvious devices in these verses. In 6:12, the expression ἀφίημι ὀφείλημα occurs twice: in verse 12b, ἀφίημι is used in connection with the verbal form of the noun ὀφείλημα (ὀφειλέταις) to describe the petitioner's forgiving act; just to mention in passing, verse 12 is the sole occurrence of the expression ἀφίημι τὰ ὀφειλήματα in the entire NT. In verses 14–15, ἀφίημι is employed in connection with παράπτωμα ("trespass," or "offence," or "sin"). Elsewhere in Matthew, ἀφίημι is employed in connection with ὀφειλήματα or with its synonyms. As examples, in 18:32 ὀφειλήματα is substituted by its feminine form ὀφειλὴν and is linked with ἀφίημι; in 18:27, ὀφειλήματα is replaced by δάνειον, which is also linked with ἀφίημι. The connection between what can be understood as "debts" and "sins" is also found elsewhere in Matthew (18:24, 28, 30, 34; 23:16, 18). This connection also emerges in Lukan tradition (Luke 7:41; 16:5, 7; 17:10). Remarkable parallels to it occur in Pauline tradition as well.[52]

The outstanding question is whether or not the meanings conveyed by ἀφίημι τὰ ὀφειλήματα and ἀφίημι παραπτώματα in these Matthean texts are the same. From the co-text of 6:12, 14–15, it is quite possible to think that these expressions most likely convey different but related meanings. Ἀφίημι τὰ ὀφειλήματα seems to suggest the idea of sins as *obligations*, whereas ἀφίημι παραπτώματα likely suggests the idea of sins as *violation* of norms. Betz has stated that, for the most part, Jewish and early Christian sources of the first-century CE connect ἀφίημι with terms for sins.[53] So, ὀφειλήματα and παραπτώματα are probably about "sins." But is this what we find in these sources?

One may begin with the LXX. As was shown in chapter 3 of this work, in LXX Gen 50:17, we have the combination ἀφίημι . . . ἀδικίαν; in the same text we also have δέχομαι . . . ἀδικίαν in the clause δέξαι τὴν ἀδικίαν τῶν θεραπόντων τοῦ θεοῦ τοῦ πατρός σου in which δέχομαι has replaced its equivalent ἀφίημι; in both cases, "sin" (ἀδικία) connotes *violation*, as opposed to *failure*. In LXX Exod 10:17, we have προσδέχομαι . . . ἁμαρτίαν in the clause προσδέξασθε οὖν μου τὴν ἁμαρτίαν in which προσδέχομαι has taken the place of its counter-part ἀφίημι; here, "sins" (ἁμαρτία) connotes *violation*. In LXX 1 Sam 15:25, we have the expression αἴρω . . . ἁμάρτημά in the clause ἆρον τὸ ἁμάρτημά μου where αἴρω has replaced its equivalent ἀφίημι; here too "sins" (ἁμάρτημα) connotes

---

52. E.g., Rom 1:14; 4:4; 8:12; 13:7–8; 15:1, 27; 1 Cor 5:10; 7:3, 36; 9:10; 11:7, 10; 2 Cor 12:11, 14; Gal 5:3; Phlm 18, cf. Eph 5:28; 2 Thess 1:3; 2:13.

53. Betz, *The Sermon*, 402; see also Bultmann, "Ἀφίημι, ἄφεσις, παρίημι, πάρεσις, κτλ.," 509–12.

violation. In LXX 1 Sam 25:28, we have the expression αἴρω . . . ἀνόμημα in the clause ἆρον τὸ ἀνόμημα τῆς δούλης σου where αἴρω has replaced its equivalent ἀφίημι; in this text, "sins" (ἀνόμημα) connotes *failure*. In LXX 1 Macc 13:39, the expression ἀφίημι . . . ἀγνοήμα καὶ ἁμαρτήμα is used; here, "sins" (ἁμάρτημά) connotes *violation*. In LXX Sir 28:2, we have the expression ἀφίημι . . . ἀδίκημα; in the same text, we also have the expression λύω . . . ἁμαρτίαν in the clause δεηθέντος σου αἱ ἁμαρτίαι σου λυθήσονται where λύω has replaced its counterpart ἀφίημι; here, "sins" (ἁμαρτία) seems to connote both *violation* and *failure*.

Secondly, the same phenomenon can be seen in the writings of Philo and Josephus. As was shown in chapter 4, Philo uses συγγνώμην ἁμαρτάνωσι, where συγγνώμη stands for its counterpart ἄφεσις[54]; in this text, "sins" (ἁμαρτάνω) seems to connote both *violation* and *failure*. Philo also employs the expression παραιτέομαι . . . ἁμαρτημάτα in the phrase παραίτησιν ἁμαρτημάτων where παραίτησις, which stands for ἄφεσις, is connected with ἁμαρτημάτα.[55] Here, the connoted meaning of both *violation* and *failure* for "sins" is probably envisaged. Josephus does use the expressions ἀφίημι . . . ἁμαρτίαν[56] and συγγνώμη . . . ἁμαρτάνω in the clause συγγνώμην αὐτῷ . . . τῶν ἡμαρτημένων, where συγγνώμη stands for its equivalent ἄφεσις[57]; while in the first passage, the connotation of *violation* for "sins" (ἁμαρτία/ἁμαρτάνω) is clear, in the second, that of *failure* is in view.

Finally, the evidence from early Christian sources include the *Didache*. In *Did*. 8.2, we find the expression ἀφίημι . . . ὀφειλήν in the clause καὶ ἄφες ἡμῖν τὴν ὀφειλὴν ἡμῶν, in which ὀφειλὴν is best understood as debts in the sense of sins; in the same passage, we have the expression ἀφίημι . . . ὀφειλέτης in the clause ὡς καὶ ἡμεῖς ἀφίεμεν τοῖς ὀφειλέταις ἡμῶν, in which ὀφειλέταις is best understood to mean debtors in the sense of sinners. In the first example, it is apparent that "debt" (ὀφειλὴ) stands for "sins" and in the second example, "debtor" (ὀφειλέτης) for "sinner." In both cases, the idea of failure to fulfill one's duties seems to be stressed. This, however, is not to reject the possibility of the connoted meaning of "actively doing something wrong" which is possibly conveyed by either ὀφειλὴ or ὀφειλέτης.

---

54. Philo, *Laws* 1.67.
55. Ibid., 2.196.
56. Josephus, *Ant*. 6.92–93.
57. Ibid., 9.214.

The survey above shows that in both Jewish and Graeco-Roman thinking, ἀφίημι is linked with terms which denote "sins." Therefore, the claim that Jewish and early Christian sources of the first-century CE connect ἀφίημι with terms for sins is grounded, given the fact that ὀφειλήματα and παραπτώματα are about sins. In Matthew, in all the occurrences of ἀφίημι τὰ ὀφειλήματα, the co-text of the sentences in which they appear seems to require that what can be referred to as *debts* be understood as sins, and debtors as sinners.

It can therefore be suggested that in 6:12 (ἀφίημι τὰ ὀφείληματὰ), in 18:27 (ἀφίημι τὸ δάνειον), and in 18:32 (ἀφίημι τὴν ὀφειλήν), the expression likely means something like remission of "sins" understood as *obligations*. It is possible to imagine that the meaning denoted by this expression seems to highlight the notion of sins as *failure* (although this does not exclude an understanding of "sins" as positively doing something wrong to one's fellow human), an idea that Warren Carter has understood to mean something like an "injustice."[58] He suggests that the language of debts in 6:12 and 18:21–35 depicts sin as an injustice; that is, not meeting one's obligations. He supports this by the Law and the Prophets. He points out, for example, that the sabbatical-regulations (Deut 15) required the cancellation of debt every seven years; he then stresses the fact that this practice ensured that none was permanently indebted, and it provided justice for the poor and needy (Deut 15:11). He also notes the connection of forgiveness and debts language in prayer which tends to recall the prophetic theme that worship and doing justice (i.e., "remitting debt; ensuring that the poor have access to resources; new social structure"[59]) are interconnected (Isa 1:10–17; 58:5–9).[60] Viewing the "debts" of both 6:12 and 18:23–35 as sin in the sense of failure or injustice is reasonable. Luz, however, thinks that this sense of the term applies to 6:12, but not necessarily to 18:23–35 because with Jesus and in Judaism "sin" is often understood not as failure but as "guilt."[61] Luz's suggestion is not persuasive enough. As was shown above, what can be referred to as "debt" in 18:23–35 is probably best understood as failure.

What is observed in the First Gospel, as far as the use of the term "debt" for sin is concerned, seems to suggest Matthew's redaction. There

---

58. Carter, *Matthew and the Margins*, 167.
59. Ibid.
60. Ibid.
61. Luz (*Matthew*, 1:322), referring to Luke 7:41–43; 16:1–8; Matt 18:23–35.

is a wider recognition in scholarship that "debts" reflects a common Aramaic metaphor for sins, a metaphor drawn from the law and commerce realm.[62] How Matthew has applied this metaphoric language in religious topic of sins and forgiveness of sins remains an outstanding question. It is possible to imagine with Jean Carmignac and many others that Matthew most likely did so to highlight the notion of sins as *failure* to fulfill what one is supposed to:

> Assimiler le péché à une dette envers Dieu, c'est en élargir notablement la notion. C'est y inclure tous les cas d'omission. C'est rappeler que tout notre être appartient à Dieu, que nous sommes obligés en tout à procurer sa gloire, que nous sommes en dette envers lui dès que nous n'agissons plus pour lui ... C'est faire écho aux paraboles où Jésus présente l'homme pécheur comme un débiteur insolvable et Dieu comme un créancier compatissant (Luc 7,41–43 et Matthieu 18,21–35.[63]

According to Carmignac, this metaphoric language in Matthew has to be interpreted within divine-human interrelationships. This reading has some merit, although one still wonders about what it does with interpersonal interrelationships. Betz's interpretation looks quite reasonable; it includes both the vertical and horizontal interrelationships. Betz has also interpreted "debts" in 6:12 to mean sins in the sense of *obligations*; he has highlighted the notion of sins as *failure*, appealing to two possible presupposed realities behind the notion of debts. The first reality is the social one that all human affairs are fundamentally those of mutual obligations, and this also does include one's relationship with God; the second is the realization that these obligations, at least to a significant degree, remain unfulfilled. Betz further argues that justice requires that one properly deals with and redeems all existing obligations; so, leaving them permanently unredeemed constitutes injustice. He goes on to suggest two ways by which one can deal with obligations: first is by having the debtor willingly or by force "pay the debt," and second by allowing the creditor to cancel the debts. He then points out that in either case the debtor is released from the obligation.[64]

---

62. For more detail and evidence in favor of this claim, see A. Watson, *The Law of Obligations in the Later Roman Republic*.

63. Carmignac, *Recherches sur le "Notre Père*," 224–25.

64. Betz, *The Sermon on the Mount*, 402.

Betz's proposal has some merits. Firstly, it sets reasonably the framework for the interpretation of the notion of debts in divine-human and human-human relationships. Second, it sees debts as *unfulfilled obligations* that require that they be resolved. And third, it acknowledges two approaches the creditor can use in handling the matter: either to force the debtor to pay the debt, or to cancel the debt. As to the framing of debts in the context of interrelationships, the question is to what extent human interrelations constitute *obligations* so as to be equated with sins. Leonardo Boff probably has a reasonable answer. He has stated that at the level of relationships, whether to God or to humans, various attitudes take shape; these attitudes are love, friendship, sympathy, cooperation, indifference, withdrawal, humiliation, arrogance, and exploitation, among many others. He then notes that there is no neutrality here. He goes on to argue that the human *ego* always manifests itself in living with others and committing oneself to them. He contends that it is within this interrelatedness that one finds an experience of indebtedness to someone else, or even of reciprocal offences committed.[65]

Clearly, Boff sees human life as consisting of an interconnected web of obligations; with regard to forgiveness, this indebtedness consists of potential reciprocal offences (or sins) committed. Betz and Boff have quite reasonably elaborated this. It is not hard to read from their conclusions the relationship between "debts" and "sins," a kind of relationship which seems to fit nicely Matthew's flow of thought in chapters 6 and 18 in which the idea of debt emerges in the context of divine-human and human-human relationships.

Summing up, in all probability, speaking from the point of view of Matthew, ἀφίημι τὰ ὀφειλήματα in 6:12 (so also 18:32 [ὀφειλή], 18:27 [δάνειον]) meant something like to "forgive debts" in the sense of remitting *sins* understood as *obligations*; but this also involves positively doing something wrong. In 6:12 what can be understood as forgiving debtors, in the phrase ἀφίημι τοῖς ὀφειλέταις, seems to stress the obligation of the wrongdoer vis-à-vis their victim. In 6:14–15, on the other hand, ἀφίημι τὰ παραπτώματα clearly means something like remission of "trespasses" understood as *violation* of something. This is probably how Matthew's readers may have understood this piece of teaching.

---

65. Boff, *The Lord's Prayer*, 87–88.

The Reading of ὡς καὶ ἡμεῖς (v. 12)

In the petition in 6:12b, the disciples are instructed to ask their heavenly Father to forgive them ὡς καὶ ἡμεῖς ἀφήκαμεν τοῖς ὀφειλέταις ἡμῶν. Temporal *deixis* is another clear rhetorical device employed by the first evangelist in 6:12 to describe the instruction given to the disciples: on the one hand there is the phrase ὡς καὶ ἡμεῖς; on the other hand, we have the aorist ἀφήκαμεν. To begin with the first point, the reading of the phrase ὡς καὶ ἡμεῖς is one of the main exegetical issues in this text. To repeat what was said earlier (ch. 2), I prefer the conditional reading of the phrase because the grammar of the text demands it and the co-text of the passage supports it; moreover, it is firmly corroborated by the expository comment in 6:14–15. Second, connected to this conditional phrase is the tense of ἀφήκαμεν. As was indicated earlier in this chapter, there are three readings of ἀφίημι in this verse. The aorist reading is to be preferred because it is attested in two most reliable uncial codices (ℵ and B). The Matthean version of the account, using the aorist tense (ἀφήκαμεν) gives the impression that God's forgiveness depends upon human's initiative, for the one praying seems to request forgiveness to the extent that they themselves ἀφήκαμεν (*have forgiven*) their debtors. The question is how God's forgiveness and human forgiveness stand together in this text.

Opinions are divided on the interrelationship just noted. There are two clear alternatives: the first is the conditional reading of the connective, and the second, the non-conditional reading of it. The non-conditional reading has been endorsed by W. Hendricksen and F. D. Bruner, among others. Uncomfortable with the conditional reading of 6:12, they have argued against this reading probably for theological reasons. Hendricksen thinks that if the conditional interpretation is to be privileged, then this would mean that our forgiving disposition earns God's forgiveness.[66] This argument is obviously biased; it is not entirely true that the conditional reading of 6:12 (so also 6:14–15) necessarily entails the interpretation that forgiving earns God's forgiveness. Bruner, on the other hand, in an attempt to avoid the expression "condition" for the clause ὡς καὶ ἡμεῖς has ended up with probably a confusing statement:

> In particular, the privilege of praying for the *Father*'s forgiveness—the meaning of the first part of the Fifth Petition—is placed by Jesus *before* the rider of *our* forgiveness of others. This means that Jesus reminds us of our standing privilege of access

---

66. Hendriksen, *The Gospel of Matthew*, 334; italics original.

to the Father *before* he reminds us of our standing responsibility of forgiving neighbours. This order, this sequence, makes me prefer the expression *"consequence"* to "condition" for the clause "as we, too, forgave those who failed us," though the consequence is close to being a condition.[67]

Bruner's argument is not persuasive enough; it seems to lack consistency. Apparently, it is grounded in the visible aspect of the syntax; the underlying idea of the syntax itself seems not to be heeded. The non-conditional reading of 6:12 (cp. 6:14–15) is on shaky ground because of the intrinsic motives of its defenders and the kind of evidence they use to secure it.

There are sound reasons to prefer the conditional reading of verse 12: the grammar of the text demands it and the co-text of the passage supports it. This reading is decisively substantiated by the explanatory comment in 6:14–15 which follows immediately the Prayer and is particularly related to the petition in verse 12; apparently implicit in verse 12, the conditional element becomes more explicit in verses 14–15, where an antithetical parallelism is used; this rhetorical device makes this reading clearer and emphasized by being stated both positively and negatively. Carmignac's comment below on this conditional reading is to the point:

> [I]l faut reconnaître que cette présentation est en accord profond avec la pensée évangélique:... Matthieu 6,14–15 reproduit sous une autre forme la même antériorité ... à la fin de la parabole du débiteur impitoyable, Jésus en dégage lui-même la leçon ...; enfin Matthieu 5,23–24 insiste plus clairement encore ... Cette antériorité est une donnée ferme et constante de l'Évangile de Matthieu.[68]

This statement recognizes the straightforward conditional reading of the text and highlights the precedence of the human act of forgiving over the divine act of it in 6:12 and beyond. As Todd Pokrifka-Joe has reasonably stated, there is no good exegetical reason to reject this straightforward reading.[69] Thoroughly related to the discussion above is the issue of the tense ἀφήκαμεν of verse 12b. This aorist ἀφήκαμεν (against the Lukan present ἀφίεμεν) clearly underpins the idea behind

---

67 Bruner, *Matthew*, 1.311.

68 Carmignac, *Recherches sur le "Notre Père,"* 231.

69 Pokrifka-Joe, "Probing the Relationship between Divine and Human Forgiveness in Matthew," 166.

the conditional phrase ὡς καὶ ἡμεῖς. As Pokrifka-Joe has also noted, with this past tense here, the petition places significant responsibility on those praying to make sure they have *already* forgiven their fellow humans if they desire to be forgiven by God.[70]

The point which seems to be emphasized by the juxtaposition of this aorist and the conditional phrase in verse 12b clearly serves to accentuate the precedence of human forgiveness over against divine forgiveness. Moreover, verse 15 presents the negative antithesis of verse 14. The terms used in this assertion are the same as those used in verse 14, as the table below shows.

Matt 6:14	Matt 6:15
Ἐὰν γὰρ ἀφῆτε τοῖς ἀνθρώποις τὰ παραπτώματα αὐτῶν, ἀφήσει καὶ ὑμῖν ὁ πατὴρ ὑμῶν ὁ οὐράνιος·	ἐὰν δὲ μὴ ἀφῆτε τοῖς ἀνθρώποις, οὐδὲ ὁ πατὴρ ὑμῶν ἀφήσει τὰ παραπτώματα ὑμῶν.

It is clear that the point which is stressed by the juxtaposition of the aorist ἀφήκαμεν (v. 12b), by the conditional phrase ὡς καὶ ἡμεῖς (v. 12b) and by the antithetical parallelism in verses 14–15 is the precedence of human forgiveness over against divine forgiveness. It is reasonable to think that for Matthew, the refusal of forgiveness toward others certainly leads to God's refusal to forgive the unforgiving person; in this sense, forgiving appears to be a moral duty from the offended person's point of view. This trend is a clear example of the notion of reciprocity in forgiveness and the link between reluctance in forgiving and the idea of judgment in Matthew.

It is striking that the notion of conditionality in divine-human forgiveness appears to be rare in biblical Judaism, as was shown earlier (ch. 4). Sir 28:1–4 is the only Jewish classic example in this regard. It is the sole apparent LXX text in which interpersonal forgiveness is stated clearly as a condition for seeking or receiving God's forgiveness. In this text, a person's forgiveness of their neighbors is connected with God's potential forgiveness of this person. As J. L. Crenshaw has commented, verses 1–4 insist that anyone who desires forgiveness from the Lord must first exercise that compassion toward their fellow human beings, including their enemies.[71] Matthew's teaching in 6:14–15 (cp. 18:32–35 [cp. Mark 11:25; Luke 11:14; Jas 2:13]) is clearly parallel to the teaching we find in Sir 28:1–4. The similarity between the Matthean material and the

---

70 Ibid.
71. Crenshaw, "The Book of Sirach," 5.772.

Sirach material has caused scholars to strongly urge that Sir 28:1–4 is a possible basis for the parable of the unmerciful debtor of 18:23–35.[72]

It is worth stressing that in both Sir 28:1–4 and Matt 6:14–15, the concept of conditionality in divine-human forgiveness emerges in the context of prayer, a fact of which Reimer shows no indication of awareness. This phenomenon is apparent in Mark 11:25 and in Luke 11:2–4, where the forgiveness teaching also occurs in the context of prayer. In Sir 28:1–7, more than just being defined as disgrace, anger, and wrath are identified with the unforgiving people. In the Sirach text, the emphasis is on God's vengeance over those who themselves take vengeance and thus clearly fail to forgive their fellow humans. It is this same emphasis which most likely underlies the teaching in Matt 6:15: "not being forgiven by the heavenly Father" may be understood as God's judgment, a phrase whose teaching is plain in 18:23–35. This would then mean that, for the first evangelist, the heavenly Father will not leave unpunished anyone who fails to forgive their fellow humans. A similar idea can be found in Ps 18:25–28, the general thesis of which appears to be that God's attitude toward his people is based upon their attitude toward him and toward others. In the general statement "with the crooked you show yourself perverse" of verse 26b, God's punishment is clearly in view. Applied to human attitudes toward others, this statement may be expanded to also include reluctance to forgive others, in which case God's punishment hangs over the individual with such a spirit. This concept of reciprocity, broadly conceived in this Psalm, abounds in the Matthean material quite specifically with the link between mercy and forgiveness (or the lack of them) and judgment (5:7, 44–45, 48; 6:12, 14–15; 7:1–2, 12; 18:32b–35), as was shown in detail in chapter 1. Further evidence for the conditional forgiveness teaching in post-biblical Judaism may include the *Testament of the Twelve Patriarchs* (*T. Gad* 6.3–7; *T. Zeb* 5.1–5; 8:1–6; *T. Jos* 18.2), rabbinic literature,[73] and Qumran (1QS and CD texts [cf. ch. 6]).

Clearly, conditionality in the teaching about divine-human forgiveness, although very rare in the Hebrew Bible, is however not absent from Jewish thought. The distinctiveness of the Matthean teaching about the

---

72. Cf. Reimer, "The Apocrypha and Biblical Theology," 277–79.

73. E.g., *b. Yoma* 9b; *b. Yoma* 86a–86b; *b. Šabb.* 151b; *b. Šabb.* 88b; *R.H.* 17a; *Meg.* 28a; *Sifre* 93b; *m. 'Abot* 3.11; *t. Yoma* 5.6ff, etc. Cf. Israel Abrahams, who has discussed most of them in "Man's Forgiveness," 1:150–167; so also Moule, "As We Forgive," 278–86.

conditional forgiveness, it has to be stressed, is its strong sense of accountability underlying forgiving or reluctance to forgive:

> 'Should you not have had mercy on your fellow slave, as I had mercy on you?' And in anger his lord handed him over to be tortured until he would pay his entire debt. So my heavenly Father will also do to every one of you, if you do not forgive your brother or sister from your heart. (18:33–35; cp. 6:15; 7:1–2; 5:7)

This emphasis is found nowhere else in the data surveyed in this study, except Sir 28:1–4 and *Ant. Rom.* 8.50.1–4. Yet, even here, the differences can still be observed. The Sirach text only states what will happen to the vengeful person: they "will face the Lord's vengeance" (v. 1). It also points to forgiving as a necessary condition for receiving God's forgiveness. It says nothing at all about what will happen to the unforgiving person.

A minority of scholars have recently argued that primary motives for forgiving are largely *self-focused*, rather than altruistic as is generally believed.[74] The difference between this proposal and what is found in Matthew is that, while this secular understanding of the motives for forgiving focuses on the forgiver's health, in this gospel, accountability before God is at the centre of the forgiving motives (18:23–35; 7:1–2; 6:14–15; 5:7). In Matthew, acts of showing mercy and forgiving are motivated by the merciful person or forgiver's identity and belonging to the kingdom.

The strategy used by Matthew in the forgiveness material in 6:12, 14–15 (and beyond) seems to suggest that through it he wanted to stress the responsibility of the offended person in forgiving. For him, it is the responsibility of the believer to forgive. This, however, does not rule out the responsibility of the offender in seeking forgiveness (cf. 5:21–26; 6:12a, where the onus is placed on the offender). Here one can recognize and situate the area of focus in Matthew's argument on the subject of interpersonal forgiveness. The question is what this really means. Betz thinks of the connection between human and divine forgiveness as the principle of justice and equity.[75] This might be true; but it needs to be verified.

The future tense in 6:14–15 (ἀφήσει [v. 14] and οὐδὲ ἀφήσει [v. 15]) is quite ambiguous. The main question is whether or not it is

---

74. Younger et al., "Dimensions of Forgiveness," 837–55.
75. Betz, *The Sermon on the Mount*, 417.

eschatological. Scholars are divided over their reading of it. Carter, for example, has taken a radical view, arguing that this tense in these verses is "logical rather than eschatological."[76] This reading tends to lose the eschatological flavour of the verb. Others, on the other hand, have argued for the eschatological orientation of the forgiveness petition[77]; this also tends to exclude the *now* reality of the action of the verb. Perhaps both aspects of the verb are in view in these verses. Betz has stated this quite nicely: "... the future tense of ἀφήσει ... points to the eschatological judgment, but the power of forgiveness as well as the acceptance of God's forgiveness are granted to the faithful even now."[78]

The Referent of γὰρ (vv. 14–15)

The concept of interpersonal forgiveness stated *implicitly* in verse 12 (cf. the conditional phrase ὡς καὶ ἡμεῖς and the aorist ἀφήκαμεν) is brought out more *emphatically* in verses 14–15 by being stated positively (v. 14) and negatively (v. 15). It is worth mentioning that the statement in these verses presents two fundamental exegetical problems. First are two main readings of ἄνθρωπος in verse 15a; of these readings, as indicated earlier in this chapter,[79] I have preferred ἀνθρώποις because this reading is attested in one of the important and most reliable uncial codex: Codex Sinaiticus. The second problem has to do with the reading of γὰρ in verse 14. The question is what the conjunction refers back to, and the implication of this: Does it refer back to verse 12 or more than that?

Opinions are divided on this question. While some think that verses 14–15 are an interpretation of verse 12,[80] others believe this verse is an implementation of the moral principle that emerges in verses 14–15.[81] A comparison between verses 14–15 and 12 gives the impression that, verses 14 and 15 logically come first. Bearing Mark 11:24 in mind, Betz has suggested that the moral rule in verses 14–15 had an independent existence prior to its inclusion in the present Matthean context.[82] This

---

76. Carter, *Matthew and the Margins*, 170.
77. E.g., R. Brown, "The Pater Noster as an Eschatological Prayer," 217–53.
78. Betz, *The Sermon on the Mount*, 416.
79. Cf. "text-critical issues in Matt 6:12, 15."
80. Strecker and Luz are among those who have taken this line.
81. Betz is among those who follow this line.
82. Betz, *The Sermon on the Mount*, 416.

has some logic in it. First is what he refers to as the "principle of reciprocity and justice."[83] The logic here goes like this. If the petitioner of verse 12a expects that their prayers will be answered, their expectation is conditional upon their own readiness to forgive (v. 12b). This would then explain the reason why verse 12 has the petition first and the declaration second, and verses 14-15 forgiveness by the disciples first and the promise of the forgiveness by God second. The second premise is what could be called a practical standard. As Betz has it, the "principle of reciprocity and justice" is set as a practical standard for the community of the disciples, a standard that comes to expression in various ways especially in the Sermon. Its logic is this: if the petition in verse 12 is an application of the principle in verses 14-15, then the issue of forgiveness does not cease when forgiveness is granted; for the disciple who is continually asking for God's forgiveness is also meant to continually offer forgiveness to others.

In fact, from a methodological point of view, Betz's proposal is open to debate; one wonders how later texts in a pericope can serve to illuminate former texts. Yet, this suggestion has some logic in it. For our part, the conditional element in 6:14-15 is explicit and emphasized rhetorically by being stated positively and negatively. It is here that the conditioned forgiveness principle appears clearly as a fact. According to these verses, only the forgiving person will be forgiven; fit to seek God's forgiveness is the disciple who has first shown readiness to forgive. The connection of 6:14-15 with the Prayer is thus twofold: semantically, it is by the catchword ἀφίημι (2x [6:12] and 4x [6:14-15]) and by the conjunction γὰρ (6:14); pragmatically, theological, liturgical, and ethical reasons surely underlie 6:12 and 6:14-15. The request in 6:12a has the act mentioned in 6:12b as its possible basis; this request and its basis as stated in 6:12 are grounded in God's grace conveyed through the idea of gratuity which can be discerned from the Prayer and from Matt 6.[84] As a principle of Jewish legal and theological thinking (Sir 28:1-4), 6:14-15 is probably also presupposed in the Sermon.[85]

---

83. Ibid.
84. So also Stiewe and Vouga, *Le Sermon sur la montagne*, 131.
85. Betz, *The Sermon on the Mount*, 416.

The Scope of Forgiveness (vv. 14–15)

Some vagueness over the object of the forgiveness required in 6:14–15 is clear. This has raised the question of whether or not forgiveness is to be confined within the circle of the Christian community. There seems to be strong evidence in support of a universalist reading of these verses. Verse 14a states the forgiving condition in general terms: ἀφῆτε ... τὰ παραπτώματα. Special reference tends to be made to the "transgressions" (παραπτώματα) of norms, not to the "obligations" (ὀφειλήματα), as in verse 12 (cp. 18:27, 32). It has been suggested that this difference is due to the nature of the source from which 6:14 derives (cf. Mark 11:25 where παραπτώματα is used).[86] In verse 14, the statement that forgiveness is to be offered to ἀνθρώποις ("people") seems to highlight the fact of the existence of Matthew's community in the midst of all humanity. In this way, the rule is thus valid not only for the members of this Christian community, but for everyone. So, it can be concluded with Betz that the demand to forgive ἀνθρώποις in 6:14 strongly suggests a universalist orientation.[87] This reading of the verse seems to square with my general view of the aim of Matthew's interpersonal forgiveness texts. Earlier in this chapter, it was suggested that Matthew possibly engaged in some sort of polemic between his Christian community and some other groups within Judaism.[88]

CONCLUSIONS

One of the main tasks in the exegesis of 6:12, 14–15 was to demonstrate how seriously Matthew highlights the notion of interpersonal forgiveness in the gospel. It was suggested that in Matt 6:12, 14–15, the emphasis on this theme is carried out in three ways. First we have the concept of reciprocity in forgiving and the link between reluctance to forgive and judgment. This concept is obvious in 6:12, 14–15 where this idea is stated clearly in two ways: (1) by means of the phrase ὡς καὶ ἡμεῖς in verse 12b; and (2) by the use of an antithetical parallelism in verses 14–15, a rhetorical device which makes obvious the consequences awaiting the potential

---

86. Ibid.
87. Ibid., 417.
88. So also Meeks, *The Moral World of the First Christians*, 137; Harrington, *God's People in Christ*, 97; Senior, *What Are They Saying about Matthew?*, 6–10; Segal, "Matthew's Jewish Voice," 35–37; White, "Crisis Management and Boundary Maintenance," 240; Duling and Perrin, *The New Testament*, 335, among many others.

unforgiving person—the consequences probably implied here but stated explicitly in 18:35.

Second is the emphasis on the responsibility of the offended person in forgiving; this emphasis is evident through the use of the past tense ἀφήκαμεν in verse 12, which clearly underscores the petitioner's prior forgiving act, and through the antithetical parallelism in verses 14–15. Third is the reinforcement of the concept of interpersonal forgiveness; this is evident (1) through the idea of interpersonal forgiveness being stated directly using ἀφίημι (4x) to describe both divine-human relationships and interpersonal relationships, (2) through the fact that the forgiveness petition in verse 12 is both *expanded* and *emphatically* stated beyond the Prayer and the Sermon (cf. 6:14–15; 18:21–35), and (3) through an antithetical parallelism in verses 14–15 (with its effects beyond this text—rhetorical device which surely serves to highlight the consequences awaiting the potential unforgiving person, cp. 18:35).

Fourth is the position of 6:12 in the Sermon and its expansion beyond the Prayer (6:14–15). The forgiveness petition in verse 12 is the only petition of the Prayer to be expanded and stated emphatically, as is evident from verses 14–15—verses which are the first evangelist's interpretation of the Prayer. Fifth is the proportion interpersonal forgiveness material occupies in and around the Prayer. This material has the lion's share: 43 of the 91 words (around 47 percent) of it is devoted to the subject of interpersonal forgiveness. This is indeed a significant proportion in a single unit. Last of all, what can be understood in terms of "forgiving debtors" in ἀφίημι τοῖς ὀφειλέταις in verse 12 seems to stress the obligation of the offender. Of note is also the possibility that in 6:12, the expression ἀφίημι τὰ ὀφειλήματα means something like "forgiving debts" in the sense of remitting "sins" understood as *obligations*. In 6:14–15, on the other hand, ἀφίημι τὰ παραπτώματα means something like remitting "sins" understood as *violation* of established norms.

6

The Rhetoric of Interpersonal Forgiveness in Matt 18:21–35

Matt 18:21–35 is the second key forgiveness text to be explored in detail for this investigation. In this text an emphasis on interpersonal forgiveness can be observed, first, through the concept of reciprocity and the link between mercy and forgiveness, together with the link between reluctance in the *praxis* of forgiveness and judgment; second, through the emphasis on the offended person's responsibility to forgive others; third, through a reinforcement of the interpersonal forgiveness concept by the use of related ideas; fourth, through strategic rhetorical positioning of interpersonal forgiveness texts within the discourse in Matt 18 and within the gospel; and fifth, through the space given to interpersonal forgiveness and related issues within the Community Discourse. In examining 18:21–35, due attention will be paid to these features, for they provide evidence for the seriousness with which Matthew takes the notion of interpersonal forgiveness. They will be pointed out and highlighted as the exegesis of the text develops. As before, in an attempt to draw a plausible overall interpretation of the discourse about forgiveness in this text, due attention will be paid to the text, the co-text, the inter-texts, and the context. The reading of this text will be done with the purpose of elucidating the meaning of ἀφίημι and describing the dynamics of both divine and human forgiveness.

The Rhetoric of Interpersonal Forgiveness in Matt 18:21-35 149

This chapter consists of six main sections: (1) the structure of Matt 18 and its flow of thought; (2) key exegetical forgiveness-related issues in Matt 18; (3) the interpretation of the parable in 18:23–35; (4) an outline of 18:23–35; (5) an exegesis of 18:23–35; (6) a brief summary of the findings of the chapter.

A PROPOSED OUTLINE OF MATT 18 AND THE FLOW OF THOUGHT IN IT

Two items are discussed under this heading: the first is a plausible outline of Matt 18, and the second presents the flow of thought in this chapter.

18:1–35	Teaching about maintenance of relationships in the community
18:1–14	Teaching about the roles of the *spiritually mature* members
18:15–20	Teaching about dealing with the *spiritually immature* members
18:15–17	Brotherly reconciliation
18:21–35	Teaching about interpersonal forgiveness
18:21–22	Peter's concern about forgiveness
18:23–35	The parable of the unforgiving debtor

This structure shows that about 60 percent of the material in this teaching material block (Matt 18) is devoted to interpersonal forgiveness and related ideas. The motif of interpersonal forgiveness runs throughout this discourse which is concerned with the preservation of the community—a main issue in the Matthean community. Matt 18:21–35 is part of the larger literary unit 18:1–35 about church life. In it a number of issues are addressed, including care for the "little ones," brotherly reconciliation, mercy, and interpersonal forgiveness. These three pieces of teaching most likely serve to warn the members of Matthew's community that they should remain united, as members of the kingdom and for their survival.

As to the flow of thought in Matt 18, the preservation of the community seems to be the central teaching of this chapter.[1] How does the interpersonal forgiveness theme fit in this central teaching? How significant is Matthew's manner of structuring his material around this central

---

1. So also Luz, *Matthew*, 2:423.

theme, and what is its significance for 18:21–35, with regard to the theme of interpersonal forgiveness?

Matthew seems to state that the disciple is a member of the wider family of the kingdom of God (18:1, 3–4, 23). As was indicated in chapter 5, this wider family finds its fuller expression in the smaller family, the church (16:18; 18:17). The members of this Christian community are the τούτων τῶν πιστευόντων εἰς ἐμέ ("those who believe in me") of verse 6. They are to consider one another as brothers and sisters (ὁ ἀδελφός σου, 18:15–17, 21), children of the same Father (cf. phrase ὁ πατήρ μου/ὑμῶν ὁ οὐράνιος in 18:10, 14, 19, 35; cp. 6:9, 14–15). As children of the *heavenly* Father and his *earthly* representatives in this community composed of both the *spiritually mature* and *immature* brethren, if the latter are to seek greatness in the kingdom of this Father of theirs (18:1), they (the *spiritually mature*) are to be primarily concerned with the preservation of the community; they are to accept greater responsibility in caring for the *spiritually immature* brethren, the "little ones." Apparently, the *spiritually mature* brethren are people who must have undergone a radical change in their lives (18:3) and are characterized by humility (18:3–4). This would be visible in their relating to and dealing with one another, most particularly with the *spiritually immature* brethren. They should be able to welcome the weaker brethren in the sense of caring for them (18:5), and make every effort not to lose even a single member, whether by their own behavior (18:6–10) or as a result of the *immature* brethren's own behavior (18:12–14; 15–17).

The *spiritually immature* brethren will potentially display their weakness to a particular *spiritually mature* brother or sister (and this may result in the former departing from the group). Yet, as part of their responsibility, the *spiritually mature* brethren are the ones to take the initiative in going to these fellow brethren in danger, at least three times, using different approaches either to retain them in the group or to bring them back to the group (18:12–17). As a means of preserving the community, and as part of their role, more *spiritually mature* brethren are to be endlessly ready to forgive the others limitlessly (18:21–22). This would confirm their understanding of their new identity in the kingdom (18:3) and confirm their place in it. As can be seen, the theme of the preservation of church community is clearly present in Matt 18; it not only flows throughout the section, but is also stressed in it. Matthew seems to say that fit for the kingdom are those who show concern for the preservation of the community and know how to relate to and deal with other members of it, more particularly the *spiritually immature* members. Concerning the perspective from which Matthew has structured his argument and the implication of this for the understanding of 18:21–35, it is quite possible that the discourse in Matt 18 focuses on the roles of the *spiritually mature* brethren toward the *spiritually immature* brethren.

EXEGETICAL ISSUES IN MATT 18

Several exegetical issues have been identified in Matt 18. Only three of them will be considered because of their direct connection with the topic under investigation. They are the relationship between repentance and forgiveness, the phrase ὁ ἐθνικὸς καὶ ὁ τελώνης and the connection between 18:15–17 and 18:21–22. In an attempt to address them, these issues will first be mentioned one after another, and then the interpretive proposals will follow.

Repentance and Forgiveness

It appears as something of a surprise to observe the lack of a direct reference to repentance in 6:12, 14–15; 18:15–17 and 18:21–22, where one would expect such a reference. Curiously, this issue seems to have not grasped the interest of scholars. Yet seeking to know the reason behind this lack, especially in an interpersonal forgiveness discourse, may help identify Matthew's overall emphasis, and provide a plausible explanation of some of the puzzles which are observed in Matt 18. Referring to these texts, scholars have suggested that repentance is assumed in them. Hagner, for example, has found support for his assumption from Luke 17:3–4, a parallel to Matt 18:21–22. Commenting on the connection between 18:15–17 and 18:21–22, he states that the difference between the former and the latter is this: in 18:15–17 the repentance of the sinning one is lacking, and in 18:21–22 it is assumed. He then makes the point that the subject in the latter is one who sins and repents.[2]

To say that repentance is lacking in 18:15–17 and that it is assumed in 18:21–22 is clearly to recognize the facts, and to state this on the basis of their Lukan parallel is to think logically. But to ask why repentance is lacking in these texts is probably to take the debate a step further. A possible answer to the question of why repentance does not appear

---

2. Hagner, *Matthew* 2:537.

explicitly in 18:15–35 is perhaps that repentance actually did not square with Matthew's argument about forgiveness in these passages, an argument which focuses on the responsibilities of his community members; that is, arguing primarily with the responsibility of the offended person in mind, Matthew did not find repentance relevant to his argument in Matt 6 and 18.

This, however, is not to say that for Matthew repentance is unnecessary for forgiveness. As indicated in chapter 1, it has been claimed that one of the crucial differences between Jesus and the Judaism of his day was Jesus' willingness to forgive in God's name without requiring prior repentance and, more determinatively, his authorization for his disciples to do likewise. E. P. Sanders, for example, has stated that Jesus invited sinners into the kingdom without requiring them to repent in the way that repentance was understood within Judaism—that is, without requirements of restitution, sacrifice, and obedience to the law.[3] Jones has criticized Sanders for seeming to imply that Jesus' message abandoned repentance.[4] Jones' criticism is probably off-target, for Sanders does not imply that Jesus' message abandoned repentance, at least as far as I understand his argument. Rather, what Sanders is trying to dismiss is the view that Jesus called for conventional rituals of repentance as a pre-condition for inclusion in the kingdom.[5] Sanders earlier noted a few repentance texts in the Synoptics, which he rapidly discussed. In his discussion of this issue, statements like the following are used: "It is emphasized that Jesus has the power to announce the forgiveness of individual's and thus to heal him . . ."; "[t]he story of the father with two sons (Luke 15.11–32), though it lacks the words, is clearly a story of repentance and forgiveness; and it makes the same point as the related parables in Luke 15:3–10: there is more joy over a repentant sinner than over the righteous who have no need of repentance."[6]

In the Synoptic gospels, clearly, Jesus' ministry is inaugurated with Jesus' announcement of the kingdom and his call to repentance. Matthew, for his part, seems not to overlook repentance; he stresses repentance as a necessary condition to enter the kingdom of heaven (3:2, 8, 11; 4:17). To be added as the evidence in this regard is 5:21–26. This passage highlights

---

3. Sanders, *Jesus and Judaism*, 207.
4. Jones, *Embodying Forgiveness*, 110.
5. Sanders, *Jesus and Judaism*, 206–7.
6. Ibid., 111–12; cf. Jones, *Embodying Forgiveness*, 111–12.

the urgency of being reconciled with an ἀδελφός in order to avoid eventual judgment. The main teaching of this passage seems to be prohibition to offend an ἀδελφός; but in the case an offence has taken place, the offender should seek reconciliation as quickly as possible, so that they may not incur judgment. Of particular significance is the fact that, in this text, the onus is placed on the offender. In this context, one may assume the idea of repentance to be incorporated in that of reconciliation. Surely, repentance is present in Matthew's thinking; it is possibly in the background in 6:12, 14-15 and 18:21-35, but the stress is much more on the responsibility of the offended person in forgiving.

Gentile and Tax Collector

The phrase ἔστω σοι ὥσπερ ὁ ἐθνικὸς καὶ ὁ τελώνης in 18:17 raises one of the exegetical issues in Matt 18. The question is what the attitude and practice described here involves: Is the expression ἔστω σοι ὥσπερ ὁ ἐθνικὸς καὶ ὁ τελώνης a formal act of excommunication of the recalcitrant ἀδελφός? Or, is it a more informal recognition that the relationship has been broken and that the offender has put him- or herself outside the community, or something else?

Luz has provided a good survey and assessment of the solutions which have been proposed. He categorizes them in four models. First is the *grace model* which suggests that verses 15-18 speak not of excommunication from the church but of winning the lost back to the church. Second is the *borderline case model*. According to this model, the church's actual law of life is the law not of exclusion but of the forgiveness that is required in the surrounding verses 10-14 and 21-22. Third is the *covenant theology model*. According to this model, within the covenant relationship established by Christ, forgiveness and the presence of the Lord are promised to the church; therefore, offences against the Father's will are especially serious, since they call into question the covenant relationship. Fourth is the *inconsistency model*. According to this model, the solution of solving the problem at hand is simply to leave the contradictions as they are in Matt 18 without trying to impose an underlying theological idea on them.[7] Luz himself takes a view which is not represented in these

---

7. (1) Pauline tradition: 2 Cor 2:5-11, which is about the expulsion of the member who insulted Paul; 1 Cor 5:1-5, which is about the expulsion of the fornicator; cf. 2 Thess 3:14-15; 1 Tim 1:20; Titus 3:10; 1 Tim 5:19-21; and (2) Johannine tradition, 3 John 10; cf. Luz, *Matthew*, 2:450-51.

models. He adopts the expulsion from the church view.[8] He probably bases his argument on the analogy found in Qumran materials (1QS 6.24–7.25) and in the early church.[9] Perhaps the weakness in Luz's view lies in building his argument, for the expulsion from the church, on an analogy.

The main question is whether Matthew depended on Qumran sources, or whether both Qumran data and the Matthean texts are parallels from a single biblical foundation, but independent of each other.[10] The latter option is probably to be preferred.[11] F. G. Martínez has studied the reciprocal relationship between six key Qumranic rebuke texts[12] and Matt 18:15–17 by comparing and contrasting the data. His aim was to determine the elements which are most likely to help in a better understanding of Matthew. Some of his conclusions on the issue of rebuke with reference to 1QS 5.25–6.1 seems to present some improbabilities. Perhaps it is necessary to explore this text first before discussing his conclusions.

> They shall rebuke one another in truth, humility, and charity. Let no man address his companion with anger, or ill-temper, or obdu[racy, or with envy prompted by] the spirit of wickedness. Let him not hate him [because of his uncircumcised] heart, but let him rebuke him on the very same day lest he incur guilt because of him. And furthermore, let no man accuse his companion before the Congregation without having admonished him in the presence of witnesses.[13]

Rebuke between the members of the community is the main concern of this text. In it are listed moral attitudes with which the rebuke between the members has to be made; they include the love of one another. The rebuke is said to be carried out not with anger, but in truth, humility, and love. Martínez has pointed to the clarity of the text according to which the obligation of rebuke is a strictly juridical obligation; for every rebuke within the community had to be made *before witnesses* and every accusation before the community assembly had to be preceded by the rebuke.[14] Martínez has remarked that the *Rabbim*, which is used in our

---

8. So also Davies and Allison, Hagner, Gundry, G. Bornkamm, to name but a few.
9. Luz, *Matthew*, 2:253.
10. Martínez, "Brotherly Rebuke in Qumran and Mt 18:15–17," 221.
11. The reasons underlying my preference for this proposal are provided in ch. 3.
12. These texts are 1QS 5.24–6.1; 9.16–18; CD 7.1–3; 9.2–8, 17–23; 20.4–8.
13. Translated by Vermes, *The Complete Dead Sea Scrolls in English*, 105.
14. Martínez, "Brotherly Rebuke in Qumran and Mt 18:15–17," 225.

text, is a more precise technical term in Qumran literature than that of "elders" used in the parallel text from 1QS. On this ground and on that of the statement in Lev 19:17, he strongly argues that an accusation before the *Rabbim* is a juridical procedure within the community; in which case, the rebuke in 1QS 5.25–6.1 is to be regarded as a juridical obligation—not to be reduced to a simple brotherly warning. He links with this the rebuke saying in 18:15–17 and suggests that the Matthean rebuke is best understood as a juridical obligation.[15]

This proposal is problematic. Firstly, it is not supported by the literary frame of Matt 18:15–17. In 18:15–17, the rebuke looks more like a question of moral or pastoral obligation, as most scholars have argued.[16] Secondly, in the Matthean text, there is no indication of the people who are potentially to play the roles of the *Rabbim* in the process of the rebuke. Unlike 1QS 5.25–6.1, in Matt 18:15–17, the rebuke is not said to be reported to church authorities and to be recorded by one of such people. Thirdly, while the purpose of the rebuke in 1QS 5.25–6.1 is for the benefit of the witness of the fault—rebuke aiming at the witness not incurring guilt because of the guilty person—in Matt 18:15–17, the rebuke is for the benefit of the guilty person, a fact that Martínez fails to emphasize. It can thus be argued that Matthew probably interpreted his sources not necessarily like others (e.g., Paul or John) may have done with theirs. So, I depart from Luz and others on the expulsion from the church view they advocate. The excommunication reading is problematic because it most likely stands against Matthew's overall teaching and focus in Matt 18, as well as his wider understanding of mission; and so, it makes it difficult to explain plausibly the relationships between pericopes within Matt 18.

A minority have taken the view that the expression ἔστω σοι ὥσπερ ὁ ἐθνικὸς καὶ ὁ τελώνης is a more informal recognition that the relationship between the offended brother or sister and the recalcitrant ἀδελφός has been broken.[17] Although it is the view of only a minority, this is an option to prefer because it seems to be in accord with Matthew's teaching and focus in Matt 18 and his theology of mission, among other things. However, the main argument of scholars who hold this latter view seems

---

15. Ibid.

16. Against Martínez (ibid., 229), who strongly argues for the juridical obligation based on Lev 19:17 and Deut 19:15.

17. Scholars who follow this line include Morris, Carter, and Nolland. For further details, see their commentaries (especially their comments on Matt 18:17) provided in the bibliography.

to be insufficient. Taking into account 18:15–17 as the only direct textual evidence to support it and Matthew's general understanding of mission, the argument seems to lack an important piece which is available in the first part of Matt 18, as will shortly be shown.

Warren Carter has argued that this option seems more in keeping with the conciliatory emphasis, and the lack of highly developed procedures. To this he adds the evidence from Matthew of Jesus being associated with tax collectors (9:9, 10–13; 11:19) and benefiting Gentiles (8:5–13; 12:18, 21; 15:21–28).[18] Similarly, John Nolland argues that the kind of shunning to which 18:17 has frequently led cannot be sustained, given Jesus' image as "friend of tax collectors and sinners" (11:9) and the evangelistic concern for those of other nations which Matthew firmly endorses.[19] Nolland's argument is clearly aware of the evidence from Matt 18 as well as Matthew's theology of mission. But it seems not to discuss adequately this latter piece of evidence. On the other hand, Carter's argument, although it takes into account both Matthew's theology of mission and 18:15–17, probably fails to take seriously the piece of evidence available in 18:1–14. How can this gap be filled? By taking into account pieces of evidence, not only from Matthew's theology of mission, but also those available in both 18:1–14 and 18:15–17. Two strands of evidence support the view that "to be for you as a Gentile and a tax collector" is not a juridical but a more informal recognition that the relationship has been broken and that the offender has put themselves outside the community.

Firstly, in Matt 18 there is a strong emphasis on preservation of the community, expressed in terms of not losing a single member of the community, *one* of the little ones. As was shown earlier (chs. 2, 5 & 6), in verse 6, there is a strong warning that *one* of the little ones should not be scandalized. In verse 10, *one* of the little ones should not be despised. The parable of the lost sheep in verses 13–14 is a strong warning to those who despise *one* of the little ones. The parable surely serves to illustrate God's judgment awaiting those who will despise *one* of the little ones; it points back to the point already made in verse 6 about the nature of the judgment awaiting people who will scandalize *one* of the little ones. The Matthean moral of the parable in verse 14, as opposed to the Lukan moral of the similar parable (15:3–7), serves to emphasize that it is not the will of God that even *one* of the little ones should be lost. Clearly, the

---

18. Carter, *Matthew and the Margins*, 368.
19. Nolland, *The Gospel of Matthew*, 748.

idea of *not to lose* even a single member of the church is emphasized in the first half of chapter 18: through the statement about welcoming *one* child (v. 5), through the prohibition of being a scandal to one of the little ones (vv. 6, 10) and through the statement about God's will regarding one of the little ones (v. 14).

Secondly, in Matthew, Jesus' sympathy with tax collectors, Gentiles, sinners, and prostitutes is clear: Jesus calls Matthew, a tax collector (τελώνης) who is now to be turned into a disciple (9:9); he was known as a friend of tax collectors and sinners (11:19) because he could eat and drink with them (9:10–13); a prophecy was made about his mission to the Gentiles and that they will hope in his name (12:18, 21, for Jesus' mission to the Gentiles, cp. 10:18; 24:14; 28:19): he heals a centurion's servant (8:5–13) and the Canaanite woman's daughter and praises her faith (15:21–28).

Matthew uses three kinds of pairing to refer to these categories of people. The first pairing is in 18:17, where Matthew uses the pairing ὁ ἐθνικὸς καὶ ὁ τελώνης ("Gentile and tax collector") and prefers the adjectival form (ὁ ἐθνικὸς) to the substantival form (τὰ ἔθνη, as in 6:32). He had already used this pairing, although not with the same construction, earlier in 5:46–47 (οἱ τελῶναι . . . οἱ ἐθνικοί); here also in 18:17 the adjectival form is used. The second pairing occurs in 9:10 and 11:19, where Matthew uses respectively τελῶναι καὶ ἁμαρτωλοὶ and τελωνῶν . . . καὶ ἁμαρτωλῶν ("tax collectors and sinners," cp. Luke 15:1; 18:9–14). The third pairing emerges in 21:31–32, where οἱ τελῶναι καὶ αἱ πόρναι ("tax collectors and prostitutes") is used. Because of Matthew's preference for the adjectival ὁ ἐθνικὸς in 5:46–47 and 18:17 to the substantive form, France has argued that this strongly emphasises that this group (Gentiles) belongs to a different category and thus reflects a traditional Jewish feeling about non-Jews.[20]

To think of the use of the adjectival as proof for the traditional Jewish feeling about non-Jews is unpersuasive. What seems, however, certain is that in 5:46–47 and 18:17, tax collectors and Gentiles are used together to represent those of whom a high standard is not to be expected, those who were regarded as at the bottom of the moral scale, as France also suggests.[21] This at least seems to be in line with the context of these two passages and also with 6:7, where οἱ ἐθνικοί clearly functions similarly. The

---

20. France, *The Gospel of Matthew*, 227.
21. Ibid., 694.

same can be also said of the "sinners" (9:10; 11:19) and the "prostitutes" (21:31–32).

These strands of evidence clearly show the traditional Jewish outlook of these categories of people, in this case Gentiles and tax collectors: they were considered outsiders and people at the bottom of moral scale. But is this the picture that Matthew thinks Jesus had of these people? Is this the picture that Matthew himself also had of these categories of people? Matthew seems to have had a different view of Gentiles and tax collectors.[22] It is possible to assume that the context of 18:17 requires that Gentiles and tax collectors be understood as objects of mission, people to be won over into the community of believers, as Carter has also suggested.[23] This would mean that the free efforts to reconcile the person outlined in 18:15–17 do not finish the process; though unspecified, restorative efforts continue.[24] Verse 17 should be interpreted in the light of the entire discourse of Matt 18 (about preservation of the community, with focus on the roles of the *spiritually mature* members) and of Matthew's wider understanding of mission (1:21; 10:18; 12:18, 21; 24:14; 28:19, let alone the three Gentile women mentioned in Jesus' genealogy in Matt 1, which probably shows Matthew's concern for mission). "Dissociation" may be suggested as a more appropriate term than "excommunication" because the former tends to fairly describe how the injurer is to behave toward the straying fellow (v. 17).

Relating Matt 18:15–17 with 18:21–22

Some scholars have identified a tension between Matt 18:15–17 and 18:21–22.[25] They wonder how one can display unlimited forgiveness (18:21–22) and yet undertake proceedings which may end in the expulsion of an ἀδελφός (18:15–17).[26] As with the two previous difficulties, this one too can be answered from what I propose as the main argument and the focus of the discourse in Matt 18. Davies and Allison, among

---

22. Against France (Ibid.) who thinks that Matthew uses these terms in their conventional Jewish sense.

23. Carter, *Matthew and the Margins*, 368.

24. Ibid.

25. Cf. Davies and Allison (*Saint Matthew*, 2:791) and Luz (*Matthew*, 2:424, 450), among many others.

26. Davies and Allison, *Saint Matthew*, 2:791.

others,[27] have addressed this problem from a certain point of view. Arguing from the basis already posed by A. Plummer,[28] they believe that the injured person who endeavors to reclaim their injurer must have already forgiven them from their heart; otherwise it would be hopeless to seek reconciliation. The injured person goes not for their own sake to seek for reparation, but for the wrong-doer's sake to win them back from evil.[29] In an attempt to defend their proposal, they firstly argue that in the Jewish tradition, reproof, and love belong together and are not perceived as antithetical, for the classic text on reproof (Lev 19:17) is followed immediately by the command to love one's neighbor as oneself (Lev 19:18). Secondly, they contend that for Matthew, membership in the Christian community disallows certain types of behavior. So, the community would cease to be if it did not insist that its members acknowledge in word and deed the lordship of Christ, with its many moral demands. They conclude by pointing out that the spirit of forgiveness cannot mean blindness and indifference to sin within the church.[30]

Davies and Allison's overall argument has some logic in it. My argument, however, cannot allow an aspect of it as is developed in the latter part. Their argument, especially in its last part, is lacking an awareness of Matthew's overall emphasis in Matt 18 (at least as understood here). It is quite possible that there is no incompatibility between 18:21–22 and 18:15–17. Verses 21–22 talk about the willingness of the injured person to grant forgiveness: it is assumed that the forgiver does not insist on their own right to redress, as France also suggests.[31] In both 18:15–17[32] and 18:21–22, the response of the one sinned against is what is in view.[33] The emphasis on both texts is likely on the injured person's responsibility toward their injurer. Therefore, the argument for a tension between verses 15–17 and verses 21–22 seems not to hold together. Neither does

---

27. E.g., France, *The Gospel of Matthew*, 699–700.

28. Plummer, *St. Matthew*, 255.

29. Davies and Allison, *Saint Matthew*, 2:791; following Plummer, *St. Matthew*, 255.

30. Davies and Allison, *Saint Matthew*, 2:791–2.

31. France, *The Gospel of Matthew*, 700.

32. According to the εἰς σὲ reading (18:15) option taken in this study; cf. ibid., 62n41.

33. Against France (ibid., 700) who thinks that in the first case what is considered is the effect on the sinner.

the hypothesis of the possibility of forgiveness denial suggested by David J. Reimer.[34]

Matthew's argument in verses 21–22, it can be confidently urged, seems to go like this: whether or not the offender repents, forgiveness is appropriate for them. Otherwise it would be hard to explain plausibly how these verses, in the light of verses 15–17, fit Matthew's argument and focus in the entire discourse of Matt 18—a chapter which is concerned with preservation of the community, focusing on the roles of the *spiritually mature* members of the community.

PARABLES' INTERPRETATION, RELATED ISSUES, AND VARIOUS EXEGETICAL POINTS ABOUT MATT 18:23–34 AS A PARABLE

Matt 18:23–35, a component of 18:21–35, is a parable. The parable *per se* begins at verse 23 and ends at verse 34; it is followed by a concluding comment in verse 35. The parable as a whole is concerned with the theme of forgiveness. Matthew's interpretation of it requires comments. This parable is an illustration of the failure to forgive others and God's response to this. It is broadly true that parables normally do contain some allegorical elements which require allegorical interpretation in the "contemporary" usage of the term; the parable in 18:23–35 is no exception. Because 18:23–35 is a parable, and there are several approaches to parable interpretation, determining a suitable approach for this study is required. I take it that the contemporary perspective is the best approach because of the kind of the evidence it uses and the ground for it. Thus, as Blomberg has stated, the correct interpretation of a parable requires recognition of the fact that certain elements in the parable are being compared to certain spiritual realities as in an allegory, with respect to one or more specific characteristics; there are usually several of these comparisons or contrasts in each parable.[35] On the other hand, there are also some elements in the parable which are to be interpreted literally.[36]

The application of the parable in verse 35 likely provides a clue for interpreting the metaphors contained in it. It has been claimed that

---

34. Reimer, "The Apocrypha and Biblical Theology," 271.

35. Blomberg, *Interpreting the Parables*, 46.

36. Both the elements that require allegorical interpretation and those that are to be interpreted literally will be shown throughout our treatment of 18:23–35.

Matthew interprets the parables' conventional metaphors allegorically without treating the entire parable as an allegory. Even if he may have added such metaphors, he remains basically within the framework of Jesus' parable.[37] As Nolland has said, to make a series of direct identifications of these metaphors in our parable is so simple; yet, though simple it may well be that, to do so helps to correctly identify the major contours of the parable.[38] Snodgrass' piece of advice on interpreting the gospels' parables is also to the point: "The parables are not equations, and that is why parables interpretation is not about listing correspondences or about tracing the reflection of a theology ... Parables must be interpreted as analogies, analogies that show *pieces* of reality but may contain other elements for a variety of purposes."[39] What this means for this study is, for example, that the βασιλεύς and κύριος in the parable is an *analogy* for God, not a *picture* of him; the δοῦλοι, σύνδουλοι, and ἀδελφοί are all analogies for the Church. This understanding is most likely to provide an adequate answer to those who find themselves uncomfortable with bringing God into the parable in 18:23–35.[40]

One of the important issues related to our parable is its function in relation to 18:21–22. The question is whether or not the parable in 18:23–34 is an illustration of 18:21–22, and whether or not there is a tension between these sets of verses. I propose that this parable is an illustration of 18:21–22. There is a connection both thematic (cf. διὰ τοῦτο in v. 23) and verbal between the parable and the verses that it follows (cf. recurrence of ἀφίημι both in vv. 21–22 and 23–35: ἀφήσω [v. 21], ἀφῆκεν [v. 27], ἀφῆκά [v. 32] and μὴ ἀφῆτε [v. 35]). To be sure, the phrase διὰ τοῦτο in 18:23 (cp. 6:25; 12:31; 13:52) seems to indicate a *connection*, and could thus be rendered "because of this," or "on account of this," or "therefore." On the other hand, it also seems to indicate the nature of this connection; that is, the parable that follows is an example or proof of the *logion* in 18:21–22.[41] However, the extent to which this parable is to be regarded as an illustration of the saying in 18:21–22 needs clarification. The parable in 18:23–35 is possibly an illustration of the negative part of the teaching contained in 18:21–22. Warranting mention is also the fact that, although

---

37. E.g., Luz, *Matthew*, 2:475 (see also n75).
38. Nolland, *The Gospel of Matthew*, 761.
39. Snodgrass, *Stories with Intent*, 71; emphasis original.
40. E.g., Schottroff is one of them; cf. *The Parables of Jesus*, 200.
41. So also Snodgrass, *Stories with Intent*, 67.

both 18:21–22 and 18:23–35 deal with the issue of forgiving others, they have different emphases. As Davies and Allison have quite reasonably noticed, while 18:21–22 are a memorable call for repeated forgiveness, 18:23–34[35] are a vivid reminder that the failure to forgive is failure to act as the heavenly Father acts (5:48).[42] So, clearly, only part of the subject of forgiveness in 18:21–22 is being singled out. Which part of this subject is singled out is debatable. Snodgrass thinks of the necessity to forgive.[43] What would happen to the potential unmerciful and unforgiving disciple is surely what is being picked up; this is what the parable seems to be all about. This is in line with the other Matthean interpersonal and related texts. In 5:7, the merciful are said to be blessed. In 6:12, it is these blessed (by implication) who are allowed to seek divine forgiveness and expect to receive it. Matt 6:14–15 elaborates the human forgiving aspect: while the positive part in 6:14 virtually repeats the idea of 6:12b, the negative part in 6:15 is singled out and taken up in 18:23–35.

Another element in the parable, which needs to be mentioned here, is how enormous almost everything is. This phenomenon is surely to cause the hearers or the listeners of the parable to be amazed. As Pierre Bonnard has also noted, at least four of these astonishing facts can be identified: the first fact is the size of the debt; the second, the king's immense generosity in cancelling the entire debt at least initially; the third, the inconceivable heartlessness of the just-forgiven debtor; and the fourth, the savage punishment by the king.[44] The size of the debt is one of the main factors in the parable which have caused scholars to doubt whether the details in the parable are true-to-life.[45]

Another important issue is to identify the point of the parable. The main question is whether this point is to be found in the first scene, in the second or in the third. As Luz has suggested, the point of the parable is to be found probably in the second and the third scenes, for the issue is concretely the requirement of mercy and forgiveness. It is primarily all about relationship with one's fellow human beings.[46] This seems to be

---

42. Davies and Allison, *Saint Matthew*, 2:794.

43. Snodgrass, *Stories with Intent*, 67.

44. Bonnard, *L'Évangile selon Saint Matthieu*, 277.

45. The following are among scholars who have satisfactorily debated this question: Derrett, *Law in the New Testament*, 32–47; De Boer, "Ten thousand Talents?," 214–32; Manson, *The Sayings of Jesus as Recorded in the Gospels according to St Matthew and St Luke*, 213.

46. Luz, *Matthew*, 2:475; see also Linnemann, *Parables of Jesus*, 112–13.

in line with Matthew's central argument in Matt 18, as will be shown in due course. However, this is not to say that the first scene (vv. 24–27) and the application of the parable (v. 35) are totally irrelevant. As Luz further notes, the content of the first scene is important for the parable; it is not simply a rhetorical device to provoke the indignation of the fellow slaves or of the readers.[47]

The contrast between the lord's mercy upon his slave and this slave's lack of mercy upon his fellow slave also deserves discussion here. It is striking that the lord in the parable chose to cancel the debt and release the debtor, at least initially (18:27). It is only later that he had to use the more severe option (18:34). The irony is that, the slave-creditor chose to have his debtor jailed (v. 34), yet this debtor belonged to the king. This unimaginable treatment of the slave by his fellow slave-creditor, as opposed to the treatment the latter himself had received from the lord, is likely the point of the parable.

OUTLINE OF MATT 18:21–35

Matt 18:21–35 forms a literary unit and is to be located within the wider literary unit 18:1–35, dealing with Jesus' teaching about church life. Three literary devices have helped in determining the boundaries of Matt 18 so as to see it as a unit. The first device is the temporal *deixis* ἐν ἐκείνῃ τῇ ὥρᾳ in 18:1; obviously, it operates as an opening discourse marker. Οὕτως in 18:35 is the second device which functions as a closing discourse marker of 18:21–35 and Matt 18 as a whole; this is confirmed by the narrative section 19:1–3 which obviously introduces another incident. The last device is the repetition of ἀδελφός in 18:21, 35: the forgiveness of the ἀδελφός is the theme in 18:21; in 18:35, the response of the heavenly Father to the disciples is based upon their readiness or reluctance to forgive their ἀδελφός. Clearly, the theme that was introduced in verse 21—in an ἀδελφός relationship setting—is now logically concluded in verse 35 within the same setting. In the face of all this, the following outline of 18:21–35 can be proposed.

  18:21–22 Query about forgiving and an answer

  18:23–34 Elaborated answer to the forgiving query

  18:35   Final answer to the forgiving query

---

47. Luz, *Matthew*, 2:475n71.

EXEGESIS OF MATT 18:21-35

As was shown earlier, 18:21-35 is located within a larger literary unit of Matt 18 concerned with the preservation of the community. This pericope is about forgiving. It can be divided into two parts, the first of which is about Peter's question and Jesus' answer (18:21-22), and focuses on the frequency of forgiving; the second concentrates on failure in showing readiness to forgive and what will befall the unforgiving person (18:23-35). The idea of punishment, which was implicit in 6:15, becomes more explicit here; it likely parallels the saying in 6:15: *not being forgiven*. The exegesis of 18:21-35 may now be undertaken. For the sake of clarity, the study of this text will be done in the sequence of three scenes, prefaced by an introduction. Due attention will be paid to the four features that have been suggested in this work as markers for the centrality of the theme of interpersonal forgiveness in the First Gospel. They will be pointed out and highlighted as the exegesis of the text proceeds. Also, we shall also seek to understand the nature of interpersonal forgiveness in this text.

Query about Forgiving and an Answer (vv. 21-22)

The first part of the pericope begins with Peter's question. The question focuses on the frequency of forgiving (18:21-22) and seems to suggest potential readiness in forgiving on Peter's part. Here the teaching of Jesus is driven by a question. Early in Matt 18, Jesus' teaching was also prompted by it (v. 1). This time it is Peter who asks the question, not the disciples as in 18:1; indeed, he is acting as their spokesperson (cp. 15:15; 16:16; 17:4). He wants to know about the boundaries of forgiveness, if at least there are any. His question is direct: Κύριε, ποσάκις ἁμαρτήσει εἰς ἐμὲ ὁ ἀδελφός μου καὶ ἀφήσω αὐτῷ; ἕως ἑπτάκις; (v. 21).

A social *deixis* can be identified in this question. A vocative is employed to describe Peter's address to Jesus. The question points back verbally to 18:15, where the expression ἁμαρτήσῃ [εἰς σὲ] is used, but probably also thematically to 6:12, 14-15, in which the forgiving disposition, as a necessary condition to receive God's forgiveness, was emphatically discussed. This makes a clear connection between Matt 6 and 18 on the issue of interpersonal forgiveness and highlights the significance of it for Matthew: in 6:12 the conditional element occurs for the first time; in 6:14-15, it is elaborated and stressed; in 18:15-17, the embodiment of its demands is likely alluded to; in 18:21-22, its practicability is affirmed. It seems to make a lot of sense that after a theoretical awareness of forgiving and its imperatives, Peter now enquires further about the practicability over the lesson already learned and surely assimilated.

Peter's question in verse 21 reads slightly differently in its partial Lukan parallel: καὶ ἐὰν ἑπτάκις τῆς ἡμέρας ἁμαρτήσῃ εἰς σὲ καὶ ἑπτάκις ἐπιστρέψῃ πρὸς σὲ λέγων, Μετανοῶ, ἀφήσεις αὐτῷ (17:4). Luke talks about the possibility of a person to sin seven times a day and turn back seven times. Obviously, in Luke the context is about forgiving those who repent and ask for forgiveness. In Matthew, the nature of the sin of this ἀδελφός is not specified. The use of παραπτώματα as the object of ἀφίημι in 6:14–15 seems to suggest that the sin in view is a general offence. Conversely, here in 18:21 it is quite clear that a personal offence is in view because the ἀδελφός is said to sin εἰς ἐμὲ; but the effect of the sin in question is potentially to affect the entire community.

Unlike the Lukan version of the account, where the context is about forgiving those who repent and ask for forgiveness, the Matthean text says nothing about the injurer's repentance. In it there is lack of a direct reference to repentance in Peter's question (v. 21); this phenomenon can be also observed in 18:15–17 and 6:12, 14–15. But in verses 21–22, it seems to many highly likely that repentance is presupposed. Whether or not this ἀδελφός has repented Matthew does not say. His silence on this in 18:21 has caused the majority of scholars to think of this case as that of a repentant ἀδελφός, and therefore to suggest that repentance is assumed.[48] The repentance reading in this verse is unlikely. It is possible to imagine that, arguing mostly from the offended person's perspective, Matthew did not find it relevant to insert repentance in his argument in Matt 18 (hence in 18:15–17, 21–22; 6:12, 14–15).

Peter wonders whether to ἀφίημι an ἀδελφός, in the sense of bearing with them, as many as ἑπτάκις ("seven times") is reasonable. The phrase ἕως ἑπτάκις is found in verse 22 in connection with ἕως ἑβδομηκοντάκις ἑπτά. In verse 22, Matthew puts these two phrases in Jesus' mouth. In 18:21–22, ἑπτάκις likely has a Jewish background. First, the word occurs in the Pentateuch: in Gen 4:15, we have a sevenfold vengeance upon Cain's murderer; in Lev 16, we have a sevenfold sprinkling of blood for the sins of the people; in Lev 26:18, 21, 24, Yahweh warns that he may chastise Israel sevenfold for their sins. Second, ἑπτάκις appears in Wisdom literature: in Prov 24:16, the righteous man is said to fall seven times

---

48. Cf. Hagner (*Matthew*, 537), among others.

(ἑπτάκις) and rises again. It is interesting that in the evidence above, there is a connection between ἑπτάκις and themes of vengeance, expiation, punishment, and forgiveness. As to the expression ἑβδομηκοντάκις ἑπτά, it occurs in LXX Gen 4:24: ὅτι ἑπτάκις ἐκδεδίκηται ἐκ Καιν, ἐκ δὲ Λαμεχ ἑβδομηκοντάκις ἑπτά, which in the Hebrew Bible reads: כִּי שִׁבְעָתַיִם יֻקַּם־קָיִן וְלֶמֶךְ שִׁבְעִים וְשִׁבְעָה.

In the LXX, ἑβδομηκοντάκις ἑπτά is the translation of שִׁבְעִים וְשִׁבְעָה, which means "seventy-seven times." In this text, there is a link between ἑβδομηκοντάκις ἑπτά and the idea of vengeance; so are both ἑπτάκις and ἑβδομηκοντάκις ἑπτά. In rabbinic literature, there is strong evidence that the Jewish sages were acquainted with the need to forgive an offender more than once. On the other hand, there are also passages which recommend limiting the forgiveness of the same sin to three times (*b. Yoma* 86b–87a). However, to take this as evidence for the argument that earlier rabbinic teaching regarded a limit of three times as sufficient is uncertain, because these pieces of evidence may represent the view of only one Jewish group. It is not unreasonable to think that in 18:21–22, which most likely echoes Gen 4:24, Matthew uses the OT text in his argument with the purpose of contrasting Lamech's vengeful spirit with the spirit which is expected from a *spiritually mature* Christian. Peter's proposal of up to seven times suggests his potential generosity in forgiving. Taking seven as the traditional number of perfection, Luz thinks that Peter's suggestion to forgive seven times (ἕως ἑπτάκις) is about whether perfect forgiveness is expected of him.[49] It is not, however, clear whether he is thinking of perfect quantity or perfect quality. Perfect quantity is most likely intended here. Because Peter's question has to do with quantity (i.e., the number of times forgiveness has to be extended rather than quality), it would perhaps be going far beyond the text itself to suggest the idea of perfection in forgiving in this text.

To Peter's question Jesus answers directly and to the point: Οὐ λέγω σοι ἕως ἑπτάκις ἀλλὰ ἕως ἑβδομηκοντάκις ἑπτά (v. 22). The formula οὐ λέγω σοι attributed to Jesus is decisive. The language in 5:21ff has allowed France to imagine that this formula intends to set Jesus' radical new standard over against the prudent conclusions of conventional wisdom.[50] Again, surely for the sake of continuity, Matthew puts the phrase ἕως ἑπτάκις in Jesus' mouth. The particle ἀλλὰ is adversative; it contrasts

---

49. Luz, *Matthew*, 2:465.
50. France, *The Gospel of Matthew*, 704–5.

ἑπτάκις with ἑβδομηκοντάκις ἑπτά. The phrase ἑβδομηκοντάκις ἑπτά is controversial. The question is whether it should be translated "seventy times and seven" (70+7), or "seventy times seven" (77x7). Some scholars prefer the former,[51] whereas others favor the latter.[52] The former is probable because of the similarity with LXX Gen 4:24, where ἑβδομηκοντάκις ἑπτά is the translation of שִׁבְעִים וְשִׁבְעָה, which means "seventy-seven times." Whichever reading of ἑβδομηκοντάκις ἑπτά one is to take, one needs to be aware of the language used here to describe Jesus' answer, the reason behind the use of this kind of language and how this OT text squares with the point Matthew is trying to make.

We most likely have here an example of hyperbole which seems to have a twofold function: the first function is to stress the contrast with Lamech's vengeance, and the second to emphasize the infinite nature of the forgiveness. As Luz has also argued, if in Gen 4:24 the issue was limiting the revenge that hangs over the bloody deeds of the descendants of Cain and Lamech, here in Matt 18:22 it is the abolition of revenge altogether.[53] Osborne has summed up this contrast quite nicely: "Lamech celebrated his vengeance; Jesus abrogates it altogether."[54] It is quite apparent that what was demanded of Peter is the "boundlessly infinite and countlessly repeated forgiveness."[55]

To sum up, Matthew's interpretation of Jesus' teaching about forgiveness in 18:21–22 is that interpersonal forgiveness is to know no limits. As France has written, if one is still counting, however "generously," one is not forgiving.[56] Whether the offender repents (which is ideal) or not (which is possible), forgiving them is a right thing to do, a reasonable act of generosity toward them. As we shall see, the teaching in the subunit 18:23–35 is Matthew's interpretation of the negative part of the teaching in 18:21–22; that is, what would happen to the potential unforgiving disciple.

---

51. The key figures of this reading include Luz, Davies and Allison, Hagner, Osborne, Nolland, France, Snodgrass, to list only a few.
52. E.g., the translators of the King James Version of the Bible, among others.
53. Luz, *Matthew*, 2:466.
54. Osborne, *Matthew*, 693.
55. Luz, *Matthew*, 2:465.
56. France, *The Gospel of Matthew*, 705.

The Unforgiving Person and God's Response (vv. 23–34)

Matt 18:23–34 contains teaching about reluctance to forgive and God's response to the unforgiving person. A parable is used to convey and stress this teaching. This parable resembles the ones in Matt 13 in that they all concern ἡ βασιλεία τῶν οὐρανῶν ("the kingdom of heaven"). As Luz has noticed, the story in the parable is concise and artistic; it is well composed throughout.[57] This will become clear in what follows. Apart from an introduction (v. 23), the parable consists of three clear scenes: the first scene takes place between the king and his slave (vv. 24–27), the second between the slave and his fellow slave (vv. 28–30), and the third once again between the king and his slave (vv. 31–34); each has almost the same form, beginning with a narrative introduction (vv. 24–25, 28, 31) and closing by describing what the creditor does with the debtor (vv. 27, 30, 34).

Introduction of the Parable (v. 23)

This introduction makes clear that the story is about the king settling accounts with his slaves. In it, two main rhetorical devices are used: first is an introductory *deixis* (διὰ τοῦτο); second is a comparison which is introduced by ὡμοιώθη. The introduction does two things: first, it connects the parable to the preceding unit (18:21–22); and second, it tells us what the story that follows is all about.

A comparison is used to describe what the kingdom is like: ὡμοιώθη ἡ βασιλεία τῶν οὐρανῶν ἀνθρώπῳ βασιλεῖ ("the kingdom of heaven is like a man, a king"). These words are found again *verbatim* in 22:2. Here in 18:23, the phrase ἡ βασιλεία τῶν οὐρανῶν returns the discourse to a motif with which it began early in the section (18:1, 3–4): the greatest in the kingdom of heaven.

The presence of kings in parables is common in the First Gospel (cf. 17:25; 22:2, 7, 11, 13; 25:34, 40). The comparison of the kingdom of heaven to a human situation already occurred in 13:24 (ὡμοιώθη ἡ βασιλεία τῶν οὐρανῶν ἀνθρώπῳ), with only one word lacking. Matthew often uses ἄνθρωπος at the start of parables (13:24, 45, 52; 18:23; 20:1; 21:33; 22:2), usually with a noun in apposition (13:45, 52; 18:23; 20:1; 22:2), almost surely to underscore the analogy between the divine and

---

57. Luz, *Matthew*, 2:468–69.

The Rhetoric of Interpersonal Forgiveness in Matt 18:21–35   169

human realms in their interrelationships within and to each other. Here in 18:23, it is certain that the meaning of the expression above is that the kingdom of heaven is like what is going to be narrated in the parable.

As another aspect of the function of the introduction of the parable, at least two interesting things can be observed in the setting of the story. First is a shift from βασιλεύς (v. 23) to κύριος in the rest of the parable; and second, the cancellation by this βασιλεύς/κύριος of the entire debt and the release of the slave-debtor (v. 27). The question is why this shift and what difference it makes. Hagner thinks of this shift as stylistic. For him, βασιλεύς does not occur again in the parable because it is not vital to it, for the evangelist inserted it to facilitate the analogy with God in verse 35; the repeated use of the title κύριος in verses 25, 27, 31, 32, 34 is thus consonant with this understanding, he suggests.[58] It is possible to imagine that by using these two terms, Matthew intended to grasp the attention of his readers about the quality of the forgiveness this debtor initially received. Perhaps of much importance is to consider the fact of settling the accounts itself. Indeed, the βασιλεύς wishes to settle accounts with his δοῦλοι. The plural form of the genitive τῶν δούλων clearly indicates that more than one slave was indebted to the king.

What is δοῦλος the image of? In biblical Jewish usage, this term seems to require religious connotations of persons who "serve" God.[59] This is probably in line with the moral of the parable in 18:35, which seems to underline the importance of human relationships. As Luz has said, the reader for whom βασιλεύς and δοῦλος are stock images of God and his people, thus, immediately thinks in terms of theological truths.[60] Although this does not need a one-to-one correspondence between the actions of the king and those of God, it does transpose the intent of the parable from the realm of human relationships alone to those of the human and divine.[61]

The action which the king is to take against his debtors is described as συνᾶραι λόγον ("settling accounts"). The word συναίρω used in verse 23 occurs only three times in the entire NT, and all in Matthew (18:23, 24; 25:19); other Matthean parables in which the kingdom is related to the settling of accounts are 24:45–51; 25:15–30. In both 18:23 and 25:19,

---

58. Hagner, *Matthew*, 2:539.
59. Luz, *Matthew*, 2:471.
60. Ibid.
61. Huffman, "Atypical Features in the Parables of Jesus," 213.

the expression συναίρω λόγον means to "settle accounts"—a combination also found in the papyri with the same meaning.[62] The question is whether the settling of accounts in 18:23 portrays the last judgement. Luz thinks that it does because for him settling accounts is a commonly used metaphor that suggests the notion of judgement.[63] Gundry has rejected this interpretation on grammatical grounds. For him, the aorist ὡμοιώθη here in verse 23 implies that this settling of accounts portrays forgiveness that has *already* taken place (cf. 7:24, 26; 25:1).[64] Perhaps Luz's option is to be preferred, because one of the three occurrences of this expression in Matthew, occurs in the context of eschatological judgement. Additionally, there are parables in Matthew in which the kingdom is related to the settling of accounts (cf. e.g., 24:45–51; 25:15–30). These parables have an eschatological flavour. Therefore, using the term συναίρω, Matthew most likely meant to point to God's eschatological judgement. But still the reality of this judgement in the Christian's daily life should not be lost: reluctance to forgive may result to the lack of God's blessing upon the unforgiving person, or to that of their spiritual growth.

Scene 1 (vv. 24–27)

Scene 1 essentially takes place between the king and one of his slaves (vv. 24–27). It focuses on the slave with the colossal debt. Because of his incapability to clear his debt, this slave begs his lord to be patient with him for the debt due. Instead, the lord unexpectedly cancels the entire debt. As already noted, the narrative story suggests that there were many slaves who were indebted to the king. Here it has to be remarked, the more indebted slave happened to be dealt with first. What happened to other debtors Matthew does not say, perhaps because it would have been hard not to cancel their debts also. A rhetorical device (repetition) is used in this parable to describe the status of these debtors. The word δοῦλος is used five times in the parable (vv. 23, 26, 27, 28, 32): it is put four times in the storyteller's mouth and once in the lord's mouth. Its translation in this parable has been heatedly debated. How one is to render it depends on how one interprets μυρίων ταλάντων (whether this expression represents 10,000 talents or a lesser sum), the sum which this δοῦλος owes the lord.

---

62. BAGD, "συναίρω, κτλ.," 964.
63. Luz, *Matthew*, 2:471.
64. Gundry, *Matthew*, 371.

Snodgrass' solution that parables are analogies, may be useful here too. But perhaps it is necessary to also discuss μυρίων ταλάντων at this point.

In the NT, τάλαντον is exclusively Matthean: it occurs 15 times, and all in Matthew. Μυρίων ταλάντων records the amount of debt: 10,000 talents. According to Josephus, the total Judean tax for one year totaled only six hundred talents; when one compares the OT sums associated with the building of Solomon's great temple (1 Chron 29:4–7), the sum of 10,000 talents may look incredible. Snodgrass has aptly questioned the tendency of thinking naively that the sum of this debt is unthinkable.[65] He has appealed to the evidence in Esther 3:9 to support his argument, a passage in which the same figure is also attested:

> If it pleases the king, let a decree be issued for their destruction, and I will pay ten thousand talents of silver (ἀργυρίου τάλαντα μύρια) into the hands of those who have charge of the king's business, so that they may put it into the king's treasuries.

In any case, still the debt in our parable clearly remains huge. J. Jeremias has observed that 10,000 talents exceeds any actual situation, and has suggested that it can only be explained if we realize that both μύρια and τάλαντα are the highest magnitudes in use (10,000 is the highest number used in reckoning, and the last is the largest currency unit in the whole of the Near East).[66] Some have worried about this unrealistic sum owed by this slave and have suggested that originally the parable referred to a smaller amount.[67] Davies and Allison, for example, think of a lesser sum which they think permits one to think of a master and a servant, and to also give the σύνδουλοι of verse 31 its natural meaning of "fellow servants."[68] Others have gone further to suggest that there may exist an oriental usage of the meaning "official." They then interpret δοῦλος in this parable as an official.[69] France provides a concise discussion of the arguments in favour of and criticism against the interpretation of δοῦλος in this pericope as an "official," and that of μυρίων ταλάντων in the sense of a lesser sum.[70]

---

65. Snodgrass, *Stories with Intent*, 68.

66. Jeremias, *Les Paraboles de Jésus*, 210.

67. De Boer ("Ten Thousand Talents?," 214–32), Manson (*The Sayings of Jesus*, 213), Davies and Allison (*Saint Matthew*, 2:798), to name but a few.

68. Davies and Allison, *Saint Matthew*, 2:797.

69. BDAG, 260; Jeremias, *Les Paraboles de Jésus*, 210, 212.

70. France, *The Gospel of Matthew*, 704n17; 705–6nn19, 21.

There is a big danger in trying to cut down the figures and to take δοῦλος in this parable to mean an official—rather than a slave—to attempt to make the story more realistic. As France reasonably points out, any attempt in trying to turn an extravagant story into a realistic scenario would surely cause one to lose much of the point of the parable.[71] It is broadly true that parables, by their nature, often employ hyperbole for effect; here we likely have a deliberate hyperbole which points to a debt that was incalculably high,[72] but not necessarily unthinkable. There are, thus, no sound reasons to require that every point of the parable corresponds to historical reality. Again, with the logic that parables should be interpreted as analogies—analogies which show *pieces* of reality but may contain other elements for a variety of purposes,[73] it is possible to imagine that in this parable, μυρίων ταλάντων means ten thousand talents, and δοῦλος a slave. Therefore, the debt of this slave was clearly so huge that it was outside his ability to repay it—not necessarily however because he was entirely without means, for it is said that the king could still sell the possessions of this debtor (v. 25b). Theoretically, slaves owned nothing; but in actual fact, some of them did own something. According to Schottroff, although slaves could have their own property and families, as in the case of the first slave, however, "their legal status still did not correspond to that of freeborn persons, nor did they have the same rights in their marriages and over their property."[74] This makes a lot of sense in this parable. What is the significance of this astronomical sum for Matthew and his audience? Why did he, to the highest degree, blow up the figure? It is possible to imagine that he did so for theological reasons: to magnify God's munificence.[75] This is believable and seems to be in line with the parable and its literary context.

It is interesting that the king himself settles accounts when one could expect this to be carried out by one of his officials. Has something given him cause for concern (cp. Luke 16:1–2)? Or is this settlement of the accounts part of a periodic pattern? The text only says that this desire of the king was from his own free will (v. 23: note ἠθέλησεν, a verb of wish); it does not give the reason for this motivation. It is almost certain

---

71. Ibid., 704n17.
72. Hagner, *Matthew*, 2:538.
73. Snodgrass, *Stories with Intent*, 71.
74. Schottroff, *The Parables of Jesus*, 197.
75. Davies and Allison, *Saint Matthew*, 2:798.

that a number of slaves have been given responsibility with considerable independence of operation for matters that involve financial transactions—a financial system managed by slaves but also involving access to coercion.[76] This responsibility was probably given to them on the basis of trust. Schottroff's suggestion that people liked to put slaves in charge of finances because they could be tortured[77] is another possibility.

The settling of accounts begins; the slaves are to be brought (προσηνέχθη) before the king in sequence (v. 23). There has been a debate among scholars as to whether προσηνέχθη implies that these debtors were brought forcibly, or whether it is simply a question of practical arrangements.[78] Jeremias has suggested that προσηνέχθη implies that the debtor was brought from jail.[79] This proposal is a speculation because in the text there is no indication that the debtors were in custody before they were brought before the king. The case of the first ὀφειλέτης with an astronomically high debt was the first presented (προσηνέχθη). The word ὀφειλέτης occurs only twice in Matthew in the forgiveness texts (6:12; 18:24). In both cases, ὀφειλέτης means something like a "debtor." However, the difference between these two texts is that in 18:24, the debtor is unable to repay his debt; whereas in 6:12, it is not clear whether or not the forgiven debtor was unable to repay his debt. In 18:24, ὀφειλέτης is explicitly connected to the idea of owing something to somebody, an idea which is perhaps implied in 6:12 where this term is first used. What effect does this have on our understanding of the subject at hand? Given that in these two texts ὀφειλέτης ("debtor") is used as the image of ἁμαρτωλός ("sinner"), it can be suggested that in them the preference for ὀφειλέτης serves to underline the fact that a sinner is someone who has an *obligation* to fulfill toward the person they have wronged. This seems to recall 6:12 where a word with the same root is used likely to stress the notion of sin as an *obligation*. Although Nolland suggests that this is probably a Semitism,[80] it is also reasonable to think that Matthew probably wanted to point to the fact that there were also other debtors.

The incapacity of this debtor to repay his debt is an obvious fact. The fact of paying the debt is described by ἀποδοῦναι (from ἀποδίδωμι).

76. Schottroff, *The Parables of Jesus*, 197.

77. Ibid.

78. Davies and Allison, *Saint Matthew*, 2:798; so Nolland, *The Gospel of Matthew*, 756.

79. Jeremias, *Les Paraboles de Jésus*, 211.

80. Nolland, *The Gospel of Matthew*, 756.

The verb ἀποδίδωμι is one of the key words of this parable; it appears in almost every verse in the parable: verses 25 (2x), 26, 28, 29, 30, 34. This fact shows how the idea of paying the debt, in the sense of fulfilling one's obligation, is central to the parable: the debtor must repay what he owes. As a result of this debtor's incapacity, the κύριος is forced to make a decision, a decision which has led John R. Donahue to think of this king as "a tyrannical gentile despot."[81] Verse 25 reads: ἐκέλευσεν αὐτὸν ὁ κύριος πραθῆναι καὶ τὴν γυναῖκα καὶ τὰ τέκνα καὶ πάντα ὅσα ἔχει, καὶ ἀποδοθῆναι. Matthew uses the verb πιπράσκω to describe what is going to happen to this debtor, his wife, his children and his property: they are to be sold and the property liquidated. This verb was already used in 13:46 in the phrase πέπρακεν πάντα ὅσα εἶχεν, a phrase similar to that of 18:25; it will be used again later in 26:9. The more common word for sell seems to be πωλέω. There is no obvious reason why Matthew has preferred the more infrequent word πιπράσκω. Perhaps he chose it for stylistic variation purposes.

The fact just described raises two questions, the first of which has to do with the background for the practice of slavery individuals because of unpaid debts; the second is whether this payment could have come close to meeting the amount of the debt. To begin with the first question, there is strong evidence that selling debtors was a common practice in the Graeco-Roman world; it was permitted by both Hellenistic and Roman laws.[82] But over time, it was limited in these laws.[83] As to Jewish law, although only one biblical text shows that thieves could be sold into slavery (Exod 22:3), there are indications that debtors were actually sold (2 Kings 4:1, Neh 5:5; Isa 50:1; Amos 2:6; 8:6). The Jewish law, however, did not permit that a Jew be sold to Gentiles. Josephus informs us that prior to the time of Herod a Jewish thief could not be sold to non-Jews.[84] With Matthew writing after the time of Herod, one wonders whether the prohibition of a Jew being sold to Gentiles was still in force in the time of Jesus, or when the First Gospel was being written.

Along with the practice of selling debtors into slavery was that of imprisoning them. The purpose of this was to compel debtors' relatives

---

81. Donahue, *The Gospel in Parable*, 75.

82. Diogenes Laetrius, *Vit.* 4.46–58; see also Deissmann, *Light from the Ancient East*, 270.

83. Luz (*Matthew*, 2:472n35) cites De Franch (*Etudes*, 61–62, 119–24), among many others.

84. Josephus, *Ant.* 16.3.

and friends to ransom them.⁸⁵ There is strong evidence that, in the East, debtors were normally thrown into prison; but beginning in the third-century bce, there were efforts to limit the practice that was becoming widespread. On the other hand, the same evidence also shows that in Jewish law the practice of imprisoning debtors does not occur, which does not necessarily mean that it did not exist at all in Hellenized Palestine.⁸⁶ What would Matthew's audience have thought of this king's origins? They would likely have thought this king to be a Gentile king, because in the world of their experience in the first-century ce, or slightly before this period, most of their earthly kings were Gentiles.⁸⁷

Is it reasonable to think of this king as a "tyrannical despot" because of his approach in recovering the loss, as Donahue has suggested? Perhaps, not really! One wonders whether this sale would make a contribution to meeting such a huge debt at all. One also wonders about the price of a slave in first-century CE. One thing, for sure, is quite clear. From the parable itself, it is genuinely true to say that even if the slave, his family, and his property were to be sold, the payment could not have come close to meeting the amount of the debt. But, as Osborne has noted, the amount recovered from the sale "would serve justice by the standards of that day."⁸⁸ This means then that the order to sell this slave, his household, and his property was part of the king's rights; and the procedure to do so was reasonable.

The slave's response to the verdict against him is interesting: πεσὼν οὖν ὁ δοῦλος προσεκύνει αὐτῷ λέγων, Μακροθύμησον ἐπ' ἐμοί, καὶ πάντα ἀποδώσω σοι (v. 26). A social *deixis* is used here to describe this slave's response. First is the body language, which is described by πεσὼν and προσεκύνει. The slave falls down before the king and beseeches him. This is a moving picture of a person in total submission to a ruler. There is evidence that in the East to prostrate before both rulers and gods was customary.⁸⁹ But what this body language, especially in its description by προσκυνέω, would have meant to Matthew and his audience needs to be determined. The co-text of the sentence and the conceptual structure of the text seem to suggest that in verse 26, προσκυνέω is best understood

---

85. The evidence for the practice of imprisoning the debtors and the purpose of the practice is provided in Luz, *Matthew*, 2:472nn35, 40–41.

86. Ibid., 2:472n42.

87. Ibid., 2:472.

88. Osborne, *Matthew*, 695.

89. Luz, *Matthew*, 2:472.

to mean something like to "beseech and pay reverence to," rather than to "worship" (other senses of the verb found elsewhere in Matthew). Hagner is of the same opinion. Appealing to the context of the parable, he suggests that here the verb probably requires a lesser sense of obeisance before a monarch.[90] Other examples of the use of προσκυνέω in Matthew with the sense of beseeching include 8:2; 9:18; 15:25 and 20:20 (although in the latter the idea of worship may be alluded to).

Second is the speech language. Two facts in this regard can be identified. The first fact is described by μακροθύμησον, and the second by ἀποδώσω. This slave appeals to his lord's patience. Μακροθύμησον occurs only twice in Matthew: in verses 26 and 29 in the phrase μακροθύμησον ἐπ' ἐμοί. The co-text of the passage seems to require that here in verse 26 μακροθυμέω be understood to mean something like to "be patient," or "bear with." It is worth noting that this slave's plea does not seek the debt to be waived, or cancelled for him; for in what follows, he goes on to make a promise. The promise itself is clearly unrealistic, given the size of the debt; one wonders whether he is sincere in making it. What is clear is that his plea seeks merely his lord's patience. The second fact is described by ἀποδώσω: the debtor promises to pay πάντα ("everything"). Πάντα is a deictic indicator here; it is emphatic because of its position in the clause in verse 26: it precedes the verb it qualifies. On hearing this debtor's proposal for repaying *everything*, Matthew's audience most likely would have laughed, because of the lack of logic in the promise, given the size of the debt. As will be seen in the second scene (vv. 28–30), this debtor's plea is similar to the other slave's plea; the sole exception is that in the second case, πάντα is lacking in the debtor's promise.

The slave-debtor's response to the lord	The slave-debtor's response to the slave-creditor
ὁ δοῦλος. . . λέγων, Μακροθύμησον ἐπ' ἐμοί, καὶ πάντα ἀποδώσω σοι (v. 26).	ὁ σύνδουλος. . . λέγων, Μακροθύμησον ἐπ' ἐμοί, καὶ ἀποδώσω σοι (v. 29).

The lord's reaction to his debtor's plea now follows: σπλαγχνισθεὶς δὲ ὁ κύριος τοῦ δούλου ἐκείνου ἀπέλυσεν αὐτόν, καὶ τὸ δάνειον ἀφῆκεν αὐτῷ (v. 27). This reaction constitutes the second amazing thing in the first scene of the parable: the lord goes far beyond the debtor's request by cancelling the whole debt. From the story, it is not hard to see the four

---

90. Hagner, *Matthew*, 2:538; so also Osborne, *Matthew*, 695.

options that the lord may have had in his power to demand repayment. It comes as something of a surprise that of these four possible options, the lord, in this scene, chooses an unexpected option: he releases the debtor and cancels the entire debt (v. 27). Matthew uses two verbs to describe this double action, the first verb being directed to the person of the debtor (ἀπέλυσεν αὐτόν), and the second to what the debtor owes him (ἀφῆκεν τὸ δάνειον). As can be observed, ἀπολυῶ is used to describe the fact that, as a *person*, the debtor is released; ἀφίημι is used to describe the fact that, as a *thing*, his debt is cancelled for him. Ἀπολυῶ with the sense of the release of person is rare in Matthew; ἀφίημι is the most common verb with this sense. But in only three occasions in Matthew, ἀφίημι can be translated by forgive with the sense of cancellation of a debt (cf. 6:12a; 18:27, 32).

Two reasons underlie the decision of the lord to cancel the debt and to release this debtor. The first reason is that he is moved by σπλαγχνισθεὶς (compassion). Σπλαγχνίζομαι, from which σπλαγχνισθεὶς derives, appears elsewhere in Matthew where, unlike here in verse 27, it applies to Jesus (9:36; 14:14; 15:32; 20:34). The second possible reason for which this king-lord decided to release the debtor and to cancel his debt is for the preservation of his honor and display of his power.[91] The honor theme as related to that of mercy may recall Seneca's linking of them.[92] The lord's feeling leads to a practical action, whatever the motivation behind this action. The first scene closes with a surprisingly happy ending: the king's unbelievable mercy on his slave debtor, releasing him, and cancelling his colossal debt. To the patience sought, the cancellation of the debt is offered instead, as an act of mercy.

Scene 2 (vv. 28–30)

The second scene takes place between a slave and his fellow slave, a scene which has been described by France as a move "from the king's audience chamber to the servants' hall."[93] In fact, this creditor-slave has just walked out from the meeting with his lord, a meeting that has just seen him re-

---

91. So also Schottroff for the idea of preservation of power (*The Parables of Jesus*, 199); but I depart from her for her suggestion that this parable does not idealize the forgiveness of debts.

92. Seneca, *Clem.* 1.9.1–7, 11; see a detailed discussion in ch. 2.

93. France, *Matthew*, 706–7.

leased and his huge debt cancelled. There are similarities and differences between the first and the second scenes: the similarities can be observed in the debtors' respective responses, and the differences in the approaches of the creditors to retrieve their respective debts.

Scene 1	Scene 2
1. Approaches of the creditors in retrieving their debts	
The lord's approach: giving of a command (ἐκέλευσεν, v. 24) The lord's final decision: (v. 27) —the release (ἀπέλυσεν) of the debtor (v. 27) —the cancellation (ἀφῆκεν) of the debt (v. 27)	The slave-creditor's approach: physical violence (κρατήσας αὐτὸν ἔπνιγεν, v. 28) The slave-creditor's final decision the throwing of the debtor in prison (ἔβαλεν αὐτὸν εἰς φυλακὴν, v. 29)
2. Responses of the debtors to the verdict	
... ὁ δοῦλος προσεκύνει αὐτῷ λέγων, Μακροθύμησον ἐπ' ἐμοί, καὶ πάντα ἀποδώσω σοι (v. 26)	... ὁ σύνδουλος ... παρεκάλει αὐτὸν λέγων, Μακροθύμησον ἐπ' ἐμοί, καὶ ἀποδώσω σοι (v. 29)

This table shows the contrast between the approach of the lord to retrieve his debt from the first slave and that of this same slave, now a creditor, to retrieve his debt from his fellow slave. It also shows another contrast between the response of the slave-debtor to the verdict of his lord-creditor and the response of the slave-debtor to the verdict of his fellow slave-creditor. The similarities are mainly found in the debtors' responses to their respective verdicts. The story in the second scene thus reads: ἐξελθὼν δὲ ὁ δοῦλος ἐκεῖνος εὗρεν ἕνα τῶν συνδούλων αὐτοῦ ὃς ὤφειλεν αὐτῷ ἑκατὸν δηνάρια (v. 28a).

A discourse *deixis* (δὲ) is employed to introduce the second scene in the parable. It serves to indicate a contrast—a contrast between the lord's approach to retrieve his debt from the first slave (cf. scene 1) and this same slave's approach to retrieve his debt from his fellow slave (scene 2), as just noted. The word ἐκεῖνος in the phrase ὁ δοῦλος ἐκεῖνος is a personal *deixis*. Here it obviously certifies that it is unmistakably the forgiven δοῦλος of verse 27 on whom the scene now focuses: it is this same slave who now proceeds to pressure ἕνα τῶν συνδούλων αὐτοῦ ("one of his fellow slaves"). The term τῶν συνδούλων which is used to describe the creditor's fellow slaves, including his debtor, is not insignificant. Luz's has argued that it is consciously chosen in order to indicate that they belonged to the same class, and thus should share a sense of solidarity.[94]

---

94. Luz, *Matthew*, 2:473n51.

The debt owed this creditor is ἑκατὸν δηνάρια ("a hundred denarii"). The term δηνάριον occurs elsewhere in Matthew (20:2, 9, 10, 13; 22:19). The δηνάριον was a Roman silver coin. It is generally admitted that it had approximately the same value as the Greek δραχμή. According to 20:1–16, it was the standard day's wage for a laborer. The question is whether or not the debt of 100 denarii was significant. Although Luz talks of 100 denarii as an amount that even a poor farmer could scrape together in the course of a year,[95] this is not to undermine the significance of the debt it represents in our parable. France has remarked that this debt is not in itself insignificant, for it probably represented some three or four months' wages.[96] This does suggest then that 100 denarii, which were owed, was not an insignificant debt *per se*; it is only a trifle compared to what the first slave owed the king, as many commentators also think.

This debtor, who is a slave and co-worker with his creditor, owes his creditor a hundred denarii. The first striking thing is his creditor's approach in demanding repayment from him: καὶ κρατήσας αὐτὸν ἔπνιγεν λέγων, Ἀπόδος εἴ τι ὀφείλεις (v. 28b). He uses physical violence as he seizes his debtor by the throat, to force him to repay. One wonders whether such an approach was acceptable in those days. Supposing it was, one may also ask why the king, to whom a huge debt was owed, never used it at least in the first instance. There is strong evidence that physical violence (including seizing the debtor by the throat) in the demand for repayment was socially unacceptable; but it was not unusual.[97] How would this creditor's behavior have sounded to Matthew's audience? They will surely be shocked for two reasons. Firstly, because this creditor had not only had his entire debt cancelled but it was a colossal debt; secondly, because of his use of physical violence against his debtor. They would surely begin to imagine a dreadful destiny for this unmerciful creditor; something of the kind of the rebuke in verses 32–33 and the subsequent punishment in verse 34 would not be a surprise at all.

It follows that under the pressure of this unmerciful creditor, the debtor makes a proposal to repay: πεσὼν οὖν ὁ σύνδουλος αὐτοῦ παρεκάλει αὐτὸν λέγων, Μακροθύμησον ἐπ' ἐμοί, καὶ ἀποδώσω σοι (v. 29). This proposal is almost the same in wording to that of this

---

95. Ibid., 2:473.

96. France, *The Gospel of Matthew*, 707.

97. Pollux, *Onomasticon* 3.116; Lucian, *Dialogi mortuorum* 2 (22).1; Plautus, *Poenulus* 789–90; Aristophanes, *Equites* 775; m. B. Batra 10.8; cf. Luz, *Matthew* 2:473n53.

slave-debtor to the lord (v. 26), except that there are three main changes in the second case, as the table below shows .

Scene 1 Slave-debtor's response to the lord's verdict	Scene 2 Slave-debtor's response to the slave-creditor's verdict
…ὁ δοῦλος προσεκύνει αὐτῷ λέγων, Μακροθύμησον ἐπ' ἐμοί, καὶ πάντα ἀποδώσω σοι (v. 26)	…ὁ σύνδουλος… παρεκάλει αὐτὸν λέγων, Μακροθύμησον ἐπ' ἐμοί, καὶ ἀποδώσω σοι (v. 29)

From the table above, it is easy to see the following. Firstly, ὁ δοῦλος is replaced by ὁ σύνδουλος. Secondly, προσεκύνει is replaced by παρεκάλει. Thirdly, πάντα is lacking in scene 2. Only two of these changes may easily be explained. Δοῦλος gives place to σύνδουλος because now the scene takes place between the slave and his fellow slave. Προσεκύνει seems to be purposely replaced by παρεκάλει in order to underscore social equality of the two characters,[98] both belonging in the same class. An additional reason, as Luz has remarked, is that in the East it was customary to prostrate only before rulers and gods.[99] It would then be strange if this debtor prostrated before his co-worker, a person of the same social status.

As can be clearly seen, the second debtor uses, where applicable, the same kind of language as that of his fellow slave used when he was in trouble. One wonders whether Jesus or Matthew was creating the parallel. This is a fictional story anyway. Of particular significant is the fact that this debtor seeks patience and promises repayment.

A social *deixis* (body and speech languages) is used to describe the second debtor's attitude vis-à-vis his creditor: he falls before his creditor, which shows how desperate he was. As to speech language, two facts can be noted, the first being described μακροθύμησον and the second ἀποδώσω. This debtor appeals to his creditor's patience and promises to repay. As discussed earlier, μακροθύμησον occurs only twice in Matthew. In verses 26 and 29, μακροθυμέω seems to mean something like to "be patient," or "bear with." As with the plea of the first debtor in the first scene, the plea of this second debtor does not seek his debt to be cancelled for him; rather, he makes a promise. Contrary to the first debtor's unrealistic promise to repay *everything* (πάντα), the promise of this second debtor is reasonable: ἀποδώσω σοι (v. 29). The plea is reasonable

---

98. So also Davies and Allison, *Saint Matthew*, 2:801.

99. Luz, *Matthew*, 2:472.

given the size of the debt: paying 100 denarii is feasible. The debt could be paid back in time, as the debtor himself did suggest. It is strange that πάντα, surprising as it was in the first scene, is absent in the second where it might have been practicable. This may suggest another strong point of contrast between the behaviour of the first debtor (duplicity) and that of the second debtor (sincerity). In any case, the question is whether or not the plea of this second debtor will be heard. This is the focus of what follows.

The creditor's response to his fellow debtor's plea reads: ὁ δὲ οὐκ ἤθελεν, ἀλλὰ ἀπελθὼν ἔβαλεν αὐτὸν εἰς φυλακὴν ἕως ἀποδῷ τὸ ὀφειλόμενον (v. 30). This response constitutes another shock in the second scene of the parable. The creditor refuses the plea for patience and the reasonable promise for repayment. As if physical violence and verbal menace were not enough, he throws the debtor in prison. This behaviour is quite strange, especially as the second debtor was someone else's slave.

The language of throwing a person into prison (βάλλω + εἰς φυλακὴν) occurs elsewhere in Matthew in connection with justice; Matt 5:25 talks of the possibility of the offender being thrown into prison should they fail to come to terms quickly with their accuser while on the way to court (cf. 5:24–26). It also occurs in Luke (12:58), John (3:24), Acts (16:23–24), and Revelation (2:10). Interestingly, in Luke this language is also used in connection with justice. This suggests that it was acceptable and within this creditor's rights to use this approach in an attempt to retrieve his debt. Osborne informs us that "[i]mprisonment was often done in case of heavy debt as a way to force the family to pay it."[100] If this is true, then the way this creditor deals with his debtor is too harsh. This way of dealing with this second debtor is quite odd given the fact that this debtor was someone's else slave. This harshness is made clearer in that, out of the three possible options in his power, as already shown, he only chooses the most extreme option. This clearly shows the kind of person he really was. Luz has suggested that if this creditor did not choose to sell his debtor into slavery it is not because he was compassionate, but because the amount owed him was less than the price of a slave; for in Judaism, the sale of a debtor into slavery was possible only when the debt was at least equivalent to the price of the slave.[101] Another alternative is

---

100. Osborne, *Matthew*, 697.
101. Luz, *Matthew*, 2:473n55.

to think that, perhaps the slave-creditor did not sell his debtor because he was already a slave.

From the second scene, it is not hard to see the contrast between the slave's behavior and the lord's behavior, and how Matthew's audience would have reacted. The audience of this story would be astonished and shocked by this creditor's lack of a sense of humanity toward his fellow debtor. They would notice that his behavior trumpets his own hypocrisy. They would not understand how he who had fallen down before his creditor, beseeching for patience as if he could repay everything, he who had benefited from an amazing grace from his creditor, could now refuse to have mercy on his fellow worker, especially for such a small debt! This leads to the last scene of the parable.

Scene 3 (vv. 31–34)

The third scene takes place once again between the king and his slave. The other slaves, having seen how their fellow slave (the creditor) had behaved toward one of them, are greatly distressed. Because of their sympathy for their fellow slave in trouble, they go to their lord and tell him what has happened. On hearing this report, the lord is so shocked that he immediately takes appropriate action against this unmerciful slave.

All that has taken place is narrated to the lord by the σύνδουλοι, who recognize the terrible hypocrisy of a man who received kindness but could not give it. What they felt over the fate of their fellow slave is described ἐλυπήθησαν σφόδρα: they were exceedingly grieved. This phrase also occurs elsewhere in Matthew, where it describes the disciples' feeling on hearing from their Lord what was to happen to him (17:23); it also occurs in LXX (Neh 5:6; Jon 4:4, 9). This description here seems to express a combination of feelings that Ceslas Spicq has aptly described as "tristesse, indignation et dégoût."[102] Whether anger is also to be read in the fellow slaves' feeling is, however, not certain. It is reasonable to think that the hearers of this parable would also naturally have the same kind of feelings.

Not only did these slaves have feelings (v. 31); they also took action: καὶ ἐλθόντες διεσάφησαν τῷ κυρίῳ ἑαυτῶν πάντα τὰ γενόμενα (v. 32). They went to their lord to inform him of what had happened. The expression διεσάφησαν... πάντα is used to describe the action of informing.

102. Spicq, *Dieu et l'homme*, 59n2.

Διασαφέω, which is used here, occurs only once in the NT, and again in Matthew, where it is used to describe the disciples' request to Jesus (13:36). Although this verb is used in a different context, in both cases it probably means something like to say point-blank, or make clear. Here in verse 31, these slaves made everything (πάντα) plain to the lord. That is, they explained exactly what had happened, providing any detail they deemed useful; they knew of the cancellation of this unmerciful slave's colossal debt. Although the text does not say that they used a spokesperson, it is not unreasonable to think that they did, supplying him with the any details he might have forgotten. For it would be strange for a crowd of slaves to come just anyhow to the king and begin to speak.

The feelings and the action of these slaves on behalf of their fellow in trouble raise two important questions. First is the kind of relationship that existed among δοῦλοι/σύνδουλοι of the same κύριος, and the extent of such relationship. Second is the extent to which a grasp of this is most likely to shed light on the audience's understanding of the unity, sympathy and action of the other slaves toward the fellow slave in trouble. What seems to be significant is that humanity underlies both their motivation and action. Perhaps through this, Matthew wanted to encourage his readers and hearers to remain united—as one family—for their survival, no matter the circumstance in which they may find themselves.

The reaction of the lord now follows, and does two things: it reminds the slave of the mercy he had received and the reason for granting it; it also describes the imminent action that the lord is now going to take against this unmerciful slave. The lord does not require any explanation from this slave. Having summoned him, he immediately addresses him thus: Δοῦλε πονηρέ, πᾶσαν τὴν ὀφειλὴν ἐκείνην ἀφῆκά σοι, ἐπεὶ παρεκάλεσάς με· οὐκ ἔδει καὶ σὲ ἐλεῆσαι τὸν σύνδουλόν σου, ὡς κἀγὼ σὲ ἠλέησα (vv. 32–33).

A social *deixis* (here a vocative) is used to introduce the lord's address to his debtor. Here we have a case of a rhetorical question, a question that does not expect an answer. This rhetorical question can be divided in two main parts. To begin with, in the first part the lord addresses the slave as a δοῦλος πονηρός ("wicked slave"). This same expression appears elsewhere in Matthew to describe the master's response to one of his slaves (25:26). This remark of the lord here in verses 32–33 comprises two parts: in the first part the lord reminds the slave that he has cancelled his entire debt, and in the second, the reason for this previous act of generosity is recalled. To begin with the first item, the reminder reads as follows: πᾶσαν τὴν ὀφειλὴν ἐκείνην ἀφῆκά σοι (v. 32). Here πᾶσαν is a discourse *deixis*. It is emphatic given its syntactical position in the clause; the lord reminds this slave of all that debt (πᾶσαν τὴν ὀφειλὴν ἐκείνην), which he cancelled for him (ἀφῆκά σοι). The word πᾶσαν, to be sure, echoes the slave's previous promise in verse 26 (πάντα ἀποδώσω σοι). The lord also adds the reason why he did so: ἐπεὶ παρεκάλεσάς με. The conjunction ἐπεὶ is probably a causal *deixis*. It seems to suggest that the lord cancelled the debt of the unmerciful slave because this slave pleaded for patience. In reality, however, the lord cancelled the debt out of pure merciful generosity, rather than because of the plea itself.

In the second part of the rhetorical question above, the lord goes on to take back the forgiveness he generously granted, as he now demands that the debt be paid in full: οὐκ ἔδει καὶ σὲ ἐλεῆσαι τὸν σύνδουλόν σου, ὡς κἀγὼ σὲ ἠλέησα (v. 33). This is a good example of the use of the concept of conditionality and the link between reluctance in showing mercy (or forgiving) and judgement. It is quite clear that the lord's own behaviour is based on the behaviour of the slave toward his fellow slave; the lord treats him as he himself has treated his fellow slave. In so doing, Matthew restates explicitly the *conditioned* forgiveness and *conditioned* mercy. This echoes the fifth beatitude in 5:7, where the concept is embodied in the "mercy for mercy" saying: "Blessed are the merciful (οἱ ἐλεήμονες), for they will receive mercy (ἐλεηθήσονται)." The disciples are to show mercy to their fellow humans if they are to expect to receive mercy from God. This principle comes to fuller expression in 6:12, 14–15 and 18:32b–35. In 7:1–2, the reciprocal principle is stated both directly with regard to judgment, and indirectly using the metaphor of measuring out commodities in the market.[103] In 7:12, this reciprocal principle seems to be established; and in 18:21–35 mercy and forgiveness are juxtaposed.[104] The call to be perfect (τέλειός) in 5:48, as the heavenly Father is perfect, also adds to the evidence.

In this vein, Davies and Allison have reasonably suggested the *imitatio Dei* motif. For them, beneath Jesus' saying in 5:7 is the idea that God, the king of all, must be imitated in his goodness: the one forgiven should have acted in kind; the one act of mercy should have begotten another.[105] Logically, because of what he had received from his lord, this

---

103. France, *Matthew*, 168, 275. So also Couroyer, "'De la mesure dont vous mesurez il vous sera mesuré,'" 366–70.

104. France, *Matthew*, 707–8.

105. Davies and Allison, *Saint Matthew*, 2:802.

slave was expected to act similarly toward his fellow slave. Sadly, he did not act as expected. E. Linnemann's comment on the character of mercy is pertinent: "Clearly mercy is essentially not something which we can accept with a feeling of relief at having got away with it once more, only to let things go on again just as we used to. It appears to have the character of an ordinance, just as justice is an ordinance."[106]

The lord is filled with anger and revokes his earlier cancellation of the slave's exorbitant debt. His verdict this time is severe as he hands this slave over to the βασανισταῖς (torturers) for an according punishment. The term βασανισταῖς is a NT *hapax legomenon*. Its use here surely serves to stress the severity of the punishment, as Davies and Allison have also suggested.[107] It has been observed that torturers, though disallowed by the Jews, were common in Roman prisons. In the case of unpaid debt, friends and relations would have accordingly been more urgent in raising money.[108] According to Josephus, Herod the Great did employ torture.[109] This slave is to be tortured until the debt was fully paid. The expression used to describe this fact is πᾶν τὸ ὀφειλόμενον (i.e., everything owed). Similar expression occurs elsewhere in Matthew (5:26) and is used of a potential brother or sister who has wronged another. It is easy to see that verse 34 is the close counterpart of verse 30, which describes in similar language this yet forgiven slave putting his fellow slave in prison until his debt was paid. It clearly teaches that as one treats others, so also will one be treated. This point is made explicit in the application of the parable in verse 35.

The enormity of the debt has led some to think that this imprisonment would have been permanent. They also think that this, together with the reference to the torturers, hint at eschatological punishment.[110] It is interesting that this wicked slave does not dare to ask for patience as he did before (18:26, 29), perhaps because he has realized how wicked he was. In Davies and Allison's words, "He knows he stands condemned."[111] Would this lord once again have mercy on him if he had asked for it? It would be strange if this slave asked for the lord's mercy once more and

106. Linnemann, *The Parables of Jesus*, 111.
107. Davies and Allison, *Saint Matthew*, 2:802.
108. Hagner, *Matthew*, 2:540.
109. Josephus, *War* 1.548.
110. Hagner (*Matthew*, 2:540), Davies and Allison (*Saint Matthew*, 2:803), among others.
111. Davies and Allison, *Saint Matthew*, 2:802.

be granted it. As one would have expected, the third scene closes with a terrible ending. The story-teller adds to it a comment to serve as the moral of the story (v. 35).

Final Answer to the Forgiving Query (v. 35)

Building upon verse 34, in verse 35 Matthew presents his own view about God's appropriate response to the disciples' unwillingness to forgive; punishment is this response. Snodgrass has argued that "[t]he focus on judgment in this parable should be compared to other parables of judgment, specially the parables of the Wheat and the Weeds and of the Rich Man and Lazarus and the parables of future eschatology."[112] This is not quite right because the judgment in this parable is not just a general judgment as is the case with these parables, but a specific one. It takes the form of punishment and applies to the unmerciful and unforgiving person. It can be linked to the situation described in other Matthean interpersonal forgiveness and related texts (5:7; 6:15; 7:1–2).

Matt 18:35 poses the fundamental question of whether the believer can still experience the judging Father as the same Father who ever forgives humans in interminable love. Related questions include the following: Can God, who has forgiven all human sins, withdraw his act of grace? Does the idea of judgment negate grace's reliability? What follows is an attempt to answer some of these questions or aspects of them.

The phrase οὕτως καὶ (v. 35) is a discourse *deixis*. Its function and the rendering of it are not obvious. Here it seems to point back not only to verse 34—where it is reported that filled with anger the lord not only revokes his earlier cancellation of the unmerciful slave's exorbitant debt, but also hands him over to the torturers—but probably also to other Matthean interpersonal forgiveness texts and related texts because of the underlying concept of reciprocity in them, together with the link of this with the idea of judgement. Because 18:35 ("So my heavenly Father will also do to every one of you, if you do not forgive... from your heart.") is an expansion of 6:14–15 ("For if you forgive others their trespasses, your heavenly Father will also forgive you; but if you do not forgive others, neither will your Father forgive your trespasses."), which is related to 5:7 ("Blessed are the merciful, for they will receive mercy.") and 7:1–2, 12 ("Do not judge, so that you may not be judged. For with the judgment

---

112. Snodgrass, *Stories with Intent*, 61.

The Rhetoric of Interpersonal Forgiveness in Matt 18:21–35

you make you will be judged, and the measure you give will be the measure you get. In everything do to others as you would have them do to you; for this is the law and the prophets."), the *logion* in 18:35 also refers to these other interpersonal forgiveness and related texts.

As to the rendering of οὕτως καὶ, the meaning Schottroff has assigned to these two words is interesting. She has translated οὕτως καὶ by a full sentence: "How is this, then, to be compared to the kingdom of God?"[113] The question is not whether it is reasonable to translate two terms by a whole sentence, but rather whether the translation provided is plausible. The translation above by Schottroff is problematic. Her approach to the parable itself may perhaps be the cause of the difficulty. The unpleasantness of the king's actions in the parable, refusing to consider further forgiveness, together with her desire to counter this impression, has led Schottroff to argue that this king is intended to portray what God is *not* like.[114] Schottroff's approach to this parable, and particularly her reading of οὕτως καὶ in verse 35 in an attempt at avoiding the straightfoward reading of the parable and the verse are altogether invalid. In 18:35 οὕτως καὶ likely means "so also."

It is interesting that the judgement is by the πατήρ μου ὁ οὐράνιος. The language of the fatherhood of God abounds in the Sermon and in the Community Discourse from which our two forgiveness texts are taken. As Gundry has said, the manner in which the heavenly Father will deal with the unforgiving disciple leaves no room for misunderstanding the parable, and therefore no excuse for failure to forgive. The expression ἀπὸ τῶν καρδιῶν ὑμῶν is important for the discussion. It also occurs in *T. Gad* 6:7: ἄφες αὐτῷ ἀπὸ καρδίας. In 18:35, it seems to express sincerity and excludes all casuistry and legalism, as France has also suggested.[115] The phrase ἀπὸ καρδίας ("from the heart") seems to show that hypocrisy has no part in the kind of forgiveness that God demands. But the warning character of the parable shows that forgiving out of obedience need not kill sincerity, for a true disciple wants to obey his master.[116] Commenting on the statement ἀπὸ καρδίας, Luz suggests that it indicates that the forgiveness of sins involves not merely that one is outwardly reconciled

---

113. Schottroff, *The Parables of Jesus*, 196.
114. A similar observation is made by Snodgrass, *Stories with Intent*, 70.
115. France, *Matthew*, 278.
116. Gundry, *Matthew*, 375.

with one's brothers and sisters but also that one affirms them completely.[117] Sincerity is thus at the core. As Luz also notes, brotherly forgiveness is no incidental matter, and unkindness among persons is a sin of no little importance. Both of them lie at the heart of one's relationship to God.[118]

CONCLUSIONS

One of the main tasks in the exegesis of 18:21–35 was to demonstrate how seriously Matthew stresses the notion of interpersonal forgiveness in his gospel. It was suggested that in 18:21–35 the emphasis on this theme is carried out in five ways. First is the strategic rhetorical position of interpersonal forgiveness texts (and texts related to the theme) and the proportion they occupy within Matthew's text. This chapter has shown that the interpersonal forgiveness theme is given the lion's share in the Community Discourse in Matt 18: about 60 percent of the material in this chapter is obviously devoted to the issues of brotherly reconciliation (vv. 15–17) and of interpersonal forgiveness (vv. 21–35); further, the fact that the parable in 18:23–35 is without parallel suggests the significance, for Matthew, of the teaching it contains.

Second is the reinforcing of the concept of interpersonal forgiveness. This is evident from the fact that this idea is stated directly by using ἀφίημι (x4) to describe both divine-human and interpersonal relationships, from the emphasis on the frequency of forgiving an ἀδελφός—a command given to the offended person; and by means of the parable, serving to highlight reluctance in forgiving together with the consequence of it.

Third is the concept of reciprocity and the link between mercy and forgiveness. This is evidenced mostly in the following three ways: (1) through the idea of *conditional* forgiveness which is used to describe divine-human and inter-human relationships; (2) through the fact that both the idea of *conditional* forgiveness and that of *conditional* mercy are juxtaposed; (3) through the link between reluctance in the *praxis* of mercy and forgiveness and the idea of punishment.

Fourth is an emphasis on the offended person's responsibility in forgiving and the link with the concept of *mature* and *immature* Christians. The co-text of 18:21–35 and the conceptual structure of it strongly

117. Luz, *Matthew*, 2:476.
118. Ibid.

suggest that the forgiving act is mainly expected of the *spiritually mature* members; in which case, forgiving an ἀδελφός is primarily part of the responsibilities of the *mature* members. Moreover, 18:21-22 suggests forgiving as an obligation for the injured person; the same is true of the parable itself. Furthermore, the absence of a direct reference to repentance in the passage surely adds to the evidence. Finally, in 18:21-35, the expression ἀφίημι τὸ δάνειον (18:27) and ἀφίημι τὴν ὀφειλὴν (18:32) means something like "remitting *debts*" (cp. 6:12). These elements all fit nicely the preservation of church cohesion that has been suggested in this study as the first evangelist's main concern in his gospel. The forgiveness pattern, in the table below, which has emerged from 6:12, 14-15 and 18:21-35 can be suggested.

Matthew
[1] A wrong is committed [2] The offender does not necessarily seek forgiveness [3] The offended person grants forgiveness as both their *responsibility* towards their fellow human and their *accountability* before their heavenly Father [4] The ultimate goal of the forgiveness demand is to bring harmony within the community.

7

Forgiveness and Connected Aspects of Matthew's Theology

PREVIOUS CHAPTERS EXPLORED THE theme of interpersonal forgiveness in various sources, namely, Graeco-Roman writings of the first-century ce, Jewish materials in Greek and the Matthean text. The table below displays a plausible outline of interpersonal forgiveness which may be identified in these documents.

Graeco-Roman Literature: Dionysius and Seneca	Jewish Literature in Greek: LXX, Philo and Josephus	Matthean Text
[1] A wrong is committed. [2] The offender, or the one acting on their behalf, seeks forgiveness; forgiveness is sought in their desperation. [3] The offended person grants forgiveness as an honourable practice, stemming from the awareness of the inclination of humans to evil and God's or deities' forgiving disposition.	[1] A wrong is committed. [2] The offender, or the one acting on their behalf, seeks forgiveness; forgiveness is sought in their desperation. [3] The offended person grants forgiveness as an honourable practice, stemming from the awareness of the inclination of humans to evil and God's forgiving disposition.	[1] A wrong is committed. [2] The offender does not *necessarily* seek forgiveness. [3a] The offended person grants forgiveness as a right thing to do, stemming from the awareness of the inclination of humans to evil and God's forgiving disposition. [3b] The offended person does potentially grant forgiveness as: their *responsibility* towards their fellow human; their *accountability* before their heavenly Father.
[4] Forgiveness granted brings harmony in the relationships between the two parties in conflict.	[4] Forgiveness granted does drive away the danger for the offender.	[4] The ultimate goal of the forgiveness demand is to bring harmony within the community.

This table shows quite clearly that there are similarities and differences between the interpersonal forgiveness rhetoric in Matthew and its rhetoric in Jewish and Graeco-Roman literature. From it, it is possible to discover that the forgiveness pattern, which emerges from Jewish literature in Greek and Graeco-Roman sources, suggests that human forgiving was widely acknowledged in the socio-religious world of the time and in society contemporary with Matthew's church. First, seeking forgiveness was part of the responsibilities of the offender; second, granting forgiveness was most likely viewed as honorable. Therefore, withholding forgiveness for whatever reason would display a lack of virtue. In Matthew, conversely, the scenario is quite different. In it a new note is sounded, as the idea of accountability before God for any reluctance to forgive others emerges; the sense of accountability before God is dominant in the forgiveness teaching in Matthew, making forgiving not *optional*.

The understanding of accountability before God (or the deities), for reluctance to forgive, is almost nonexistent in both the Graeco-Roman and Jewish sources surveyed. The Marcius' account (*Ant. Rom.* 8.50.1–4) is probably the only clear example in Dionysius. Jewish sources surveyed in chapter 4 also showed that this notion is very rare, Sir 28:1–4 being the sole clear example. This suggests that in both Graeco-Roman and Jewish thinking, the offended person was not necessarily bound to forgive. Although the Dionysius and Sirach texts contain the idea of accountability in forgiveness, still nothing quite exact is said of what will happen to the potential unforgiving person. The actively vengeful of Sir 28:1, to be understood as anybody who fails to forgive their fellow humans, is said to face God's vengeance. In Matthew, most importantly, what will happen to them is clearly stated: they will be punished; and it is punishment which is the main concern in 18:23–35, as was shown in chapter 6 of this work.

For Matthew, however, forgiving is not merely an appropriate moral act, or an honorable practice; rather it is primarily an *obligation* which lies squarely upon the shoulders of the offended person; it is "a must." This is affirmed quite strongly throughout the gospel in its use of the language of forgiveness and related concepts (5:7, 38–48; 6:12b, 14–15; 7:12; 18:12–14, 15–17, 21, 33); the texts in brackets were surveyed elsewhere in this work.

For Matthew, withholding forgiveness would be subject to retribution. The particularity of Matthew with regard to the rhetoric of interpersonal forgiveness lies precisely in the emphasis he has placed on the punishment which will befall the potential unforgiving disciple (18:23–35, cp. 6:15). In Matthew's view, reluctance or failure to forgive brings God's punishment. Surely Matthew has underscored the idea of accountability in forgiving more than any biblical writers. This emphasis should be recognized and stressed in teaching and preaching about forgiveness and its practice in communities of believers in all contexts.

This last chapter of the work is structured around four main sections. The first section compares the teaching about interpersonal forgiveness in 6:12, 14–15, in 18:21–35 and in other Matthean interpersonal forgiveness texts and related passages. The second section explores this teaching and Matthew's message more holistically. The third relates the findings of this study to the contemporary church in all contexts. The fourth discusses the contribution of this work in Matthean scholarship, presents conclusions and lays out a couple of points for further study.

INTER-TEXTUAL SYNTHESIS OF MATT 6:12, 14–15; 18:21–35 AND OTHER MATTHEAN INTERPERSONAL FORGIVENESS TEXTS

The thesis propounded in this work is that interpersonal forgiveness is quite central to the message in Matthew. It also ventures an understanding of the nature of human forgiving in it. The evidence for the emphasis on this theme in the First Gospel includes the following fivefold pattern: first is the concept of reciprocity and the link between mercy and forgiveness, together with the link between reluctance in the *praxis* of them and the idea of judgment; second is the emphasis on the responsibility of the offended person in forgiving, and the link of this with the concept of the *spiritually mature* and *immature* Christian; third is a reinforcement of the concept of forgiveness by the use of related concepts; fourth is the strategic rhetorical positioning of interpersonal forgiveness texts (and related texts) within the Matthean text; and fifth is the proportion these texts occupy within the Sermon and the Community Discourse.

As was shown in chapter 2 of this work, this pattern is observed more or less throughout the gospel. Most interestingly, the elements of it altogether are incorporated in 6:12, 14–15 and 18:21–35. In exploring them, these features were pointed out and highlighted. In this vein, this final section draws upon chapters 1, 5, and 6, tying up the various theoretical strands on the subject of interpersonal forgiveness in 6:12, 14–15 and 18:21–35.

Matt 6:12, 14–15

What the study holds in store with regard to 6:12, 14–15 is discussed in what follows. For the sake of convenience and clarity, the findings are given in the scheme of the pattern that was suggested as the evidence for the prominence of the interpersonal forgiveness theme in Matthew.

The Concept of Reciprocity and the Link between Mercy and Forgiveness

The concept of reciprocity is obvious in 6:12, 14–15. In this text, this idea is stated quite clearly in three ways: first, by means of the phrase ὡς καὶ ἡμεῖς (v. 12); second, by the use of an antithetical parallelism in verses

14–15, a rhetorical device which likely serves to stress the consequences awaiting the potential unforgiving person—the consequences implied here but stated explicitly in 18:35; third, by the way in which conditional forgiveness is employed in 6:12, 14–15 to characterize divine-human and interpersonal relationships, as a clear expression of the conditional mercy of 5:7,[1] where showing mercy is said to be expected of the disciple if they are to expect to receive mercy from God.

The Emphasis on the Offended Person's Responsibility to Forgive and the Link of This with the Concept of "Spiritually Mature and Immature" Christians

The emphasis on the responsibility of the offended person to forgive and the link of this with the concept of *spiritually mature* and *immature* Christians is another clear evidence for the prominence of the theme in Matthew. The logic here is this. Because 18:21–35 is an expansion of 6:14–15 (cp. 5:7; 7:1–2, 12; 18:15–17), and given the fact that Matt 18 as a whole is about *mature* and *immature* Christians (according to the understanding of the present author), what is being said of 18:21–35 also applies to 6:12, 14–15.

In 6:12, 14–15, the phenomenon described above is expressed in two main ways. Firstly, although both the responsibility of the offender for seeking forgiveness and that of the offended person for granting forgiveness are equally stated, the latter feature receives much more stress. This is clear from 6:12a (1x, cp. 5:23–25 through the language of brotherly reconciliation) and 6:14–15 (2x and emphasis of 18:12–14 [seeking the erring sheep language], 18:15–17 [brotherly reconciliation language], 18:21, 33). Secondly, this trend can be found in verse 12 where the past tense ἀφήκαμεν is used to underline the petitioner's prior forgiving act. It is worth mentioning that, out of nine Matthean interpersonal forgiveness and related occurrences, in only one of them the responsibility of the offender for seeking forgiveness is in view; all the rest of these occurrences are concerned with the responsibility of the offended person to show mercy, for loving enemies, for not retaliating, for being perfect and forgiving (5:7; 5:38–48; 6:12, 14–15; 7:12; 18:12–17, 21, 33).

---

1. Cf. discussion in ch. 2 of this work under "the concept of reciprocity and the link between mercy and forgiveness" on pp. 30–36 above.

Reinforcing the Concept of Interpersonal Forgiveness

A reinforcement of the concept of interpersonal forgiveness appears in 6:12, 14–15. In this text, this trend is evidenced, firstly, when the idea of interpersonal forgiveness is stated quite directly using ἀφίημι (4x) to characterize both divine-human and interpersonal relationships; secondly, by the fact that the forgiveness petition in verse 12 is not only *expanded* but also *emphatically* stated around the Prayer (6:14–15) and beyond the Sermon (18:21–35); and thirdly, by an antithetical parallelism in verses 14–15 with its effects beyond this text.

Strategic Rhetorical Positioning within the Matthean Text

Matt 5:7 and 7:12 more or less form an *inclusio* about the first block of teaching material. The teaching material block in Matt 5–7, in which this *inclusio* along with other interpersonal forgiveness and related texts emerge, is placed at the beginning of Jesus' ministry in Galilee. Matt 6:12, 14–15 is placed at about the centre of the Sermon. On top of that, the positioning of the forgiveness petition in verse 12 within the Prayer is also compelling. Furthermore, while the saying in verse 14 is Matthew's re-arrangement of his Mark's narrative (cp. Mark 11:25), verse 15 is part of his special material.

Proportion of Interpersonal Forgiveness and Related Texts within the Sermon

Interpersonal forgiveness and related passages occupy a good proportion in the Sermon. The Sermon contains a large number of passages on forgiveness and tangential subjects related to it: 392 of the 1,990 words of the material in it are devoted to brotherly reconciliation (5:21–26), non-retaliation (5:38–42), loving enemies (5:43–47; 7:12), being perfect (5:48), forgiving (6:12, 14–15) and not judging others (7:1-2). This percentage (about 20 percent) is not insignificant, especially in a discourse in which various issues are being addressed. Additionally, within the Sermon, the interpersonal forgiveness texts altogether in and around the Prayer have the lion's share: 43 of the 91 words (around 47 percent) of this material is devoted to the subject of forgiving. That is also surely a high proportion within a single unit dealing with various issues.

Matt 18:21–35

As was the case with 6:12, 14–15, here again for the sake of convenience, the findings from 18:21–35 are presented in the format of the pattern that was suggested as the evidence for the prominence of the interpersonal forgiveness theme in Matthew.

The Concept of Reciprocity and the Link between Mercy and Forgiveness

The concept of reciprocity and the link between mercy and forgiveness is evident in 18:21–35; this is apparent in three ways. Firstly, through the idea of *conditional* forgiveness which is employed to characterize divine-human and interpersonal relationships. Secondly, through the fact that the ideas of *conditional* forgiveness and *conditional* mercy are juxtaposed (πᾶσαν τὴν ὀφειλὴν ἐκείνην ἀφῆκά σοι, ἐπεὶ παρεκάλεσάς με [v. 32b]; οὐκ ἔδει καὶ σὲ ἐλεῆσαι τὸν σύνδουλόν σου, ὡς κἀγὼ σὲ ἠλέησα [v. 33]). Third, through the express link between reluctance in exercising mercy and forgiveness, and the idea of punishment (οὕτως καὶ ὁ πατήρ μου . . . ποιήσει ὑμῖν ἐὰν μὴ ἀφῆτε . . . [v. 35]). From this, it is not unreasonable to equate the *conditional* mercy of 5:7 with the *conditional* forgiveness of 6:12, 14–15; 18:23–35, as well as with 5:48 and 7:1–2, 12.

The Emphasis on the Offended Person's Responsibility to Forgive and the Link with the Concept of Spiritually "Mature and Immature" Christians

The emphasis described in the heading is another further obvious evidence for the prominence of the forgiveness theme in the First Gospel. Perhaps the following three considerations in this regard may prove effective in describing the phenomenon in Matt 18. Firstly, in this chapter, the forgiving act is expected of each member of the community, but most particularly of the *spiritually mature* members. Here forgiving an ἀδελφός is primarily part of the responsibilities of the *mature* members. Forgiving others seems to be contained in the motif of caring for the "little ones," which is apparently predominant in this first half of the chapter. The motif of caring for the "little ones" is plain and emphasized through the repetition of ἑνὸς (or ἕνα) ἓν τῶν μικρῶν τούτων in verses 6–14. In verse

6, for example, ἕνα τῶν μικρῶν τούτων is connected with σκανδαλίζω to underscore that *one* of the "little ones" is not to be scandalized. In verse 10, ἑνὸς τῶν μικρῶν τούτων is connected with the negative form of καταφρονέω (μὴ καταφρονήσητε) to stress that *one* of the "little ones" should not be despised. The parable of the lost sheep in verses 12–14 is a strong warning to those who despise *one* of the "little ones," already both mentioned and stressed in verse 10. This caring includes the seeking of the ἀδελφός (vv. 15–17), forgiving them limitlessly (vv. 21–22), forgiving them from the heart (v. 35).

Secondly, in 18:21–22 granting forgiveness looks more like an obligation for the injured person; and it is striking that Peter's question to Jesus does not have repentance (or related concepts) as prerequisite(s). Thirdly, this same pattern characterizes the teaching in 18:23–35, a teaching built upon the *logion* in 6:15. The teaching in this parable emphasizes what the potential unforgiving disciple will incur: punishment. A possible link between 18:28–35; 6:15; 5:21–23 (about not retaliating) and 7:1–2 (about prohibition to judge others) may thus be proposed, as was suggested elsewhere in this work[2]: the unmerciful debtor in 18:28–30, his punishment in 18:32–34 and in the moral of the parable (18:35) seem to be closely linked with the reluctance to forgive and its subsequent consequence, suggested by the *logion* in 6:15 ("neither will your Father forgive your trespasses").

Reinforcing the Concept of Interpersonal Forgiveness

A reinforcement of the concept of interpersonal forgiveness is introduced again in 18:21–35. This phenomenon is evident in three ways. First, the idea of interpersonal forgiveness is stated quite directly by using ἀφίημι (4x) to express both divine-human and interpersonal human relationships. Second is an emphasis on the frequency of forgiving an ἀδελφός, a command given to the offended person. Third, a parable is used—a parable which clearly serves to highlight the consequences of reluctance in forgiving, as is evidenced by the language of judgment in verse 35.

---

2. See p. 57–67 above.

Strategic Rhetorical Positioning of the Community Discourse within the Gospel

The Community Discourse in Matt 18 is a section which forms part of the larger literary unit 18 about church life. This section, which contains the second key Matthean forgiveness passage (18:21–35), deals with the maintenance of relationships in the believing community. The section in question occurs toward the end of Jesus' ministry in Galilee and at the beginning of his ministry in Judea. The parable in 18:23–35 is without parallel in the gospels; it is something the first evangelist has put together from various traditions. It is possible to think that the location of the material in this section, having to do with the preservation of the community, should be regarded as a leading concern in the Matthean community. Matthew, it can be reasonably argued, has placed this material in its current location to warn the members of his community that whatever plan the devil may try to bring against them (cf. 13:39), they should remain united.

Proportion within the Community Discourse

Interpersonal forgiveness texts and related passages occupy a significant proportion in the Community Discourse: about 60 percent of the material in it is devoted to the subjects of reconciliation (18:15–17), forgiving and showing mercy (18:21–35). This is even without the "little ones" texts. This percentage is indeed a good proportion in a single unit dealing with various topics.

Exegetical Synthesis of Matthean Interpersonal Forgiveness Texts

Matthew's interpretation of Jesus' teaching about forgiveness in 6:12, 14–15 and 18:21–35 can be now brought together. The forgiveness discourses in 6:12, 14–15 and 18:21–35 are complementary; in both discourses the forgiveness dynamics are the same. One of the basic assumptions of this study is that God's grace is the key to understating the Matthean teaching on the subject of interpersonal forgiveness.[3] It can therefore be argued that Matthean demands, including the demand to forgive, are grounded

---

3. The role of grace in Matthew's theology as related to ethical demands in the gospel is discussed in more detail later in this chapter.

in Matthew's theology of God's grace expressed in terms of God's fatherly care for those who are his children. In Matthew's view, the grace of God that the believers have experienced ought to generate from them similar acts of generosity toward not only the members of the Christian community, but also toward humankind (cf. 6:14, where the demand to forgive ἄνθρωποι seems to suggest a universalist orientation).

In 6:12b, the conditional element in divine-human forgiveness is apparent in the phrase ὡς καὶ ἡμεῖς ἀφήκαμεν, which seems to highlight the human forgiving act. Indeed, the clause which precedes this phrase is an appeal for God's forgiveness, an appeal which is grounded in God's sovereign generosity in providing to *all* the needs of his creation including the unrighteous (e.g., the context of the Sermon, 5:45 and 6:26–30). It is with this reality in mind (6:8; cp. 6:18, 33) that in 6:12–13, the petitioner directs their concerns for food, forgiveness, deliverance, and guidance, to the Πάτερ ἡμῶν ὁ ἐν τοῖς οὐρανοῖς (6:9).

Matt 6:12, 14–15 provides a dynamic of forgiveness. At the divine-human relation level, one distinctive forgiveness pattern is clear: it is the responsibility of the offender for seeking forgiveness (cf. the request in v. 12). This teaching seems to echo the saying in 5:23–26 where the seeking of reconciliation with an ἀδελφός is part of the responsibility of the offender; the context of this *logion* in that text requires that the seeking of reconciliation language be linked with the idea of repentance. Regarding 6:12a, the obligation of the potential sinner to seek forgiveness is obvious. Speaking from the perspective of God, the granting of the forgiveness sought appears merely as a possibility—not an externally imposed obligation; this is firmly grounded in the biblical tradition according to which God's promise of anything depends on his own free will. Yet, because of his character, as affirmed in Matt 6, Matthew's readers know that they can rely on God for all their concerns, including their desire for forgiveness. On this ground, they can come before God with their plea for forgiveness with full confidence; they are on firm ground as they seek God's favor on these specific concerns of theirs.

At the level of human interpersonal relationships, forgiving clearly appears as an obligation for the offended person. Without the prior fulfillment of this obligation by the petitioner, appealing for forgiveness for one's sins (let alone to expect to be answered) is pointless. Given the fact that in divine-human relation the offender is responsible for seeking forgiveness from their victim, certainly, the same attitude is to be expected of their offender in interpersonal relationships (cf. 5:23–26).

On the other hand, one observes that Matthew has given more space to the responsibility of the offended person in forgiving, as the following statistics show: 7 *logia* are concerned with the responsibility of the offended person in forgiving against 1 which is about the responsibility of the offender in seeking forgiveness/reconciliation. To consider a few examples, the statement in 6:12b reminds the Father of what the petitioner has already performed vis-à-vis their debtor(s), a fact which is highlighted in the protasis in 6:14–15; in 18:12–14, the responsibility of the offended person is embodied in the initiative of the shepherd going after the straying sheep; in 18:15–17, this responsibility is evidenced in the offended person being enjoined to go several times after their offender; in 18:21, it is plain in Peter's proposal; and in 18:33, it is found in the lord's rebuke to his unmerciful debtor. As can be seen, the two forgiveness texts in Matthew are integrally connected to each other; both texts lay a strong emphasis on the offended person's responsibility to forgive, an emphasis which is found nowhere elsewhere in the NT and beyond (at least in the data surveyed, Sir 28:1–4 and *Ant. Rom.* 8.50.1–4 being only an exception).

FORGIVENESS TEACHING AND MATTHEW'S THEOLOGY

The study of the Matthean interpersonal forgiveness and related texts altogether raises a number of theological concerns. The main question is how Matthew's teaching about interpersonal forgiveness, as affirmed in these texts, can be linked with his message viewed holistically. I will here restrict myself to the first evangelist's teaching about forgiveness and his theology of God, his Christology and soteriology, and his teaching about interpersonal forgiveness as related to his theology of grace, righteousness and discipleship.

Forgiveness and God

In the First Gospel, the notion of forgiveness is linked with that of God as king and father. To begin with, the notion of God as king appears to be central to Matthew's thinking. Matthew uses this metaphor—a "predominant relational metaphor used of God in the Bible," according to Marc

Zvi Brettler[4]—frequently. The kingdom of heaven/God (ἡ βασιλεία τῶν οὐρανῶν/τοῦ θεοῦ) was at the very centre of the message of the Matthean Jesus (4:23; 9:35; cp. 6:11; 12:28). The gospel of the kingdom of heaven/God is the gospel that was to be preached throughout the whole world to all the nations (24:14). The *present* reality of this kingdom (ἤγγικεν γὰρ ἡ βασιλεία τῶν οὐρανῶν) is a dominant motif in Matthew. The teaching about this aspect of the kingdom appears at the very beginning of Jesus' ministry (4:17) and continues throughout (10:7: Ἤγγικεν ἡ βασιλεία τῶν οὐρανῶν; 12:28: ἄρα ἔφθασεν ἐφ' ὑμᾶς ἡ βασιλεία τοῦ θεοῦ; 19:14 by implication). In 13:11, we are informed about Jesus' proclamation of τὰ μυστήρια τῆς βασιλείας τῶν οὐρανῶν ("the mysteries of the kingdom of heaven").

Four more texts in the gospel may serve to strengthen our argument; these texts, it has to be highlighted, have no parallels in the other Synoptics. First is Matt 5:35; in this text, Jerusalem is described as "the city of the great king," that is "God's city" (cf. Ps 48:2). Second is Matt 18:23–35; the parable of the unmerciful slave in this text likens God to "a king who wished to settle accounts with his slaves." Third is Matt 17:24–27, which is the temple tax account. As Allison has reasonably suggested, "Jesus' pronouncement regarding the temple tax in this text presupposes that, in one important respect, God relates to the disciples just as earthly kings relate to their children."[5] Jesus' question and Peter's answer in verses 25b–26 are worth quoting: "What do you think, Simon? From whom do kings of the earth take toll or tribute? From their children or from others?" When Peter said, "From others," Jesus said to him, "Then the children are free." Fourth is Matt 22:1–14; the parable of the wedding banquet also likens God to a king.

As to the notion of God as father, we noted earlier (ch. 5) how central this notion is in the First Gospel. God's fatherly care and aid for all needs is clear in Matthew. Mohrlang is probably correct when he writes that "of all the synoptic writers it is Matthew that draws the most winsome picture of God as a kind and caring heavenly Father, concerned to meet the everyday needs of his children . . .; indeed it is to him that disciples are invited to look for *all* their needs . . ."[6] To be sure, the idea of God as father abounds in Matthew. In 6:9–15, for example, this no-

---

4. Brettler, *God Is King*, 160.
5. Allison, *Constructing Jesus*, 245.
6. Mohrlang, *Matthew and Paul*, 80; italics original.

tion is central, πατήρ being a key term in this text. At the beginning of the pericope (v. 9), the disciples are instructed to address God as their Father in heaven (Πάτερ ἡμῶν ὁ ἐν τοῖς οὐρανοῖς). The pericope ends with the fatherhood of God (ὁ πατὴρ ὑμῶν ὁ οὐράνιος/ὁ πατὴρ ὑμῶν, vv. 14–15). The same is true of Matt 6, as a whole, which begins by referring to God as the Father in heaven (τῷ πατρὶ ὑμῶν τῷ ἐν τοῖς οὐρανοῖς [v. 1]), and concludes with him as the disciples' heavenly Father (ὁ πατὴρ ὑμῶν ὁ οὐράνιος [vv. 26, 32]). Within this framework, the fatherhood of God language abounds. God is again referred to as Father (ὁ πατήρ σου/ ὑμῶν and τῷ πατρί σου [vv. 4, 6, 8, 18]): he is a Father who is in secret (vv. 6, 18), who can see into the secrets of his children (vv. 4, 18) and can reward his children (vv. 1, 4, 6, 18); he always knows and hears the pleas of his children before they ask him (vv. 7–8, 18, 33); he cares for his children and for his creation and provides for them (vv. 26–30); he cares for them and for the creation and provides for them altogether (6:6–13, 25–30; cp. 7:7–11; 10:20, 29–32; 18:10–14, 19–20; 24:20; 26:36–44). An aspect of God's fatherly care and aid includes God's readiness to deliver his children from the evil one (6:13). Martin Stiewe and François Vouga have reasonably described this action of God as "l'expression de l'esprit de la gratuité et du don."[7] The experience and promise of God and Jesus' continual presence, as an expression of God's grace, also strongly adds to the evidence. More or less at the beginning of Matthew, God is said to be himself with his people (including the disciples) in Jesus' presence (cf. Jesus' name Ἐμμανουήλ, 1:23; cp. 8:25; 14:30; 18:20; 28:20).

The notions of the kingship and fatherhood of God in the First Gospel provide us with this picture of God: a gracious, merciful, loving and forgiving king and father. These attributes of God, it has to be said, seem to be so interwoven in the gospel that one cannot easily separate them neatly. The first evangelist seems to view God as a gracious king and father as an expression of his grace toward his people and children.[8] The portrait of God as a merciful and forgiving king and father thus abounds in the First Gospel (6:12, 14; 9:2–8, 13; 12:7; 18:23–35). The concepts of mercy and forgiveness are both and together more prominent in Matthew than in the whole of the rest of the NT.[9] The payment of a full day's wage to laborers who have worked only one hour is such an act of

---

7. Stiewe and Vouga, *Le Sermon sur la montagne*, 128–33.
8. This notion is discussed in detail elsewhere in this chapter.
9. The evidence for this is provided in ch. 2 of this work.

God's mercy (20:1–16). Jesus' attention to the children (παιδία) and the "little ones" (μικροί [Matt 18]), to the blind and the lame in the temple (21:14–16) also add to the evidence. We also have the picture of God as a loving person. In Matthew, God's love is described as being beyond boundaries; it is beyond racial differences or social rank. In 2:1–12, for example, God brings Gentile wise men to worship Jesus. He chooses Galilee of Gentiles as the place for Jesus to begin his earthly ministry (4:15–16). He elicits the faith of the Roman centurion (8:5–13) and that of the Canaanite woman (15:21–28). For Matthew, the love of God/Jesus to the world is the model *par excellence* of the love of the disciples to the least of their brothers and sisters (25:31–46), which might seem to indicate the *immature* church members.

To expand on the forgiving character of God a bit further, for Matthew, readiness to forgive appears to be one of the distinctive characteristics of God in the gospel: God is always disposed to forgive humans. His readiness to forgive has to do with his character; it is an expression of his genuine grace, mercy and generosity toward mankind (5:7, 45, 48; 6:12, 14; 18:27, 33) without favoritism: as noted already, he makes his sun rise not only on the good but also on the evil; he sends the rain not only on the righteous but also on the unrighteous (5:45). For Matthew, God's willingness to forgive *all* and welcome sinners into his kingdom was central to Jesus' teachings (9:9–13; 11:19; 22:1–10). In 6:12, the disciples are on firm ground when they come before their Father with their plea for forgiveness; they are indeed assured of God's ongoing forgiveness provided that they extend the same forgiveness to others (cf. 6:14).[10] This understanding of Matthew is rooted in Jewish tradition. The belief in readiness to forgive as integral to God's character abounds in Jewish writings: the LXX,[11] Philo,[12] and Josephus,[13] among others. The idea that the gods are disposed to forgive human beings is present in Graeco-Roman thinking.[14] The most obvious implication of this is that whether in Jewish or in Graeco-Roman ideas, God and the deities are the models *par excellence* for human readiness to forgive. The members of Matthew's group,

10. On this Stanton has written, "They know they can seek God's forgiveness only if they are willing to forgive others" (*The Gospels and Jesus*, 12).

11. Exod 34:6–7; Num 14:18–19; Pss 25:18; 32:1,5; 85:2; Isa 33:24; 55:7; Sir 28:1–4.

12. Philo, *Laws* 1:235–6; 2:196; *Punishments* 166–7.

13. Josephus, *Ant.* 6.92–93; *War* 5.416–7.

14. E.g., Dionysius, *Ant. Rom.*8.50 (a detailed discussion of this section is provided in ch. 3).

as Christians, were called to exercise forgiveness to everyone in response to God's forgiving grace which they had already received and had been experiencing. In other words, in Matthew, the demand for interpersonal forgiveness presupposes the reality of God's initial merciful grace.

Forgiveness and Christology

In Matthew, forgiveness is linked to Christology. The teaching about interpersonal forgiveness and the demands of it in this gospel are to be understood in the light of the royalty of Jesus. The Matthean Jesus makes it clear that forgiving one's fellow human is as important as seeking God's forgiveness; for him these two realities are inseparable. This is what Jesus primarily taught through his life and death. Jesus enacted forgiveness in many ways, one of which is his table fellowship with tax collectors and sinners. As L. G. Jones has written, table fellowship was seen as a sign not only of communion among people but also of communion in the sight of God. The logic thus goes that because the cultically impure ones were welcomed at Jesus' table, they were implicitly included in a relationship of communion with God himself.[15]

In both the two main texts discussed in this work, the evangelist links forgiveness to Jesus' ministry as a whole. In 6:9–15, for example, Jesus is portrayed as a teacher. In it forgiveness appears as one of the most important topics taught by Jesus during his earthly ministry. This is obvious both in the immediate literary context of the passage (Matt 6) and in the wider context of it (the Sermon [5–7], which presents the teaching of Jesus on various matters, the primary audience of the teaching being his disciples [5:1–2]).[16] In 6:12–14, human sinfulness is clearly presupposed (cp. 7:11; 15:19–20). Matt 18:21–35 emerges in the context of Jesus' teaching, which Matthew has organized in a series of teachings to support his own understanding of Church life (Matt 18). While in 18:21–22 Jesus teaches that forgiveness is to be granted limitlessly, in 18:23–35, he emphatically not only teaches that forgiveness will be denied those unwilling to extend it to others, but also they will face God's punishment (cp. Sir 28:1–4). In 18:15–17, Jesus' teaching on reconciliation stresses

---

15. Jones, *Embodying Forgiveness*, 121.

16. There is a debate about the primary audience of this teaching. The question is whether the teaching was intended primary to the crowds or to the disciples. I prefer the latter option for the arguments provided in ch. 5 of this work in this respect.

the role of the offended person for taking the first step; treating the offender as "a Gentile and tax collector" is suggested as the last thing to do, that is, after all the procedures for reconciliation had been exhausted.

Besides, for the Matthean Jesus, given human sinfulness, admission to the kingdom is only possible because of divine forgiveness. God's willingness to forgive all and to welcome sinners into his kingdom is evidently central to Jesus' teachings (9:9–13; 11:19; 22:1–10). On one occasion, Jesus himself pronounced the forgiveness of sins (9:2). More than just pronouncing it, Jesus did possess the authority to forgive sins (9:6). Furthermore, Jesus demonstrated an ongoing willingness to forgive failings of the disciples. He assured them of God's forgiveness (6:12) provided that they extend the same forgiveness to others (6:14). In fact, forgiving was Jesus' way of life; this is an active demonstration of God's willingness to forgive (6:14) which is grounded in his mercy (5:45, 48). Jesus expects the same of his disciples on the same ground of mercy (5:7; 18:33); so too, those willing to forgive will be forgiven (6:14, cp. Mark 11:25; Sir 28:2).

Forgiveness, Grace, Soteriology, and the Kingdom

In Matthew, the concept of forgiveness is linked with soteriology and (as has already been noted) with the notion of God's grace. References to the soteriological significance of Jesus' life and death are the first evidence in this regard. In 1:21, we are told that Jesus "will save his people from their sins (τῶν ἁμαρτιῶν); in 26:28, we note most particularly the phrase εἰς ἄφεσιν ἁμαρτιῶν; in the middle of the Sermon, in the Prayer, the forgiveness of sins motif (6:12) occurs, a motif which is highlighted in 6:14–15, anticipating the parable of 18:23–35. Several times in the narrative material, the forgiveness of sins is underscored (9:1–8; 12:31–32). Matt 9 contains an account of a miracle performed by Jesus, an account which stresses the Son of Man's power to forgive sins (ἀφιέναι ἁμαρτίας, v. 6). It is worth noting that in this account, ἀφίημι ἁμαρτίας is one of the key expressions: it is repeated three times (v. 2: ἀφίενταί σου αἱ ἁμαρτίαι; v. 5: ἀφίενταί σου αἱ ἁμαρτίαι; and v. 6: ἀφιέναι ἁμαρτίας). In 26:28, the forgiveness of sins is explicitly identified as the purpose underlying Jesus' outpouring of his blood in death; this purpose and sacrifice are indirectly stated in 1:21 in which it is clearly said of Jesus that he will save his people from their sins, and also stated indirectly in 20:28 which speaks of the Son of Man giving his life as a ransom for many. Thus, from the beginning, the narrative is focused on forgiving sins. As Hagner has also clearly stated, "It is indeed the forgiveness of sins that constitutes the essence of grace . . . [T]hat is precisely what the gospel, the story of Jesus, is all about."[17]

Secondly, the gospel of the kingdom (4:23; 9:35; 24:14) is another piece of evidence for the relationship between forgiveness, grace and soteriology. The arrival of the kingdom of heaven is one of the features which are highlighted in the teaching in Matthew. This feature is closely linked to soteriology. The teaching over this aspect of the kingdom appears at the very beginning of the ministry of Jesus (4:17; 10:7; 12:28; 19:14).

The selection of the individual disciples is another piece of evidence. In Matthew, Jesus' sympathy with tax collectors (οἱ τελῶναι), Gentiles (οἱ τελῶναι . . . οἱ ἐθνικοὶ/τὰ ἔθνη), sinners and prostitutes (αἱ πόρναι) is quite clear: Jesus calls Matthew, a tax collector (τελώνης) who is now to be turned into a disciple (9:9); the disciples had experienced God's grace by their initial calling, as well as in their walk with the earthly Jesus. Jesus was known as a friend of tax collectors and sinners (11:19) because he could eat and drink with them (9:10–13). A prophecy was made about his mission to the Gentiles and that they will hope in his name (12:18, 21; for Jesus' mission to the Gentiles, cp. 10:18; 24:14; 28:19). He also heals a centurion's servant (8:5–13) and the Canaanite woman's daughter, and praises her faith (15:21–28).

On top of that, the recurring theme of God's mercy and forgiveness (6:12–14; 9:2–8, 13; 12:7; 18:23–27, 32–35; 21:31) is further clear evidence; this theme is reflected in the demand for human mercy and forgiveness (6:12–15; 9:13; 12:7; 18:21–35). As pointed out in the previous section, the idea of mercy is much more prominent in Matthew than in any other gospel. The experience and promise of God and Jesus' continual presence, as an expression of God's grace, also adds to the evidence. Almost at the beginning of Matthew (1:23), a promise is given that God himself will be with his people in Jesus' presence. Jesus is always among his disciples to serve, help and bless them in their life of discipleship (8:25; 14:30; 18:20; 28:20).

---

17. Hagner, *Righteousness in Matthew's Theology*, 106.

Forgiveness, Righteousness, and Discipleship

The notions of forgiveness, righteousness and discipleship are also effectively linked in Matthew's thinking. This link, however, is not quite so obvious; it thus requires elucidation. In an attempt to elucidate it, righteousness will be first examined, then its relationship with the notions of discipleship and forgiveness.

Righteousness, to be sure, is a most important theme in the First Gospel. The term δικαιοσύνη, which is used to convey the idea of it, occurs seven times in the gospel—more than in any other gospels. Five of its seven occurrences in Matthew are in the Sermon. The meaning of the term in the gospel has been heatedly discussed, as is evidenced by recent publications on the subject.[18] The views on the subject can be grouped in three possible categories. The first category argues that in Matthew, δικαιοσύνη refers consistently and exclusively to the obedience of demand.[19] The second category has it that in Matthew, δικαιοσύνη refers to the righteousness that is a gift dependent upon God's saving activity.[20] The third category, in an attempt to circumvent the two possible extremes, has argued that underlying the demand for δικαιοσύνη in Matthew is an element of presupposed gift, or that included in the gift is also an element of demand.[21] This perspective has the merit of identifying where the centre of gravity of the debate lies and spells it out, as well as proposing a solution which is more plausible.[22]

In Matthew, forgiveness appears as an expression of righteousness. Mercy was the focal point of the Matthean Jesus' message, which shows what it meant to fulfill the law (5:17–20; 9:13; 12:7; 25:31–46). Matthew speaks of the priority of mercy over sacrifice (9:13; 12:7; 23:23). In the miracle narratives, he shows that the mercy of the Son of Man corresponds to the mercy which is demanded of people (9:27–31; 12:7–14). Yet, mercy is said to have been forgotten by the scribes and Pharisees (23:23), which would amount to a judgment on them (25:31–46). A demand for righteousness (δικαιοσύνη) is thus made to disciples that their

---

18. E.g., Strecker, *The Sermon on the Mount*; Przybylski, *Righteousness*; France, *Matthew*; Hagner, *Righteousness in Matthew's Theology*, among many others.

19. Can be included in this category Przybylski, Strecker, Luz, Dupont, Hill, Davies and Allison, among others.

20. Fiedler and Giesen are among the defenders of this viewpoint.

21. Hagner, "Righteousness in Matthew's Theology," 108.

22. See especially the flow of Hagner's argument in ibid., 112–18.

righteousness should exceed that of the scribes and the Pharisees (5:20), righteousness of which acts of mercy are the expression, as is evidenced by 9:13; 23:23; 25:31–46. In these three references, the motif of mercy is connected with that of righteousness; in 5:7, it is possible to suggest this link from the framework of the beatitudes. Because of the concept of reciprocity and the link between mercy and forgiveness in the Sermon (Matt 5–7) and in the Community Discourse (Matt 18) and beyond, what is being suggested with regard to the link between righteousness and mercy may apply to its link with forgiveness.

Interpersonal Forgiveness, Discipleship, and Ethics

In the First Gospel, interpersonal forgiveness is linked to the notions of discipleship and ethics; it is all about the *imitatio Dei/Christi*: God and Jesus being depicted in Matthew as a gracious, merciful, loving and forgiving king and father (king/prince for Jesus), this has practical consequences on God's subjects and children (Jesus' followers and his brothers and sisters). It has been observed that Matthew's understanding of discipleship is one of the points which still seem to be unclear as far as the theology of Matthew is concerned.[23] It is not the intent of this section to engage in this complex debate; others have thoroughly discussed this issue.[24] My concern with regard to discipleship lies with what Matthew thinks a disciple ought to be, and thus to find out how this relates to his understanding of interpersonal forgiveness.

As was discussed earlier in this work (ch. 2), in Matthew the concept of the fictive kinship of Christians with God is embedded in the idea of the fatherhood and kingship of God and that of the *imitatio Dei/ Christi*. Thus, the *good seed* is likened to the children of the kingdom (13:24–30, 38), and the one who *does the will* of the heavenly Father and to whom entering the kingdom has been promised (7:21), together with the *righteous* who will shine like the sun in the kingdom of their Father (13:43), those likened to the *little children* to whom high priority in coming to Jesus has been given, those at Jesus' right hand who are declared "blessed" by his Father and who are welcomed by Jesus to inherit the kingdom prepared for them from the foundation of the world (25:34), are all without doubt Christians. It is thus reasonable to imagine that those

---

23. Luz, "The Disciples in the Gospel according to Matthew," 115.

24. E.g., ibid., 115–164.

who do the will of this gracious, merciful, loving and forgiving Father (which is also the will of Jesus) and abide to his commands definitely belong to the kingdom.

As was shown earlier in this chapter, what the idea of the fatherhood of God might have meant to Matthew and his readers and hearers is an interesting question. Two possible interpretations have been proposed. Antony J. Saldarini has observed that the community to and for which Matthew wrote was a community with a strong sense of group cohesion, emphasised in the use of kinship language to describe its members. He argues that at the core of Matthew's identity is the relationship of Jesus to God as Son and the analogous relationship of his disciples to God as sons and servants.[25] Saldarini's observation points to identity as the meaning of the fictive kinship in Matthew. For him, the kinship language in this gospel serves to highlight Jesus and the believers' identity with God as both sons and servants. To this aspect of meaning John K. Riches has added another: "commitment." He traces the notions of fictive kinship from Philo, who speaks of all humans as judged worthy of kinship with God because in principle they share the gift of reason.[26] From this parallel, he suggests that for Matthew, the central mark of the members of his community, which makes them brothers and sisters of Jesus—and who therefore share kinship with each—is doing the will of the heavenly Father. He goes on to argue that there is a clear sense in which those who become brothers and sisters of Jesus by doing God's will leave their former ways behind them and become members of a new family centred on Jesus.[27]

These two features of the meaning of kinship in the First Gospel are not mutually exclusive; they are helpful because they may shed some light on our understanding of what the notion of fatherhood of God may have meant to Matthew's recipients. It can be suggested that both Matthew and his audience likely understood their being children of God to mean their *identity* and their *commitment* to doing God's will. This would be reflected in their mutual relationships: just as their Father is always gracious, loving, merciful and ready to forgive, among other things, so too should they be as the children of such a father; just as it is not the will of

---

25. Saldarini, *Matthew's Christian-Jewish Community*, 94–99.
26. Cf. Philo, *De Abrahamo* 41.
27. Riches, *Conflicting Mythologies*, 209–10.

the Father that "one of these little ones" should be lost (18:14), so too they should long for community cohesion, and so on.

The *imitatio Dei/Christi* is the second possible concept which contains the idea of fictive kinship of Christians with God. The fundamental issue in this regard is how one should treat others, as members of the kingdom. As Allison has reasonably suggested, the main focus seems to be on "abandoning animosity and demonstrating unexpected generosity."[28] The *imitatio Dei* in the First Gospel includes being merciful (18:33), loving (5:44-45; cp. 22:34-40), perfect (5:48) and forgiving (18:32b). The *imitatio Christi* aspect can be found in the way in which Matthew has tried to relate the mission of the disciples to that of Jesus: as Jesus is meant *primarily* to preach to Israel (9:35), so the disciples are sent *primarily* to Israel (10:5-6); as Jesus has power to heal diseases (4:24; 9:35), so have the disciples (10:1); as Jesus shows mercy and forgives sins (9:2-8,10-13), so the disciples are expected to (6:12; 9:13; 18:27, 32b-33). To extend this aspect a bit further, in the First Gospel, the call to exercise mercy and forgiveness toward others is grounded in God's and Jesus' person and character. So, God's mercy and forgiveness exemplified in Jesus' person, life and ministry constitutes a good reason and provides a paradigm for the disciples to teach and practice mercy and forgiveness.

The central point of the Matthean teaching about discipleship is probably the necessity for a radical obedience to Jesus' commandments and the demands of them, some of which are listed above. Disciples are those who have radically conformed to Jesus' teaching and commandments (28:19). In Matthew's view, a disciple is somebody to whom Jesus' commandments have been taught, and of whom obedience to their demands is expected. A change of one's way of life is thus required from a disciple of Jesus. This may involve persecution and death (5:10-12), measuring the cost of one's job (9:9), family (10:34-39), economic security (19:16-30), possessions (8:18-22; 23:34-36), and social status (10:24-25). Therefore, being a true disciple equates with being a Christian and member of the new people of God. It is clear that, in Matthew, the Christians' mercy, love and forgiveness are modeled on God's mercy, love and forgiveness. Christians are called to love others, including their enemies as God/Jesus loves the righteous and the unrighteous; they are called to be merciful as God/Jesus is merciful (5:7); they are called to forgive people as God/Jesus forgives them (6:12, 14; 9:2, 6; 12:7, 31-32;

---

28. Allison, *Studies in Matthew*, 322.

18:21–22, 27, 33; 26:28); they are therefore called to be perfect as God/Jesus is perfect (5:48). Although important qualifications need to be surely made because God is God and humans are humans, for the first evangelist, God's and Jesus' mercy, love, and forgiveness provide the paradigm for how his community was to understand its vocation in the kingdom.

IMPLICATIONS OF THE STUDY FOR THE CHURCH

What can be drawn from the overall investigation into the significance of interpersonal forgiveness in Matthew, for its possible implications for the church worldwide? I would like to suggest that, for Christian theological discourse about forgiveness to be enriched, with the ultimate purpose of the transformation of the church and society through Christ, the teaching and practice of forgiveness should be informed by Matthew's voice. This would mean at least four things.

Emphasis on Forgiving

The teaching and practice of interpersonal forgiveness, that is informed by Matthew's voice, means seeking to make a clear distinction between the responsibilities of each party in forgiveness, and to recognize Matthew's primary focus on the responsibility of the offended person toward the offender. In Matthew, Jesus' life, teaching and ministry are an urgent call upon the community of the *forgiven* people to seek and grant forgiveness. As Jones has stated, the fundamental orientation of Christian life is that we are *forgiven* sinners.[29] And so, *forgiveness*, for which in his discussion F. Gerald Downing has coined the term "forgiven-ness,"[30] should characterize the lives of Church members across the world. But, in Matthew, the responsibility of the offended forgiven Christian toward the offender predominates. This is not without significance. The fact that the first evangelist gives more space to the responsibility of the offended person in forgiving seems to strongly suggest that he was extremely concerned about the possibility of his community members' unwillingness to forgive their fellow brethren.

This fact needs to be spelled out and underscored in the teaching and preaching of forgiveness worldwide. Christians, to be sure, are enabled by

29. Jones, *Embodying Forgiveness*, 148.
30. Downing, *Making Sense in (and of) the First Christian Century*, 77.

Jesus' love to forgive others (9:2; cp. references to Jesus' association with the sinners) because it is as sinners that they learn to better understand themselves as sinners who have been *forgiven*. It is reasonable to think that, according to Matthew, for those who have experienced God's forgiveness and have thereby been initiated into God's kingdom, reluctance or failure to forgive is equally scandalous; it is scandalous and virtually *unthinkable* (18:23–33). What seems to be virtually *unthinkable* seems to have *unfortunately* happened and continued to happen within Matthew's church, as the prominence of the interpersonal forgiveness theme in the gospel seems to suggest. Likewise, reluctance in forgiving seems to be unfortunately observed among Christians in all contexts.

Whether or not it makes sense to forgive somebody who has not repented, or is not ready to repent at all, the primary focus of the offended people should be to engage as individuals in communal practices of forgiveness that would reflect God's forgiving character (18:23–35; 5:7, 44–45, 48; 6:14; 9:13; 23:23), whatever good reasons we may have to withhold forgiveness. In situations of persistent abuse and recurring violence, this would require the offended person to reclaim the significance of loving enemies (5:42–48) and renunciation of violent revenge (5:38–41) as an indispensable feature of the craft of Christian forgiveness. As Jones has correctly put it, Christians should not confront this perplexing and troubling reality by failing to continue to insist on the precedence of God's forgiveness to our forgiveness and repentance. But if, and insofar as, people fail to respond to forgiveness with repentance, then perhaps the best that can be done is to acknowledge that they are enemies of the cross of Christ—but enemies whom we are nonetheless called to learn to love,[31] to pray for, feed and give something to drink (Rom 12:17–21). As Miroslav Volf has reasonably suggested, repentance should not be regarded so much a prerequisite of forgiveness; rather, repentance should be regarded as result of forgiveness,[32] which should cause the unrepentant person to come to their senses. So, Christian theological discourse about forgiveness should seek to distinguish clearly between the responsibilities of both parties involved in conflict, and based on the Matthean forgiveness teaching stress the responsibility of the offended party.

---

31. Jones, *Embodying Forgiveness*, 160.
32. Volf, "Forgiveness, Reconciliation, and Justice," 875–76.

The Demand for Satisfaction/Reparation

This teaching and practice of interpersonal forgiveness that is informed by Matthew's voice means not insisting over much upon satisfaction (or reparation) as a prerequisite (or corroboration) for granting forgiveness. In fact, one of the amazing things in the First Gospel is the evangelist's silence on the demand for satisfaction or reparation, as a prerequisite or corroboration for granting forgiveness. Unlike Matthew, the teaching about this aspect of forgiveness is attested in Graeco-Roman materials surveyed. In these materials, this demand sometimes varies; it is dependent upon who the offended person is. This may suggest that in the Graeco-Roman society of Matthew's time, the prerequisite for forgiving was probably not clearly defined. Thus, one can only speculate that satisfaction or reparation—as either a prerequisite or corroboration for forgiveness—was possibly for the offended person to decide. To be sure, in Jewish scriptures there is attestation of a penalty for stealing (e.g., Exod 22:1–4), which seems to be echoed in Luke 19:8. This is sometimes suggested as evidence for the gospel teaching demanding reparation. The Lukan text, however, has nothing to do with forgiveness.

A possible question to be raised could be what to do if the case has been taken to the court. The lack in Matthew of the demand for reparation (or satisfaction) as prerequisite (or corroboration) for granting forgiveness is likely not without significance. Christian theological rhetoric of forgiveness worldwide should carefully take note of Matthew's silence on this issue, a silence which can be viewed as one of the elements of Matthew's distinctiveness on the subject of interpersonal forgiveness, and to encourage offended people not to insist too much on their rights in seeking justice for the offences done against them.

Motivations in Forgiving

This teaching and practice of interpersonal forgiveness that is informed by Matthew's voice means being fairly aware of the final motivations underlying forgiving. Some of the questions people ask in the context of "post-conflict period" are these: Why forgive? What are the advantages in forgiving? Giving a possible answer to these questions, it is necessary to first of all consider inquiring about Matthew's view on the motivations underlying interpersonal forgiveness. The question raised earlier was whether Matthew viewed forgiving as *primarily* altruistic, or as a *self-oriented* process, or both. As was noted earlier (ch. 5), a few scholars have recently argued that primary motives for forgiving are largely *self-focused*.[33] The difference between this hypothesis and what can be found in Matthew is that, while this understanding of the motives for forgiving focuses on the forgiver's health, in the First Gospel, accountability before God is at the centre of the forgiving motives (18:23–35; 7:1–2; 6:14–15; 5:7). Acts of showing mercy and forgiving in it are motivated by the merciful person or forgiver's identity and belonging to the kingdom. An echo of this can be found in Jewish and Graeco-Roman thoughts.[34] The distinctiveness with Matthew, it has to be highlighted, is the fact that for him clearly believers forgive *primarily* for their own benefit—not merely because of the other. They forgive *primarily* to maintain their relationship and fellowship with their heavenly Father, so that they may be blessed by him. On the other hand, they also forgive out of fear of potential punishment. The Christian rhetoric of forgiveness should take seriously this teaching provided in Matthew.

Interpersonal Forgiveness and Retaliation

The teaching and practice of interpersonal forgiveness that is informed by Matthew's voice means promoting the culture of non-violence and peacemaking. Matthew links the idea of non-retaliation to the notions of loving enemies and peacemaking; so doing, he contrasts the *talionis* principle (5:21) with the love commandment (5:38–48). The most pressing concern for our purposes is how the people (including Christians) respond or ought to respond in the face of the wrong done to them. From experience, people respond differently to aggression. There are two clear approaches, one of which is appealing to justice and the other to take the matter in one's own hands (i.e., revenge). There are cases where under the impulsion of anger, and given the hugeness of injuries, some Christians have sought revenge (or tried to), sometimes not considering the appeal for forgiveness by the offender. Second, although probably unfamiliar, there have been cases where the injured individuals have managed their

---

33. Younger et al., "Dimensions of Forgiveness," 837–55.

34. For Jewish thought, see, e.g., *T. Gad* 6.3–4, 6–7. For Graeco-Roman thought, see, for example, Seneca, *Clem.* 1.9.1–7, 11, which narrates an incident between Augustus and Cinna; in this text, the idea of interpersonal forgiveness is linked with the notions of honor and friendship. For a development of the idea of friendship, see Plutarch, *Moralia: How to Profit by One's Enemies* 91a–b.

anger and resentment and have ignored what has happened, going on granting forgiveness to their offender(s). What possible answer does Matthew provide to this issue?

Whether the wrongs done are specified or unspecified, major or minor, or whether the offender repents or not, rather than seeking revenge, Matthew seems to strongly urge that Jesus' followers should be able to move out of themselves and be ready to forgive anyway. The Matthean teaching seems to take a bit further Jewish teaching on forgiveness. Although, for sure, the law of retribution legislated by the conditions described in the Pentateuch[35] was given to Jewish people, there are several cases of vengeance in Jewish scriptures. Gen 50:17 is one of the LXX good examples of the relationship between forgiveness and vengeance. This passage gives an account of the offender fearing a possible victim's revenge for the wrong done to him in the past. In the story, we note the initiative of the offender imploring forgiveness from the victim, an initiative which can be regarded as an act of repentance. 1 Sam 25:26–28 is another clear example. This passage narrates the story of David and Abigail/Nabal. David seeks help from Nabal; the latter seems to have retorted abusively. Abigail, Nabal's wife, being aware of her husband's discourtesy toward David, ventures to take the matter in her own hands as if she was the author of the offence. As a result of her approach, the life of Nabal is spared, at least this time, as David's anger against him is driven away. In this account, Abigail's approach that seeks forgiveness clearly drives away the offended David's vengeful spirit.

Additionally, God is sometimes also revealed in Jewish writings as the God who takes revenge over his enemies and also as the God who avenges his people. When the notion of vengeance applies to God, it clearly takes a positive connotation since God is holy. But this concept has a negative connotation when it is applied to humans. Human vengeance is negative in nature, for usually it achieves almost nothing good to the retaliator; rather, it essentially seeks to satisfy one's anger. What happened, for example, to the Jews when they went on to take revenge against Antiochus Epiphanes and his army (the Syrians) is probably one of good illustrations; the Jews were humiliated. In their battle with the Syrians, they were killed in great number, their city plundered and their sanctuary lay deserted for almost three and a half years.[36] How Abraham

---

35. Cf. Exod 21:24; Lev 24:20; Deut 19:21.
36. Josephus, *War* 5.394.

chose to handle the situation in which he found himself speaks volumes. When Abraham was offended by Pharaoh, as the latter carried off Sarah, he refrained from retaliating. Yet, he could have taken revenge on the ravisher, having enough mighty people under him.[37]

This piece of teaching on non-retaliation is surely echoed in Matt 5:43–48 (cp. Rom 12:17–21). The Matthean passages demanding the love of enemies and peacemaking (5:43–48), extending mercy and forgiveness (5:7; 6:14–15; 18:23–35), and reconciliation (5:23–24; 18:15–17) should be read in this vein. Matthew's teaching on non-retaliation should be incorporated in theological discourse about interpersonal forgiveness.

All taken together, this is the kind of message the contemporary churches in all contexts do need to be constantly reminded of, a message to be spread among the communities across the world torn by recurrent conflicts and wars. The four points proposed above, if taken seriously and both enacted and incorporated in teaching and preaching, are most likely to fill the gap that has been observed in Christian theological discourse about forgiveness in churches of the wider world. In this way, the potential danger of the interpreter, ending up with unbalanced or unsound theological conclusions—at high risk of doing no justice to Matthew's overall understanding of the issue of forgiveness and forgiveness-related issues—would be most likely averted.

CONTRIBUTION, CONCLUSIONS, AND WAY FORWARD

This work is a contribution to Matthean scholarship, specifically in the area of the debate about the position of Matthew in the development of early Christianity and Judaism. This study has ventured to answer the question of what contribution Matthew expected his gospel to make to the internal and external problems that his Christian community was facing, and to suggest what values he commends to his community. Three points may suffice to show aspects of this contribution. The first and main contribution of this study is in providing fresh evidence for the prominence of the theme of interpersonal forgiveness in the First Gospel. This author suggests that the teaching about this subject in both the Sermon (Matt 5–7) and the Community Discourse (Matt 18) stands as a major and largely innovative contribution to the development of the moral consciousness in this newly formed Christian group. This author

---

37. Ibid., 5.379–381.

is unaware of interest having been previously shown in this topic in NT scholarship generally and in Matthean scholarship in particular. There is no literature available that has attempted to demonstrate the centrality of this theme in Matthew. The survey of scholarship (cf. ch. 1) showed that interpersonal forgiveness is not on the list of what scholars think to be the most prominent themes in Matthew. They consider the key themes in this gospel to include: (1) the role of the Torah in its relation to Jesus and his teaching; (2) hostility toward the Jewish leadership; (3) identity, self-definition, and the future of God's covenant people; (4) forgiveness of sins; (5) righteousness; (6) discipleship and community; (7) and reward and judgment.[38]

There is no doubt about these as key issues in the gospel. Most of them are, to a greater or lesser extent, subjects of full scale discussions in the gospel itself, some running as themes throughout the text. Each of these issues has received due attention in Matthean scholarship, except the theme of interpersonal forgiveness. Just to take one example, in J. A. Overman's *Matthew's Gospel and Formative Judaism*, this theme of interpersonal forgiveness never appeared on his list of key issues which he regards as central in Matthew. Although he acknowledges interpersonal forgiveness as a prominent issue in Matt 18, it is still unclear whether for him this is amongst the most prominent themes in the entire gospel. In the paragraph in which a few Matthean forgiveness passages are drawn into discussion, Overman focuses his attention on ὀφειλήματα/ἁμαρτιας— not on ἀφίημι.[39] Affirming forgiveness of *sins* as a prominent theme in Matthew[40] is not quite the same as affirming the centrality of the *interpersonal* forgiveness theme in this gospel. These are clearly two distinct notions; each of them deserves due attention to be explored as a theme on its own right. On the other hand, acknowledging the prominence of this theme in Matthew,[41] without attempting to validate this claim is clearly only scratching the surface of the matter; while concentrating exclusively on the meaning of forgiving in this gospel[42] is too restrictive.

---

38. E.g., Przybylski, *Righteousness in Matthew and His World of Thought*; France, *Matthew*; Luz, *The Theology of the Gospel of Matthew*; Overman, *Matthew's Gospel and Formative Judaism*; Deines, "Not the Law but the Messiah"; Stanton, "Matthew as Interpreter of the Sayings of Jesus," 257–72; M. Brown, "Matthew," *NIDB*, 3:844.

39. Overman, *Matthew's Gospel and Formative Judaism*, 90, 103, 108, 113.

40. Like Overman and Deines, among others.

41. Like Luz, Hagner, France, Betz, Davies and Allison, among many others.

42. Like Moule for whom forgiving in the First Gospel is about ability to receiving

Our findings, drawn from the entire study (and most particularly from chapters 2, 5, and 6), show clearly that the theme of interpersonal forgiveness is quite central to the message in Matthew. This is made clear: (1) by the concept of reciprocity and the link between mercy and forgiveness, together with the link between reluctance in the *praxis* of them and the idea of judgment; (2) by the emphasis on the responsibility of offended person in forgiving and the link between this and the notion of the *spiritually mature* and *spiritually immature* Christians; (3) by a reinforcement of the forgiveness concept by the use of related concepts; (4) by the strategic rhetorical positioning of interpersonal forgiveness and related passages within Matthew's text; and (5) by the proportion these texts occupy within the Sermon and the Community Discourse. Matthew focused on interpersonal forgiveness because of the circumstances faced by his community; the marginal group, newly separated from Judaism, struggled to find its new identity in the midst of the crisis which followed from the events of 70 CE and tried to survive in a hostile world. He was thus offering the members of this community moral guidance and spiritual encouragement—a component of which is the teaching about forgiving others, including one's enemies.

The findings also show something about the nature of forgiving in Matthew. In this gospel, what can be referred to as "forgiving" has the following possible meanings. On the one hand, "forgiving debts" (ἀφίημι τὰ ὀφείληματὰ [6:12; 18:27, 32]) means something like letting go *failures*; whereas, "forgiving sins or trespasses" (ἀφίημι τὰ παραπτώματα/ αἱ ἁμαρτίαι [6:14–15; 9:2, 5, 6]) means something like letting go the wrong acts done. On the other hand, "forgiving debtors" (ἀφίημι τοῖς ὀφειλέταις) means something like releasing people who have *failed* to meet their obligations. The implication of this is that, for Matthew, forgiving a person is something like giving up or letting go bitterness for the injury (or wrongdoing) they have caused, or for their failure to meet their obligation. It is a sort of "moving past" their transgression, or failure, by ceasing to harbor bitterness and refraining from retaliating—the final endeavor being potentially to be able to restore a disrupted (or a broken) relationship. This meaning can also be found in Graeco-Roman and Jewish literature surveyed.

The second main contribution of the present study is that it has attempted a complex link between the concept of the "little ones" in Matt

---

divine forgiveness.

18:1–14 and that of *spiritually mature* and *immature* Christians in Matt 18, together with the preservation of the community (which is a major concern in Matt 18) and the issue of interpersonal forgiveness in the First Gospel as a whole. Rather than simply recognizing the centrality of the idea of the "little ones" in Matt 18, this study has taken the issue a stage further. As to the notion of *spiritually mature* and *immature* Christians in Matt 18, this has been explored in this work as an unexploited topic in Matthean studies.

The third main contribution is that this study has taken into account the evidence provided in Jewish and Graeco-Roman literature in Greek, as the background against which Matthew's text on the subject at hand is to be read. These sources include the LXX, the writings of Philo and Josephus, together with those of Dionysius and Seneca. These data altogether have formed the background for the Matthean interpersonal forgiveness texts and related texts. They have helped this study in three main ways: first, to situate the theme of interpersonal forgiveness in the first-century CE discourse in Graeco-Roman and Jewish writings of the time, and ascertain the nature of interpersonal forgiveness; second, to find out how the act of forgiving is viewed in secular and Jewish writings of that time, and whether this act is associated with demands; third, to discern motives behind the act of forgiving and whether what is awaiting the unforgiving person is a concern in these sources.

All taken together, these findings may lead to some revised views among scholars on these key themes, and to a potential reconsideration of the right place of the theme of interpersonal forgiveness in their scheme of Matthean key themes.

As a way of conclusion, this investigation ventured in an exploration of the theme of interpersonal forgiveness theme in Matthew, and argued that the concept of interpersonal forgiveness is central to the message in this gospel. Its main foci have consisted in showing that this concept is quite central to the message in the First Gospel. It also ventured an understanding of the nature of interpersonal forgiveness in it. Five strands of evidence for this hypothesis have been proposed. A few tasks were set for this project, one of which was to explore the rhetoric of interpersonal forgiveness in some Graeco-Roman and Jewish literature in Greek (chs. 3 & 4), as the background against which the Matthean material was to be read. The reading of these materials was done with the main purpose of describing the dynamics of interpersonal forgiveness, or divine forgiveness (or both), where applicable. Searching the discourse meaning of ἀφίημι (and its cognate) and related terms as well as their Latin equivalents in these data was part of the procedure in this respect.

The second task set for the present project was to sketch all the Matthean forgiveness passages that use the technical term ἀφίημι and forgiveness-related ideas (ch. 2). As an aspect of this task, 6:12, 14–15 and 18:21–35 were singled out for a thorough examination in chapters 5 and 6. These texts were deemed most relevant because, first, they are the only Matthean texts in which the idea of interpersonal forgiveness is stated explicitly. Second, in them the five strands of evidence proposed appear to be included altogether. As was with the Graeco-Roman and Jewish literature in Greek, the reading of Matthew's text was done with the purpose of describing the dynamics of divine and human forgiveness. Searching the discourse meaning of ἀφίημι in it was also part of the process. The third and last task was to discuss whether, or how, the rhetoric of interpersonal forgiveness in 6:12, 14–15 relates to (or differs from) its rhetoric in 18:21–35 and other Matthean interpersonal forgiveness-related texts, and to find out how this rhetoric fits in Matthew's flow of thought in the gospel as a whole (ch. 7).

Discourse analysis was used because it likely offers an effective way of drawing attention to the text: it proceeds from the detail to the whole discourse. Four areas of concern in it were considered: the text, the co-text, the inter-texts, and the context. In discussing the two key Matthean forgiveness texts, the focus was on personal *deixis*, social *deixis*, temporal *deixis*, and discourse *deixis*. Every particular word, expression or idea in 6:9–15 and 18:21–35 was taken seriously as part of the entire discourse. More precisely, the study was concerned with how a particular word, expression or concept in these two texts functions in the whole discourse. Further, the study was concerned with whether or how the two key Matthean passages relate to (or differ from) each other and to other Matthean interpersonal forgiveness texts, and how both fit in Matthew's flow of thought in the gospel. Discourse analysis has proven very helpful in reading Matthew's texts. Far from being a model with a potential for taking the text away from the people, as some may think, this study has shown that this model can successfully bring the text to the people.

It is the hope of this author that this work may now claim to be able to act as a theological resource in NT exegesis and for the church and theological schools in the wider world. It should, however, be acknowledged that this work did not cover all the issues appertaining to the interpersonal forgiveness theme in Matthew. Only the most pressing problems deemed most relevant for our purposes were considered. To mention only two possible areas of inquiry for further study, the following can be proposed. First is the relationship between Matthew's view on the community of believers as members of the kingdom and his Christology and aspects of his theism and the ethical implications of this. How are the believers, as members of the kingdom, to behave in response to the character of God as king and father as well as the royalty of Jesus with regard to forgiving? Second is the relationship between reluctance in forgiving (6:15; 18:28–35) and the work of the evil one (6:13). A possible question to ask is how reluctance in forgiving relates to the work of the devil, who in 6:13, is portrayed as the one from whom the disciples are to be delivered. Is reluctance or failure to forgive part of this captivity?

Bibliography

Aarde, Andries van. "Jesus' Mission to All of Israel Emplotted in Matthew's Story." Paper presented at Annual Meeting of the Society of Biblical Literature, Philadelphia, PA, 2005. Online: www.sbl-site.org/assets/pdfs/aarde_jesus.pdf.

Abrahams, Israel. "God's Forgiveness." In *Studies in Pharisaism and the Gospels*. 1:139-49. Cambridge: Cambridge University Press, 1917.

———. "The Lord's Prayer." In *Studies in Pharisaism and the Gospels*. 2:94-108. Cambridge: Cambridge University Press, 1924.

———. "Man's Forgiveness." In *Studies in Pharisaism and the Gospels*. 1:150-67. Cambridge: Cambridge University Press, 1917.

Aitken, James K. "Jewish Tradition and Culture." In *The Early Christian World*, edited by Philip F. Esler, 1:80-110. London: Routledge, 2000.

Aland, Barbara, et al., editors. *The Greek New Testament*. 4th rev. ed. Stuttgart: Deutsche Bibelgesellschaft, 1993.

Aland, Kurt, editor. *Synopsis Quattuor Evangeliorum*. 3rd rev. ed. Stuttgart: Deutsche Bibelgesellshaft, 1985.

Alexander, Loveday C. A. "Relevance of Greco-Roman Literature and Culture to New Testament Study." In *Hearing the New Testament: Strategies for Interpretation*, edited by Joel B. Green, 109-26. Grand Rapids: Eerdmans, 1995.

Allison, Dale C., Jr. "Matthew: Structure, Biographical Impulse and the *Imitatio Christi*." In *The Four Gospels 1992*, edited by Festschrift Frans Neirynck, et al., 2:1203-21. Leuven: Leuven University Press, 1992.

———. *Reconstructing Jesus: Memory, Imagination, and History*. London: SPCK, 2010.

———. *Studies in Matthew: Interpretation Past and Present*. Grand Rapids: Baker Academic, 2005.

Augsburger, David. *The Freedom of Forgiveness: Seventy Times Seven*. Chicago: Moody, 1970.

Aquino, Karl, et al. "When Push Doesn't Come to Shove: Interpersonal Forgiveness in Workplace Relationships." *Journal of Management Inquiry* 12 (2003) 209-16.

Assohoto, Barnabé, and Samuel Ngewa. "Genesis." In *African Bible Commentary*, edited by Tokunboh Adeyemo, 9-84; Nairobi: WorldAlive, 2006.

Bailey, Kenneth E. *Jesus through Middle Eastern Eyes: Cultural Studies in the Gospels*. London: SPCK, 2008.

Balch, David L., editor. *Social History of the Matthean Community: Cross-Disciplinary Approaches*. Minneapolis: Fortress, 1991.

Baker, Don. *Forgive and Restore: The Healing Touch of Church Discipline*. Basingstoke, UK: Marshall, Morgan & Scott, 1986.

Barth, G. "Matthew's Understanding of the Law." In *Tradition and Interpretation in Matthew*, edited by Günther Bornkamm et al., 58–164. New Testament Library London: SCM, 1963.

Bauckham, Richard. "The Relevance of Extracanonical Jewish Texts to New Testament Study." In *Hearing the New Testament: Strategies for Interpretation*, edited by Joel B. Green. Grand Rapids: Eerdmans (1995) 90–108.

Bauer, David R. *The Structure of Matthew's Gospel: A Study in Literary Design*. JSNTSup 3. Sheffield: JSOT Press, 1988.

Bauer, Walter A. *Greek-English Lexicon of the New Testament and Other Early Christian Literature*. 3rd ed. Translated and revised by F. W. Danker. Chicago: University of Chicago Press, 2000.

Beam, Fred. "The Price of Prison." *Helps for Bible Preachers*. Bristol: AIM, 2001.

Beardslee, W. A. "Recent Literary Criticism." In *The New Testament and Its Modern Interpreters*, edited by Eldon J. Epp and G. W. MacRae, 175–98. Atlanta: Scholars 1987.

Beare, Francis W. *The Gospel according to Matthew*. Oxford: Blackwell, 1981.

Best, Ernest. "Mark's Use of the Twelve." In *Disciples and Discipleship: Studies in the Gospel according to Mark*, 131–61. Edinburgh: T. & T. Clark, 1986.

Betz, Hans D. *The Sermon on the Mount: A Commentary on the Sermon on the Mount, including the Sermon on the Plain (Matthew 5:3–7:27 and Luke 6:20–49)*. Edited by Adela Yarbo Collins. Minneapolis: Fortress, 1995.

Biggar, Nigel. "Forgiveness in the Twentieth Century." In *Forgiveness and Truth: Explorations in Contemporary Theology*, edited by Alistair McFadyen and Marcel Sarot, 181–217. Edinburgh: T. & T. Clark, 2001.

Black, Stephanie L. *Sentence Conjunctions in the Gospel of Matthew: Καὶ, δὲ, τότε, γάρ, οὖν and Asyndeton in Narrative Discourse*. JSNTSup 216. Sheffield: Sheffield Academic, 2002.

Blomberg, Craig L. *Interpreting the Parables*. Leicester: Apollos, 1990.

———. *Matthew*. The New American Commentary 22, edited by David S. Dockery. Nashville: Broadman, 1999.

———. *Preaching the Parables: From Responsible Interpretation to Powerful Proclamation*. Grand Rapids: Baker Academic, 2004.

Boff, Leonardo. *The Lord's Prayer: The Prayer of Integral Liberation*. Maryknoll, NY: Orbis, 1983.

Bonnard, Pierre. "Composition et signification historique de Matthieu XVIII." In *De Jésus aux Évangiles: tradition et rédaction dans les Évangiles synoptiques*, edited by I. de la Potterie, 130–40. Gembloux, France: Duculot, 1967.

———. *L'Évangile selon Saint Matthieu*. 3rd ed. Commentaire du Nouveau Testament. 2ème série. Geneva: Labor et Fides, 1992.

Bonhoeffer, Dietrich. *Le prix de la grâce*. Neuchâtel: Delachaux et Niestlé, 1967.

Borgen, P. "Philo of Alexandria: A Critical and Synthetical Survey of Research since World War II." *ANRW* 2:21/1 (1991) 97–154.

———. "Philo of Alexandria." In *Jewish Writings of the Second Temple Period*, edited by M. Stone. Philadelphia: Fortress (1985) 233–82.

Boring, Eugene M. "The Gospel of Matthew." In *The New Interpreter's Bible: New Testament Survey*, edited by L. E. Keck, 34–61. Nashville: Abingdon, 2005.

Bornkamm, Günther. "The Authority to 'Bind' and 'Loose' in the Church in Matthew's Gospel." In *The Interpretation of Matthew*, 2nd ed., edited by Graham N. Stanton: 101–114. Studies in New Testament Interpretation. Edinburgh: T. & T. Clark, 1995.

Boucher, Madeleine. *The Mysterious Parable: A Literary Study*. CBQMS. Washington: CBAA, 1977.

Bovon, François. "The Synoptic Gospels and the Noncanonical Acts of the Apostles." *HTR* 81, no. 1 (1988) 19–36.

Braund, Susanna M. *Seneca: De clementia*. Oxford: Oxford University Press, 2009.

Brooke, George J. *The Dead Sea Scrolls and the New Testament*. London: SPCK, 2005.

Brown, Jeannine K. "Matthew's 'Least of These' Theology and Subversion of 'Us/Other' Categories." Paper presented at Society of Biblical Literature, Contextual Biblical Interpretation, Atlanta, GA, November 22, 2010.

Brown, Raymond E. "The Paternoster as an Eschatological Prayer." In *New Testament Essays*, 217–53. London: Chapman, 1967.

Browning, W. R. F. "Philo." In *Dictionary of the Bible*. No pages. Oxford Reference Online: http://www.oxfordreference.com/views/ENTRY.html?subview=Main&entry=t94.e1469.

Brownlee, W. H. *The Dead Sea Manual of Discipline: Translation and Notes*. In BASOR Supplementary Studies 10–12 (1951).

Bruner, Frederick D. *Matthew: A Commentary*. Vol. 1. Rev. exp. ed. Grand Rapids: Eerdmans, 2004.

———. *Matthew: A Commentary*. Vol. 2. Rev. exp. ed. Grand Rapids: Eerdmans, 2004.

Buhler, Rich. *Pain and Pretending*. Nashville: Nelson, 1991.

Bullinger, Ethelbert W. *Figures of Speech Used in the Bible*. 1898. Reprint, Grand Rapids: Baker, 1968.

Carmignac, Jean. *Recherches sur le "Notre Père."* Paris: Letouzey et Ané, 1969.

Carson, D. A. *Matthew*. Expositor's Bible Commentary. Grand Rapids: Zondervan, 1984.

Carter, Warren. *Matthew and the Margins: A Socio-Political and Religious Reading*. JSNTSup 204. Sheffield: Sheffield Academic, 2000.

———. *Matthew: Storyteller, Interpreter, Evangelist*. Peabody, MA: Hendrickson, 2004.

Charlesworth, James H., editor. *The Old Testament Pseudepigrapha*. Vol. 2. London: Longman & Todd, 1983.

Cohen, Shaye J. D. *From the Maccabees to the Mishnah*. Philadelphia: Westminster, 1987.

Copper, John M., and J. F. Procopé. *Seneca: Moral and Political Essays*, edited by John M. Copper and J. F. Procopé. Cambridge: Cambridge University Press, 1995.

Cotterell, Peter, and Max Turner. *Linguistics and Biblical Interpretation*. London: SPCK, 1989.

Couroyer, Bernard. "'De la mesure dont vous mesurez il vous sera mesuré.'" *Revue Biblique* 77 (1970) 366–70.

Cousland, J. R. C. *The Crowds in the Gospel of Matthew*. NTSup 102. Leiden: Brill, 2002.

Craske, Jane. "Forgiveness in Context." In *Forgiveness and Truth: Explorations in Contemporary Theology*, edited by Alistair McFadyen and Marcel Sarot, 125–30. Edinburgh: T. & T. Clark, 2001.

Crystal, David, editor. *A Dictionary of Linguistics and Phonetics*. 5th ed. Oxford: Blackwell, 2003.

Daube, David. "Sin, Ignorance and Forgiveness in the Bible." In *Biblical Law and Literature*, edited by Calum Carmichael, 375–89. Studies in Comparative Legal History 3. Berkeley: Robbins, 2003.

David, Roman, and Susane Y. P. Choi. "Forgiveness and Transitional Justice in the Czech Republic." *Journal of Conflict Resolution* 50 (2006) 339–67.

Davies, W. D., and Dale C. Allison Jr. *A Critical and Exegetical Commentary on the Gospel according to Saint Matthew* Vols. 1–2. Edinburgh: T. & T. Clark, 1988, 1991.

———. "Reflections on the Sermon on the Mount." *SJT* 44 (1991) 283–309.

De Boer, Martinus C. "Ten Thousand Talents? Matthew's Interpretation and Redaction of the Parable of the Unforgiving Servant (Matt 18:23–35)." *CBQ* 50 (1988) 214–32.

Deines, Roland. "Not the Law but the Messiah: Law and Righteousness in the Gospel of Matthew—An Ongoing Debate." In *Built upon the Rock*, edited by Daniel M. Gurtner and John Nolland, 53–84. Studies in the Gospel of Matthew. Grand Rapids: Eerdmans, 2008.

Deissmann, Adolf. *Light from the Ancient East*. Translated by Lionel R. M. Strachan. London: Hodder & Stoughton, 1927.

Delobel, Joel. "The Lord's Prayer in the Textual Tradition." In *The New Testament in Early Christianity*, edited by Jean-Marie Sevrin, 293–309. Bibliotheca Ephemeridum Theologicarum Lovaniensium 86. Leuven: Leuven University Press, 1989.

Derrett, J. Duncan M. *Law in the New Testament*. London: Longman & Todd, 1970.

Dionysius of Halicarnassus. *The Roman Antiquities* 3. Vol. 2, edited by T. E. Page, E. Capps, and W. H. D. Rouse. Translated by E. Cary. LCL. London: Heinemann, 1939.

———. *The Roman Antiquities* 8. Vol. 5, edited by T. E. Page et al. Translated by E. Cary. LCL. London: Heinemann, 1945.

———. *The Roman Antiquities* 10. Vol. 6, edited by T. E. Page et al. Translated by E. Cary. LCL. London: Heinemann, 1947.

Djaballah, Amar. *Les paraboles aujourd'hui: visages de Dieu et images du Royaume*. Sentier, Québec: Clairière, 1994.

Donahue, John R. *The Gospel in Parable: Metaphor, Narrative, and Theology in the Synoptic Gospels*. Minneapolis: Fortress, 1988.

Dorff, Elliot N. "The Elements of Forgiveness: A Jewish Approach." In *Dimensions of Forgiveness: Psychological Research and Theological Perspectives*, edited by Everett L. Worthington Jr., 29–55. Philadelphia: Templeton, 1998.

Downey, G. *A History of Antioch in Syria from Seleucus to the Arab Conquest*. Princeton: Princeton University Press, 1961.

Downing, F. Gerald. *Making Sense in (and of) the First Christian Century*. JSNTSup 197. Sheffield: Sheffield Academic, 2000.

Drury, John. *Tradition and Design in Luke's Gospel: A Study in Early Christian Historiography*. London: Darton, Longman & Todd, 1976.

Duling, Dennis C., and Norman Perrin. *The New Testament: Proclamation and Parenesis, Myth and History*. 3rd ed. Fort Worth: Harcourt, 1994.

Dumais, Marcel. *Le Sermon sur la montagne: état de la recherche: interprétation bibliographique*. Sainte-Foy, Québec: Letouzey et Anné, 1995.

Dunn, James D. G. *Jesus' Call to Discipleship*. Understanding Jesus Today. Cambridge: Cambridge University Press, 1992.

Durham, John I. *Exodus*. World Biblical Commentary 3. Nashville: Nelson, 1987.

Ellingworth, Paul. "Forgiveness of Sins." In *Dictionary of Jesus and the Gospels*, edited by Joel B. Green, Scot McKnight, and I. Howard Marshall, 241–43. Downers Grove, IL: InterVarsity, 1992.

Enright, Robert D., and Catherine T. Coyle. "Researching the Process Model of Forgiveness within Psychological Interventions." In *Dimensions of Forgiveness: Psychological Research and Theological Perspectives*, edited by Everett L. Worthington Jr., 139–61. Philadelphia: Templeton, 1998.

Enright, Robert D. *Forgiveness Is a Choice: A Step-by-Step Process for Resolving Anger and Restoring Hope*. Washington DC: APA, 2001.

Enslin, Morton. *Christian Beginnings*. New York: Harper & Brothers, 1938.

Esler, Philip F., editor. *Modelling Early Christianity: Social-Scientific Studies of the New Testament in Its Context*. London: Routledge, 1995.

Exline, Julie J., et al. "Forgiveness and Justice: A Research Agenda for Social and Personality Psychology." *PSPR* 7, no. 4 (2003) 337–48.

Farmer, William R. "The Patristic Evidence Reexamined: A Response to George Kennedy." In *New Synoptic Studies*, edited by William R. Farmer, 2–15. Macon, GA: Mercer University Press, 1983.

Farrer, Austin M. "On Dispensing with Q." In *The-Source Hypothesis: A Critical Appraisal*, edited by Arthur J. Bellinzoni Jr., 321–56. Macon, GA: Mercer University Press, 1985.

Feldman, Louis H., and G. Hata, editors. *Josephus, the Bible and History*. Detroit: Wayne State University Press, 1989.

Fokkelman, J. P. *Narrative Art and Poetry in the Books of Samuel: A Full Interpretation Based on Stylistic and Structural Analysis*. Vol. 2. SSN 23. Assen, Netherlands: Van Gorcum, 1986.

Foster, Paul. *Community, Law and Mission in Matthew's Gospel*. WUNT 2/177. Tübingen: Mohr/Siebeck, 2004.

France, R. T. *The Gospel of Matthew*. NICNT. Grand Rapids: Eerdmans, 2007.

———. *Matthew: Evangelist and Teacher*. Exeter, UK: Paternoster, 1989.

Fromentin, Valérie. *Denys d'Halicarnasse: Antiquités Romaines*. Vol. 1. Paris: Belles Lettres, 1998.

Garland, David E. *Reading Matthew: A Literary and Theological Commentary*. Macon, GA: Smyth & Helwys, 2001.

Gibbs, Jeffrey A. *Matthew 1:1–11:1: A Theological Exposition of Sacred Scripture*. Concordia Commentary. Saint Louis: Concordia, 2006.

Gilbert, M. "La Loi du talion." *Christus* 31 (1984) 73–82.

Glancy, Jennifer A. "Slaves and Slavery in the Matthean Parables." *JBL* 119, no. 1 (2000) 67–90.

Goodacre, Mark S. *The Case against Q: Studies in Markan Priority and the Synoptic Problem*. Harrisburg, PA: Trinity, 2002.

———. *Goulder and the Gospels: An Examination of a New Paradigm*. JSNTSup 133. Sheffield: Sheffield Academic, 1996.

———. *The Synoptic Problem: A Way through the Maze*. London: T. & T. Clark, 2001.

Gore, C. *The Sermon on the Mount: A Practical Exposition*. London, 1896.

Gould, James. "The Catechetism's Understanding of Grace." *Anglican Theological Review* 91, no. 3 (2009) 373–94.

Goulder, Michael D. *Midrash and Lection in Matthew*. London: SPCK, 1974.

Green, Joel B. "Discourse Analysis and New Testament." In *Hearing the New Testament: Strategies for Interpretation*, edited by Joel B. Green, 175–96. Grand Rapids: Eerdmans, 1995.

Guelich, Robert A. *The Sermon on the Mount: A Foundation for Understanding*. Waco: Word, 1982.

Gundry, Robert H. *Matthew: A Commentary on His Handbook for a Mixed Church under Persecution*. 2nd ed. Grand Rapids: Eerdmans, 1994.

———. "A Responsive Evaluation of the Social History of the Matthean Community in Roman Syria." In *Social History of the Matthean Community: Cross-Disciplinary Approaches*, edited by David L. Balch, 62–67 Minneapolis: Fortress, 1991.

Guthrie, Donald. *New Testament Theology*. Leicester, UK: InterVarsity, 1981.

Hagner, Donald A. *Matthew 1–13; 14–28*. Word Biblical Commentary 33A–33B. Dallas: Word, 1993, 1995.

———. "Righteousness in Matthew's Theology." In *Worship, Theology and Ministry in the Early Church*, 101–20. JSNTSup 87. Sheffield: JSOT Press, 1992.

Harrington, Daniel J. *God's People in Christ*. Philadelphia: Fortress, 1980.

Hatch, Edwin and Henry A. Redpath, editors. *A Concordance to the Septuagint and the Other Greek Versions of the Old Testament (Including the Apocryphal Books)*. 2nd ed. Grand Rapids: Baker, 1998.

Hauerwas, Stanley. *The Peaceable Kingdom*. Notre Dame: University of Notre Dame, 1983.

Hays, Richard B. *The Moral Vision of the New Testament: Community, Cross, New Creation*. Edinburgh: T. & T. Clark, 1997.

Heller, Thomas, Stephen Krasner, and John McMillan. "A Trust Fund for Ituri," 2003. Paper presented at the Center for Democracy, Development and the Rule of Law, Stanford University, December 7, 2003. Online: http://facultygsb.stanford.edu/mcmillan/personalpage/documents/Ituri.pdf (site discontinued).

Hendricksen, William. *The Gospel of Matthew*. New Testament Commentary. Edinburgh: Banner, 1976.

Hill, David. *The Gospel of Matthew*. New Century Bible. London: Marshall, Morgan & Scott, 1972.

Hobbs, Edward C. "A Quarter-Century without 'Q.'" *PSTJ* 33:4 (1980) 10–19.

Holman, C. Hugh. *A Handbook to Literature*. 3rd ed. New York: Odyssey, 1972.

Holmes, Michael W. *The Apostolic Fathers: Greek Texts and English Translations*. 3rd ed. Grand Rapids: Baker, 2007.

Houlden, J. L. *Ethics and the New Testament*. Harmondsworth, UK: Penguin, 1973.

Houston, James M. "Forgiveness." In *Baker Encyclopedia of the Bible* 1:810–12.

Huang, S. T. and Robert D. Enright. "Forgiveness and Anger-related Emotions in Taiwan: Implications for Therapy." *Psychotherapy* 37 (2000) 71–79.

Huffman, N. A. "Atypical Features in the Parables of Jesus." *JBL* 97 (1978).

Hultgren, Arland J. *The Parables of Jesus: A Commentary*. Grand Rapids: Eerdmans, 2000.

Hurtado, Larry W. "Genre Gospel." In *Dictionary of Jesus and the Gospels* 1:276–82.

———. "New Testament Studies in the 20th Century." *Religion* 39 (2009) 43–57.

Jastrow, Marcus. *A Dictionary of the Targumim, the Talmud Babli and Yerushalmi, and the Midrashic Literature*. Vol. 1. 1989. Reprint, New York: Judaica.

Jaworski, Adam, and Nikolas Coupland. "Discourse Analysis and Conversation Analysis." In *The Linguistics Encyclopedia* 114–19.

Jeffers, James S. *The Greco-Roman World of the New Testament Era: Exploring the Background of Early Christianity*. Downers Grove, IL: InterVarsity, 1999.

Jeremias, Joachim. *Les Paraboles de Jésus*. Puy-Lyon, France: Mappus, 1962.

Johnson, Luke T. "The New Testament's Anti-Jewish Slander and the Conventions of Ancient Polemics." *JBL* 108 (1989) 419–41.

Johnson, Sherman E. and George A. Buttrick. "The Gospel according to St. Matthew." In *The Interpreter's Bible* 7:231–625.

Jones, L. Gregory. *Embodying Forgiveness: A Theological Analysis*. Grand Rapids: Eerdmans, 1995.

Josephus. *Jewish Antiquities: Books V–VIII*. Edited by G. P. Goold. Translated by H. St. J. Thackeray LCL 281. Cambridge, MA: Harvard University Press, 1988.

———. *Jewish Antiquities: Books IX–XI*. Edited by T. E. Page, E. Capps, and W. H. D. Rouse. Translated by Ralph Marcus. LCL 326. London: Heinemann, 1937.

———. *The Jewish War: Books IV–VII*. Edited by G. P. Goold. Translated by H. St. J. Thackeray. LCL 210. Cambridge, MA: Harvard University Press, 1997.

Kahlefeld, Heinrich. *Paraboles et leçons dans l'Évangile* 2. Translated by Georges Bret. Lectio Divina 56. Paris: Cerf, 1970.

Kant, Immanuel. *Religion within the Limits of Reason Alone*. Translated by T. M. Green and H. H. Hudson. New York: Harper & Row, 1960.

Kee, H. C. "Testaments of the Twelve Patriarchs: A New Translation and Introduction." In *The Old Testament Pseudepigrapha* 1, edited by James H. Charlesworth. London: Darton, Longman & Todd (1983) 775–828.

Kimelman, Reuven. "Birkat Ha-Minim and the Lack of Evidence for an Anti-Christian Jewish Prayer in Late Antiquity." In *Jewish and Christian Self-Definition*, edited by E. P. Sanders, 2:226–44. London, SCM, 1981.

Kingsbury, J. Dean. "The Plot of Matthew's Story." In *Interpretation* 46 (1992) 45–59.

Kissinger, Warren S. *The Parables of Jesus: A History of Interpretation and Bibliography*. London: Scarecrow, 1979.

Klein, Ralph W. *1 Samuel*. World Biblical Commentary 10. Waco: Word, 1983.

Kloppenborg, John S. "On Dispensing with Q? Goodacre on the Relation of Luke to Matthew." *New Testament Studies* 49, no. 2 (2003) 210–36.

———. *Q, the Earliest Gospel: An Introduction to the Original Stories and Sayings of Jesus*. Louisville: WJK, 2008.

Kraft, Charles H. *Deep Wounds, Deep Healing: Discovering the Vital Link between Spiritual Warfare and Inner Healing*. Ann Arbor, MI: Servant, 1993.

Lenski, R. C. H. *The Interpretation of St. Matthew's Gospel*. Minneapolis: Augsburg, 1943.

Liddell, Henry G. and Robert Scott. *A Greek-English Lexicon*. 9th ed., revised and augmented by Henry Stuart Jones. Oxford: Clarendon, 1968.

Linnemann, Eta. *Parables of Jesus: Introduction and Exposition*. London: SPCK, 1966.

Luz, Ulrich. "The Disciples in the Gospel according to Matthew." In *Studies in Matthew*, translated by Rosemary Selle, 115–42. Grand Rapids: Eerdmans, 2005.

———. *Matthew 1–7; 8–20; 21–28: A Commentary*. 3 vols. Hermeneia. Minneapolis: Fortress, 2001, 2005, 2007.

———. *Studies in Matthew*. Grand Rapids: Eerdmans, 2005.

———. *The Theology of the Gospel of Matthew*. New Testament Theology, edited by J. D. G. Dunn. Translated by J. Bradford Robinson. Cambridge: Cambridge University Press, 1995.

Mackintosh, H. R. *The Christian Experience of Forgiveness*. London: Nisbet, 1927.
Malina, Bruce J. and Richard L. Rohrbaugh. *Social-Science Commentary on the Synoptic Gospels*. 2nd ed. Minneapolis: Fortress, 2003.
Manson, T. W. *The Sayings of Jesus as Recorded in the Gospels according to St. Matthew and St. Luke*. London: SCM, 1949.
Marguerat, Daniel. *Le jugement dans l'Évangile de Matthieu*. 2è éd. Le Monde de la Bible 6. Geneva: Labor et Fides, 1995.
Marshall, Howard I. *The Gospel of Luke*. NIGTC. Carlisle, Cumbria: Paternoster, 1978.
Marty, Martin E. "The Ethos of Christian Forgiveness." In *Dimensions of Forgiveness: Psychological Research and Theological Perspectives*, edited by Everett L. Worthington Jr., 9–28. Philadelphia: Templeton, 1998.
Martin, R. P. "Reconciliation and Forgiveness in Colossians." In *Reconciliation and Hope*, edited by R. Banks, 104–24. Grand Rapids: Eerdmans, 1974.
Martínez, Florentino García. "Brotherly Rebuke in Qumran and Mt 18:15–17." In *The People of the Dead Sea Scrolls: Their Writings, Beliefs and Practices*, edited by Florentino García Martínez and Julio Trebolle Barrera, translated by Wilfred G. E. Watson, 221–32. Leiden: Brill, 1995.
———. *The Dead Sea Scrolls Translated: The Qumran Texts in English*. 2nd ed. Translated by Wilfred G. E. Watson. Leiden: Brill, 1996.
Massaux, Edouard. *Influence de l'Évangile de Saint Matthieu sur la littérature chrétienne avant Saint Irénée*. Bibliotheca Ephemeridum Theologicarum Lovaniensium 75. Leuven: Leuven University Press, 1986.
Matthews, P. H., editor. *Oxford Concise Dictionary of Linguistics*. Oxford: Oxford University Press, 1997.
McCarthy, Michael. "Discourse Analysis." In *The Oxford Companion to the English Language*, edited by Tom McArthur, 316–17. Oxford: Oxford University Press, 1992.
McCullough, E., Steven J. Sandage, and Everrett L. Worthington Jr. *To Forgive Is Human*. Downers Grove, IL: InterVarsity, 1997.
McDonald, H. D. *Forgiveness and Hope*. Richmond, Virginia: Knox, 1961.
Meeks, Wayne A. *The Moral World of the First Christians*. Library of Early Christianity 6. Philadelphia: Westminster, 1986.
Metzger, Bruce M. *A Textual Commentary on the Greek New Testament*. 2nd ed. Stuttgart: German Bible Society, 1994.
Mohrlang, Roger. *Matthew and Paul: A Comparison of Ethical Perspectives*. SNTSMS 48. Cambridge: Cambridge University Press, 1984.
Montefiore, Claude G. *The Synoptic Gospels*. Vol. 2. 2nd ed. New York: Ktav, 1968.
Morris, Leon. "Forgiveness." In *Dictionary of Paul and His Letters*, edited by Gerald F. Hawthorne, Ralph P. Martin, and Daniel G. Reid, 311–13. Downers Grove, IL: InterVarsity, 1993.
———. *The Gospel according to Matthew*. Grand Rapids: Eerdmans, 1992.
Mortureux, Bernard. *Recherches sur le "De clementia de Sénèque."* New ed. Latomus Collection 128. Brusells: Latomus, 1973.
Moule, Charles F. D. "'. . . As We Forgive. . .': A Note on the Distinction between Deserts and Capacity in the Understanding of Forgiveness." In *Essays in New Testament Interpretation*, 278–86. Cambridge: Cambridge University Press, 1982.

Moulton, W. F., editor. *A Concordance to the Greek Testament according to the Texts of Westcott and Hort, Tischendorf and the English Revisers*. 5th ed. Edinburgh: T. & T. Clark, 1978.
Murray, John. "A Lesson in Forgiveness." *Writings of John Murray* 3. Edinburgh: Banner of Trust, 1982.
Nave, Guy D., Jr. *The Role and Function of Repentance in Luke-Acts*. Academia Biblica 4. Atlanta: SBL, 2002.
Neirynck, Frans F. *Evangelica I: Gospels Studies—Études d'Évangile*. Collected Essays. Leuven: Leuven University Press, 1982.
———. *Evangelica II*. Collected Essays from 1982 to 1991, edited by F. Van Segbroeck. Leuven: Leuven University Press, 1991.
Neirynck, Frans F., et al., editors. *The Four Gospels 1992*. Vol. 2. Leuven: Leuven University Press, 1992.
Nestle-Aland, K., et al. *Novum Testamentum Graece*. 27th rev. ed. Stuttgart: Deutsche Bibelgesellschaft, 2001.
Newman, Louis E. "The Quality of Mercy: On the Duty to Forgive in the Judaic Tradition." *Journal of Religious Ethics* 15, no. 2 (1987) 168.
Nida, Eugene A. *Componential Analysis of Meaning: An Introduction to Semantic Structures*. The Hague: Mouton, 1975.
Nida, Eugene A., and William D. Reyburn. *Meaning across Cultures*. American Society of Missiology Series 4. Maryknoll, NY: Orbis, 1981.
Nolland, John. *The Gospel of Matthew*. NIGTC. Grand Rapids: Eerdmans, 2005.
———. *Luke 1–9:20*. World Biblical Commentary 35A. Dallas: Word, 1989.
Oepke, Albrecht. "Παῖς, παιδίον, παιδάριον, τέκνον, τεκνίον, βρέφος, κτλ." In *TDNT* 5:636–54.
Omanson, Roger. *A Textual Guide on the Greek New Testament*. New York: UBS, 2006.
O'Neill, J. C. "The Lord's Prayer." *JSNT* 51(1993) 3–25.
Osborne, Grant R. *Matthew*. Zondervan Exegetical Commentary: New Testament. Grand Rapids: Zondervan, 2010.
Osten-Sacken, P. von der. "Ἐλάχιστος, κτλ." In *EDNT* 1:426–27.
Overman, J. Andrew. *Church and Community in Crisis: The Gospel according to Matthew*. New Testament in Context. Valley Forge, PA: Trinity, 1996.
———. *Matthew's Gospel and Formative Judaism: The Social World of the Matthean Community*. Minneapolis: Fortress, 1990.
Patte, Daniel. *The Gospel according to Matthew: A Structural Commentary on Matthew's Faith*. Philadelphia: Fortress, 1987.
Peli, Pinchas H. *Soloveitchik on Repentance*. New York: Paulist, 1984.
Philo, Judaeus. *On Rewards and Punishments* 166. Vol. 8. Edited by T. E. Page, E. Capps, and W. H. D. Rouse. Translated by F. H. Colson. LCL. London: Heinemann, 1939.
———. *On the Special Laws* 1–2. Vol. 7. Edited by T. E. Page, E. Capps, and W. H. D. Rouse. Translated by F. H. Colson. LCL. London: Heinemann, 1937.
Plummer, Alfred. *An Exegetical Commentary on the Gospel according to St. Matthew*. London: Elliot, 1909.
Pokrifka-Joe, Todd. "Probing the Relationship between Divine and Human Forgiveness in Matthew." In *Forgiveness and Truth: Explorations in Contemporary Theology*, edited by Alistair I. McFadyen, Marcel Sarot, and Anthony Thiselton, 165–72. Edinburgh: T. & T. Clark, 2001.

Porter, Stanley E. "Discourse Analysis and New Testament Studies: An Introductory Survey." In *Discourse Analysis and Other Topics in Biblical Greek*, 14–35. JSNTSup 113. Sheffield: Sheffield Academic, 1995.

Rajak, Tessa. *Josephus: The Historian and His Society*. 2nd ed. London: Duckworth, 2002.

Redlich, E. Basil. *The Forgiveness of Sins*. Edinburgh: T. & T. Clark, 1937.

Reed, Jeffrey T. "Discourse Analysis." In *Handbook to Exegesis of New Testament*, edited by Stanley E. Porter, 189–217. Leiden: Brill, 1997.

Reimer, David J. "The Apocrypha and Biblical Theology: The Case of Interpersonal Forgiveness." In *After the Exile: Essays in Honour of Rex Mason*, edited by John Barton and David J. Reimer, 259–82. Macon, GA: Mercer University Press, 1996.

———. "Stories of Forgiveness: Narrative Ethics and the Old Testament." In *Reflection and Refraction: Studies in Biblical Historiography in Honour of A. Graeme Auld*, edited by Robert Rezetko, Timothy H. Lim, and W. Brian Aucker, 359–78. Leiden: Brill, 2007.

Repschinski, Boris. *The Controversy Stories in the Gospel of Matthew: Their Redaction, Form and Relevance for the Relationship between the Matthean Community and Formative Judaism*. FRLANT 189. Göttingen. Vandenhoeck & Ruprecht, 2000.

Richards, Jack C., John Platt, and Heidi Platt, editors. *Longman Dictionary of Language Teaching and Applied Linguistics*. 2nd ed. Essex, UK: Longman, 1993.

Riches, John K. *Conflicting Mythologies: Identity Formation in the Gospels of Mark and Matthew*. Studies of the New Testament and Its World. Edinburgh: T. & T. Clark, 2000.

———. *Matthew*. New Testament Guides, edited by A. T. Lincoln. Sheffield: Sheffield Academic, 1996.

Ropes, James H. *The Synoptic Gospels*. Cambridge, MA: Harvard University Press, 1934.

Rotter, Joseph C. "Letting Go: Forgiveness in Counseling." *Family Journal* 9 (2001) 174–77.

Saldarini, Antony J. *Matthew's Christian-Jewish Community*. Chicago: University of Chicago Press, 1994.

Sanders, E. P. *Jesus and Judaism*. London: SCM, 1985.

Sanders, E. P., and Margaret Davies. *Studying the Synoptic Gospels*. London: SCM, 1989.

Sanders, T., and J. Sanders. "Text and Text Analysis." In *Encyclopedia of Language and Linguistics* 12:597–607.

Schoedel, William R. "Ignatius and the Gospel of Matthew." In *Social History of the Matthean Community: Cross-Disciplinary Approaches*, edited by David L. Balch, 129–77. Minneapolis: Fortress, 1991.

Schottroff, Luise. *The Parables of Jesus*. Translated by Linda M. Maloney. Minneapolis: Fortress, 2006.

Schweizer, Eduard. *The Good News according to Matthew*. Translated by E. Green. London: SPCK, 1975.

Scott, Bernard B. *Hear Then the Parable: A Commentary on the Parables of Jesus*. Minneapolis: Fortress, 1989.

———. "The King's Accounting: Matthew 18:23–34." *JBL* 104, no. 3 (1985) 429–42.

Segal, Alan F. "Matthew's Jewish Voice." In *Social History of the Matthean Community: Cross-Disciplinary Approaches*, edited by David L. Balch, 3–37. Minneapolis: Fortress, 1991.

Seneca. *De clementia*. In *Moral and Political Essays*, edited and translated by John M. Cooper and J. F. Procopé. Cambridge University Press: Cambridge, 1995.

Senior, Donald. "Directions in Matthean Studies." In *The Gospel of Matthew in Current Study*, edited by David E. Aune, 5–21. Grand Rapids: Eerdmans, 2001.

———. *Matthew*. Abingdon New Testament Commentaries. Nashville: Abingdon, 1998.

———. *What Are They Saying about Matthew?* New York: Paulist, 1983.

Shults, F. LeRon, and Steven J. Sandage. *The Faces of Forgiveness: Searching for Wholeness and Salvation*. Grand Rapids: Baker, 2003.

Silva, Moisés. *Biblical Words and Their Meaning: An Introduction to Lexical Semantics*. Rev. exp. ed. Grand Rapids: Zondervan, 1994.

Sim, David C. *The Gospel of Matthew and Christian Judaism: The History and Social Setting of the Matthean Community*. Edinburgh: T. & T. Clark, 1999.

———. "The Social Setting of the Matthean Community." *HTS* 57, nos. 1–2 (2011) 268–80.

Smedes, Lewis B. *The Art of Forgiving*. New York: Ballantine, 1996.

———. "Stations on the Journey from Forgiveness to Hope." In *Dimensions of Forgiveness: Psychological Research and Theological Perspectives*, edited by Everett L. Worthington Jr., 341–54. Philadelphia: Templeton, 1998.

Snodgrass, Klyne. *Stories with Intent: A Comprehensive Guide to the Parables of Jesus*. Grand Rapids: Eerdmans, 2008.

Snyman, Andries H. "A Semantic Discourse Analysis of the Letter to Philemon." In *Text and Interpretation: New Approaches in the Criticism of the New Testament*, edited by P. J. Hartin and J. H. Petzer, 83–99. Leiden: Brill, 1991.

Spicq, Ceslas. *Dieu et l'homme*. Lectio Divina 29. Paris: Cerf, 1961.

Stanley, Charles. *Forgiveness*. Nashville: Nelson, 1987.

Stanton, N. Graham. *A Gospel for a New People: Studies in Matthew*. Edinburgh: T. & T. Clark, 1992.

———. *The Gospels and Jesus*. Oxford: Oxford University Press, 1989.

———. "Matthew as Interpreter of the Sayings of Jesus." In *The Gospel and the Gospels*, edited by Peter Stuhlmacher, 257–72. Grand Rapids: Eerdmans, 1991.

Stark, Rodney. "Urban Chaos and Crisis." In *Rise of Christianity: A Sociologist Reconsiders History*, 147–162. Princeton: Princeton University Press, 1996.

Sternberg, M. *The Poetics of Biblical Narrative: Ideological Literature and the Drama of Reading*. Indiana Studies in Biblical Literature. Bloomington: Indiana University Press, 1987.

Stiewe, Martin and François Vouga. *Le Sermon sur la montagne: un abrégé de l'Évangile dans le miroitement de ses interprétations*. Geneva: Labor et Fides, 2002.

Strecker, Georg. *The Sermon on the Mount: An Exegetical Commentary*. Translated by O. C. Dean Jr. Edinburgh: T. & T. Clark, 1988.

Streeter, B. H. *The Four Gospels: A Study of Origins*. 2nd rev. ed. London: Macmillan, 1930.

Stuart, Douglas. "Malachi." In *The Minor Prophets: An Exegetical and Expositional Commentary* 3, edited by Thomas E. McComiskey, 1245–1396. Grand Rapids: Baker, 1998.

Swinburne, Richard. *Responsibility and Atonement*. Oxford: Clarendon, 1989.

Talbert, Charles H. *Reading the Sermon on the Mount: Character Formation and Ethical Decision Making in Matthew 5–7*. Grand Rapids: Baker Academic, 2004.

Taylor, Vincent. *Forgiveness and Reconciliation*. 2nd ed. London: Macmillan, 1946.
Telfer, William. *The Forgiveness of Sins: An Essay in the History of Christian Doctrine and Practice*. London: SCM, 1959.
Thompson, William G. *Matthew's Advice to a Divided Community: Mt. 17,22–18,35*. Analecta Biblica. Rome: Biblical Institute, 1970.
Tuckett, C. M. *Q and the Early History of Early Christianity: Studies on Q*. Edinburgh: T. & T. Clark, 1996.
———. "The Q Hypothesis: A Good Hypothesis?" An unpublished paper on Debate on Q, 30th Annual Conference in Bangor, North Wales, 2010.
———. *The Revival of the Griesbach Hypothesis*. Cambridge: Cambridge University Press, 1983.
Turner, David L. *Matthew*. Baker Exegetical Commentary on the New Testament. Grand Rapids: Baker Academic, 2008.
Via, Dan O., Jr. "Ethical Responsibility and Human Wholeness in Matthew 25:31–46." *HTR* 80 (1987) 79–100.
Volf, Miroslav. *The End of Memory: Remembering Rightly in a Violent World*. Grand Rapids: Eerdmans, 2006.
———. *Exclusion and Embrace: A Theological Exploration of Identity, Otherness, and Reconciliation*. Nashville: Abingdon, 1996.
———. "Forgiveness, Reconciliation, and Justice: A Theological Contribution to a More Peaceful Social Environment." *Millennium: Journal of International Studies* 29, no. 3 (2000) 861–77.
Watson, Alan. *The Law of Obligations in the Later Roman Republic*. Oxford: Clarendon, 1965.
Watson, Francis. "Q as Hypothesis: A Study in Methodology." *NTS* 55 (2009) 397–415.
Wenham, Gordon J. *Genesis*. World Biblical Commentary 2. Nashville: Nelson, 1994.
Werren, Wim J. C. "The Macrostructure of Matthew's Gospel: A New Proposal." *Biblica* 87 (2006) 171–200.
Whiston, William. *The Works of Josephus*. Complete and Unabridged. New ed. Peabody, MA: Hendrickson, 1987.
White, L. Michael. "Crisis Management and Boundary Maintenance: The Social Location of the Matthean Community." In *Social History of the Matthean Community: Cross-Disciplinary Approaches*, edited by David L. Balch, 211–47. Minneapolis: Fortress, 1991.
Williams, Rowan. *Resurrection*. New York: Pilgrim, 1982.
Willmer, Haddon. "Jesus Christ the Forgiven: Christology, Atonement and Forgiveness." In *Forgiveness and Truth: Explorations in Contemporary Theology*, edited by Alistair McFadyen and Marcel Sarot, 15–29. Edinburgh: T. & T. Clark, 2001.
Worthington Jr., E. L., J. W. Berry and L. Parrott. "Unforgiveness, Forgiveness, Religion, and Health." In *Faith and Health*, edited by T. G. Plante and A. Sherman, 107–38. New York: Guilford, 2001.
Worthington, Everett L., Jr. *Forgiveness and Reconciling: Bridges to Wholeness and Hope*. Downers Grove, IL: InterVarsity, 2003.
Young, Brad H. *The Parables: Jewish Tradition and Christian Interpretation*. Peabody, MA: Hendrickson, 1998.
Younger, Jarred W., et al. "Dimensions of Forgiveness: The Views of Laypersons." *Journal of Social and Personal Relationships* 21, no. 6 (2004) 837–55.

Zerwick, Max, and Mary Grosvenor. *A Grammatical Analysis of the Greek New Testament.* Rome: Biblical Institute Press, 1981.

Index of Subjects

accountability, 16–18, 35–36, 143, 189, 191–92, 214
accounts, 8, 83
    the settling of, 168–70, 172–73, 201
aggression, 47, 214
allegory, 160–161
analogy(ies), 154, 161, 169, 171–72
anger, 11, 14, 16n55, 43–46, 56, 67–68, 71, 80, 83, 85, 96–98, 113, 142–43, 154, 182, 185–86, 214–15
    of God, 105, 111
antithesis(es), 43, 45, 47–49, 55, 55n65, 56, 60, 128, 141
avenge, 112–13, 215

Beatitudes, 13, 15, 31, 49, 54, 54n59, 55, 128, 208
Bible, 11, 17, 17n60, 100–101, 121n18, 142, 166, 167n52, 200

centrality, 2, 7, 18, 23, 30, 52, 123, 129, 164, 217, 219
cheek
    slap on the right cheek, 47
    turning of the other cheek, 47
Christians, 11, 37, 40–42, 49, 60, 119–21n16, 123, 146n88, 189, 194, 196, 204, 208, 210–12, 214, 218–19
    spiritually immature, 24, 30, 37, 40–42, 60, 123, 189, 194, 196, 218–19
    spiritually mature, 24, 30, 37, 40–42, 60, 123, 189, 194, 196, 218–19
Christology, 2, 200, 204, 221
clemency, 78, 80–82, 84, 105

commitment, vii–viii, 115, 209
community, 2, 3, 4, 5, 12, 14, 40, 41–42, 46, 47n46, 48–49, 51, 55n67, 58, 58n71, 67, 119, 119n5, 120–22, 122n24, 123–26, 145, 149–56, 158–59, 164, 189, 191, 196, 198, 209, 209n25, 210–11, 216–19, 221
    Jewish, 101, 119, 121, 166
    Jewish-Christian, 5, 119n5, 209n25
Community Discourse, 30–31, 52, 58–59, 60–61, 126, 148, 187–88, 193, 198, 208, 216, 218
compensation. *See* reparation
concept(s), 7, 10–11, 24–25, 27, 29–30, 34–37, 40, 42, 48–49, 60, 62, 76, 80, 83, 86, 89, 98, 109, 115, 117, 123, 142, 144, 146–48, 184, 186, 188, 192–94, 194n1, 195–97, 202, 208, 210, 215, 218–20
conditionality, 1, 7–8, 10–12, 22–23, 33–34, 97, 100, 141–42, 184
conflict(s), vii, 2–3, 8, 22, 47, 90, 95, 119, 121–22, 191, 212–13, 216
context(s), 3, 7–9, 11–12, 14, 16, 17, 22, 25–28, 40, 45, 49–50, 58, 62, 66–67, 72, 74, 83, 88, 90–91, 93–94, 97, 102–3, 105–6, 109–110, 112, 117, 124, 131, 138, 142, 144, 148, 153, 158, 163, 165, 170, 172, 176, 183, 192, 199, 204, 212–13, 216, 220
co-text, 24, 26, 33, 62, 70, 72, 88, 91–93, 96–97, 102–3, 105, 109, 111,

117–18, 131, 133, 136, 139–40, 148, 176, 189
creditor(s), 137–38, 163, 168, 176, 178–82
criticism, 19, 21, 23, 49, 80, 119, 152, 171
  redaction, 127
  source, 132

debt(s), viii, x, 21, 46, 133–38, 162, 170–72, 174, 176–77, 179, 181–84, 186
  cancelling the, 163, 169, 173, 175, 177, 178, 179, 184
  remitting, 189
debtor(s), 10, 12, 135–38, 162–63, 168–70, 172–75, 175n85, 176–83, 200
  release the, 163, 169, 177
  unmerciful, 35, 41, 141, 197, 200
  unforgiving, 149
deixis, 26, 168
  causal, 184
  discourse, 25, 178, 184, 186, 220
  personal, 25, 132, 178, 220
  social, 25, 164, 175, 180, 183, 220
  temporal, 25, 129, 139, 163, 220
denarii, 179, 181
disciple(s), 15, 19, 31–33, 37, 39, 40, 48–51, 53–54, 59n72, 122, 124, 128–29, 132, 139, 145, 150, 152, 157, 163–64, 182–84, 186, 188, 194, 201–3, 204n16, 205–8, 208n23, 209–10, 221
  unforgiving, 33, 162, 168, 187, 197
discipline, 4, 42, 78
discipleship, 3, 53, 200, 206–8, 210, 217
discourse, 8, 18, 22, 25–26, 28, 39–40, 49, 52–53, 62, 103, 117, 128, 128n43, 129, 131, 148–49, 151, 158–59, 160, 168, 195, 211–12, 216, 219–220
  analysis, 24, 25, 26, 26n83, 26n87, 27, 27n88–89, 220
  marker, 129, 163

emphasis, 3n7, 5, 7, 11–15, 24, 30, 32, 34, 37, 45–46, 52n56, 57, 60, 66, 116–17, 119, 123, 126, 142–43, 146–48, 151, 156–57, 159–60, 160n39, 188–89, 192–94, 196–97, 200, 211, 218
eschatology, 186
excommunication, 153, 155, 158
exegesis, 2, 7, 24–25, 117, 129, 132–33, 146, 148–49, 164, 188, 220

failure(s), 1, 6, 41, 72, 134–37, 160, 162, 164, 192, 212, 218, 221
father(s), 5, 10–11, 30, 42, 49–50, 55n62, 89–91, 99, 105–6, 108–10, 113, 139, 150, 152–53, 186–87, 197, 200–203, 208–10
  Apostolic, 46n44
  in heaven, 124, 202
  heavenly, 17, 32, 35–36, 48–49, 56, 139–40, 142–43, 150, 162–63, 184, 186–87, 189, 191, 201–2, 208–9, 214
  and king, 32, 42, 49, 106, 109, 200, 202, 208, 221
fatherhood, 49–50, 106, 109, 129, 187, 202, 208–9
fear, 90–91, 93, 98–99, 116, 120, 214
  of judgment, 13–14
First Gospel. *See* Gospel of Matthew
forbearance, 76, 80, 85–86, 102–3, 106, 111–12, 115
forgive, 1, 4–7, 12, 15–16, 18–20, 22, 22n74, 23n77, 30–31, 33, 35–37, 41, 45, 49, 60, 66–68, 71–73, 76–77, 79, 83, 85–86, 90–93, 97, 99, 104, 107, 109–10, 126, 139, 141–42, 142n73, 143, 145–46, 150, 152, 162–63, 166, 177, 186, 192, 194, 196, 198–99, 200, 203, 203n10, 205, 209, 210, 212–15
  debt(s), 22, 33, 107, 138, 147, 177n91, 218
  failure to, 11, 98, 100, 160, 162, 164, 187, 192, 212, 221
  offender, 166

reluctance to, 60, 73, 143, 163, 168, 170, 186, 191–92, 197, 211–12, 221
sin(s), 205
sinners, 210
forgiven
  person/people, 73, 211
  sinners, 211
forgiveness
  conditional, 142–43, 188, 194, 196
  conditioned, 31, 145, 184
  divine/God's, 6, 10, 12, 27, 34–35, 62, 70, 141, 162, 191, 202–5, 208–9, 212, 217, 219
  divine-human, 17, 22, 33, 33n6, 34, 97, 100, 117, 139, 140n69, 141–43, 148, 199, 220
  interpersonal, vii, ix, 1–12, 15–18, 22–25, 27–29, 30, 32–34, 37, 42–43, 46–47, 51–54, 56, 58–64, 69–70, 72–76, 78, 88–89, 91n9, 94–101, 107–8, 115, 117–19, 123, 125–26, 128–29, 132–33, 141–44, 146–51, 164–65, 167, 186–88, 190–98, 200, 204, 208, 211–14, 214n34, 216–22
  and judgment, 117, 148
  and justice, 9, 16n54, 19, 19n67, 21, 23, 36n15
  of sin(s), 3–4, 5n14, 102, 109, 137, 188, 205–6, 217
forgiver, 28, 36, 73, 85, 88, 143, 159, 214
forgiving, 6, 9, 10, 15, 16–18, 21–24, 28, 32–33, 36, 41, 49, 57, 60, 64, 70, 73, 81, 85–86, 90, 96–98, 100, 104, 106–8, 115–17, 126, 134, 138–41, 143, 145–47, 153, 162–67, 184, 186, 188–89, 191–98, 200, 205–6, 210–14, 217, 217n42, 218, 221
debtor(s), 138, 139, 147, 169, 218
human, 6–7, 18–19, 22, 34,62, 88, 140–41, 162, 191, 193, 199, 204, 211
sin(s), 206, 218

generosity, 22, 84, 96, 99, 103–4, 109, 116, 162, 166–67, 184, 199, 203, 210
gospel(s), 1n1, 21, 28, 30, 34, 37–38, 40, 46, 52–53, 56, 58, 60–61, 101, 117, 119, 128, 131, 133, 143, 146, 161, 188–89, 192, 198, 204, 206–210, 212–14, 216–20
  of the kingdom, 15, 206
  Synoptic, 19, 48n51, 152, 201
Gospel of Matthew, vii, ix, 2, 2n3, 3, 3n4, 3n6, 4n9, 4, 6n20, 7, 9, 13, 15, 18, 22, 25, 31nn1–2, 32, 32n3, 36, 38, 41, 43, 44n36, 45, 45n41, 46n42, 47nn45–46, 48–49, 49n52, 51, 53n58, 54, 55n67, 106, 119n5, 120, 120n13, 121n19, 124n30, 125, 127n33, 127nn37–38, 128n39, 136, 139n66, 156n19, 157n20, 159n27, 159n31, 161n38, 164, 167n50, 167n56, 168, 172n70, 173n78, 174n80, 175, 179n96, 193, 196, 200–2, 207–10, 213–14, 216–17, 217nn38–39, 217n42, 219
grace, 9, 12, 14, 14n48, 15, 15n50, 21, 23, 76, 105, 153, 182, 186, 198n3, 200, 205–6
  divine/God's, 51, 124, 145, 198–99, 202–6
  and mercy, and generosity, 203
guilt,18, 66, 70, 91, 94, 136, 154–55
guilty, 19, 21, 66–67, 113, 155
  person, 78, 83, 155
guiltlessness, 81

hapax legomenon, 32, 185
harmony, 46, 85, 126, 189, 191
hatred, 48, 56, 91, 120

identity, 3, 6, 37–38, 48, 52–53, 119–20, 123, 123n29, 126, 143, 150, 209, 214, 217–18
imitate, 49, 70, 185
imitatio Dei/Christi, 32, 48, 48n51, 49, 185, 208, 210

implication(s), 6, 11, 17, 28, 36, 50–51, 63, 64, 81, 133, 144, 151, 162, 201, 203, 211, 218, 221
initiative, 33, 41–42, 46, 71, 83, 86, 95–96, 99, 106, 110, 125, 139, 150, 200, 215
injurer, 16, 125, 158–60, 165
injuring
  party, 67, 71, 73
  person, 104, 116
injustice, 66, 136–37
insult(s), 43–45, 47, 94
interpretation, 1, 3, 12, 24–25, 27, 44, 57–58, 117, 126–27, 132, 137–39, 144, 147–49, 160, 160n36, 161, 167, 170–71, 198, 209
interrelationship(s), 8, 28, 33, 70, 88, 132, 137–39, 169
inter-text(s), 25, 62, 88, 117, 148, 220

Judaism, 2–3, 3n4, 3n6, 4n9, 9, 11, 19, 19n65, 35, 40, 91, 101, 119, 119n5, 121–22, 136, 141–42, 146, 152, 152n3, 152n5, 182, 216–17, 217nn38–39, 218
judgment, 10–11, 13–14, 24, 30–31, 36, 38, 43, 45–46, 50, 55, 57, 60, 69n19, 124, 141, 146, 153, 156, 184, 186–87, 193, 197, 207, 218
  divine/God's, 10, 35, 44, 47, 124, 142, 156
  eschatological, 13–14, 144, 185
  and reward. *See* reward(s)
  and salvation, 52
justice, 20–21, 38, 48, 52, 136–37, 145, 175, 181, 212n32, 213–14, 216
  and equity, 143

king(s), 38, 66, 69n19, 75–76, 80n64, 93–95, 106, 109, 110–11, 113, 162–63, 168–69, 170–75, 177–79, 182–83, 187, 201, 201n4, 221
  and father, 32, 42, 49, 106, 109–10, 200, 202, 208
kingdom, 13–15, 19, 41, 49–50, 60, 124, 126, 143, 149, 150, 152, 168, 170, 201, 203, 205–6, 208–9, 211, 214, 221

  of the Father, 50, 150, 208
  of God, 150, 187, 201, 212
  of heaven, 19, 47, 50, 152, 168–69, 201, 206
  heavenly, 124

letting go, 1, 84, 86, 115, 218
lex talionis, 47–48
limitless, 126, 150, 197, 204
"little ones," the, 37, 39–42, 59, 90, 123–26, 149–50, 156–57, 196–98, 203, 210, 218–19
love, x, 11, 15–16, 27, 49, 51, 84, 91, 138, 154, 159, 186, 203, 210–12, 214
  for/of enemies, 43, 48–49, 53–55, 55n65, 58–60, 125, 194–95, 212, 214, 216
  and mercy. *See* mercy
logia, 41, 58, 61, 200
logion, 5, 41, 45, 49, 58, 161, 187, 197, 199

Matthean (Christian) community, 2nn2–3, 6, 38, 41, 47–48, 55, 59–61, 117, 119, 119n6, 119n9, 121–23, 121n17, 122, 122n23, 126, 146, 149–50, 159, 198, 216
Matthew's gospel. *See* Gospel of Matthew
measure(s), 50, 121, 187
measure for measure, 43, 50
member(s), 7, 12, 40, 41–42, 49–56, 60, 71, 73, 101, 109, 124–26, 146, 149–52, 153n7, 154, 156–60, 189, 196, 198–99, 203, 209–11, 218, 221
merciful, 17, 30–32, 35, 41, 49, 55n62, 67, 83, 105, 109, 111, 114, 122, 126, 143, 184, 187, 202, 204, 208–10, 214
mercifulness, 74
mercy, 6, 10, 17, 27, 29–32, 35, 42–43, 48–51, 53–55, 70, 75–76, 78, 80, 84–85, 91, 94, 96–97, 99, 106, 114, 143, 149, 163, 177, 182–87, 194, 198, 205–8, 210
  conditional, 188, 194, 196

Index of Subjects   241

conditioned, 31, 184
divine/God's, 6, 32, 34, 105, 109, 112, 203, 210–211
divine/God's, and forgiveness, 7, 15, 206
and forgiveness, 7, 24, 30, 32, 34–36, 41, 60, 96–97, 142–43, 148, 163, 184, 188–89, 193, 194n1, 196, 202, 208, 210, 214, 216, 218
forgiveness, and judgment, 142
and generosity, 96, 103, 109
human, 34
human, and forgiveness, 206
metaphor(s), 31, 44, 49, 137, 161, 170, 184, 200
metaphoric, 137
minority, 2, 20, 123, 132, 143, 155
motif(s), 3–5, 42–43, 45, 49, 98, 101, 149, 168, 185, 196, 201, 205, 208

non-retaliation, 27, 43, 47, 59–60, 125, 195, 214, 216
non-violence, 214

obligation(s), 1, 11–12, 16, 41, 73, 87, 100, 104, 134, 136–37, 137n62, 138, 146–47, 154–55, 155n16, 173–74, 189, 192, 197, 199, 218
offence(s), 17, 20, 45–46, 51, 64–66, 68, 70, 72–73, 91, 95–96, 100, 103–4, 106, 109, 114, 134, 138, 153, 165, 213, 215
offended, 45, 92n10, 93, 213–16
    party, 12, 67, 72–73, 109, 115, 212
    person/people, 7, 12, 24, 30, 37, 41, 45–46, 51, 59–60, 70, 83, 85–87, 91n9, 93, 99–100, 103–4, 107, 115–17, 125, 141, 143, 147–48, 152–53, 165, 189, 191–94, 196–97, 199–200, 205, 211–13, 218
offender(s), 11–12, 18–20, 41–43, 45–46, 51, 64–65, 78, 81, 83, 85–86, 91, 93, 95, 98–100, 104–7, 115–16, 125–26, 143, 147, 153, 156, 160, 166–67, 181, 189, 191, 194, 199–200, 205, 211, 214–15
offending, 55, 104, 125
    party, 12, 73, 91, 96, 109, 115

person, 86
parable(s), 10, 31, 35, 37n19, 38n22, 39n25, 40n30, 42–43, 42n34, 45–47, 49, 52, 56, 59, 100n25, 123n29, 124, 142, 149, 152, 156–57, 160–63, 160n35, 161, 161n40, 163n46, 168–72, 169n61, 170–72, 172n74, 173n76, 174, 174n81, 175–77, 177n91, 178–79, 181–83, 185–89, 185n106, 187n113, 197–98, 201, 205
    interpretation, 160–61
pardon, 65, 77, 77n56, 78–82, 102–5, 107, 111
patience, 84, 103, 176–77, 180–82, 184, 186
peace, 21, 65, 73, 95, 105–6
peacemaking, 48, 56, 214, 216
perfect, being, 43, 48, 53, 56, 59–60, 122, 125–26, 194–95
pericope(s), 26, 43, 61, 132, 145, 155, 164, 172, 202
practice(s), 7, 32, 58, 75, 85–86, 101, 107, 116, 136, 153, 174–75, 175n85, 191–92, 210–14
Prayer/the Lord's Prayer, 6, 6n18, 12, 22, 22n76, 31, 33, 57, 60, 107, 117, 129, 131–32, 136, 142, 145
prayer(s), 5, 11, 22, 53, 56, 68, 70–71, 97–98, 104–6, 111–12, 129, 136, 142, 145
praxis, 24, 30, 34, 60, 88, 148, 189, 193, 218
preservation, 114, 177, 177n91
    of the community, 42, 123, 126, 149–50, 156, 158, 160, 164, 189, 198, 219
preserving the community, 150
prominence, 2, 4, 13, 37, 40, 132, 193–94, 196, 212, 216–17
punishment, 10, 13, 19, 35, 35n12, 44–45, 77–78, 81, 100, 105–6, 162, 164, 166, 180, 185–86, 189, 192, 196–97, 214
    eschatological. *See* judgment
    divine/God's, 142, 192, 204
    and reward. *See* reward

Index of Subjects

Qumran, 142, 154, 154n10, 155, 155n14

rebuke, 41, 154, 154n10, 155, 155n14, 180, 200
reciprocity, 24, 30, 34–36, 48, 60, 97, 117, 141–42, 145–46, 148, 186, 188, 193, 194n1, 196, 208, 218
reconciliation, vii, 12, 19, 19n67, 20, 27, 41, 43, 45–49, 50–51, 55–56, 59–60, 64–65, 69–73, 105–6, 114–15, 125, 153, 159, 198–200, 204–5, 212n32, 216
   brotherly, 42, 51, 53, 59–60, 123, 125–26, 149, 188, 194–95, 199
   and peace, 96
reluctance, 11, 24, 30, 34–36, 41, 60, 70, 73, 117, 141–43, 146, 148, 163, 168, 170, 184, 188–89, 191–93, 196–97, 212, 218, 221
reluctant, 60, 81
remission, 76, 85–86, 115
   of a deserved punishment, 77, 81,
   of a penalty, 78
   of the sins/trespasses, 104, 136, 138
reparation, 18, 21–22, 87, 107, 116, 159, 213
repentance, 9, 17–19, 20–23, 71, 73, 92, 103–4, 109, 111–12, 112n52, 114–15, 152–53, 165, 189, 197, 199, 212, 215
reprobation, divine, 44
responsibility, 7, 11–12, 16, 18, 18n63, 23–24, 30, 33, 37, 41–42, 45, 60, 91n9, 99, 107, 115–17, 124–25, 140–41, 143, 147–48, 150, 152–53, 160, 173, 189, 191, 193–94, 196, 199, 200–212, 218
retaliate, 35, 47, 67, 83, 85
retaliating, 111
   non-/not, 49, 122, 126, 194, 197, 216, 218
retaliation, 35n12, 48, 53, 55n65, 56, 98, 112, 116, 214
revenge, 67, 70, 83–84, 167, 212, 214–15
   inflicting, 82
   limiting, 48, 167

pursuing, 83
seeking, 113, 115–16, 214–15
taking, 1, 113, 215–16
reward(s), 48–49, 202
   and judgment, 3, 217
   and punishment(s), 13–14, 101
rhetoric, 9, 23, 28, 62–63, 73–74, 86, 88–89, 91, 94, 100, 106–7, 115–17, 148, 163, 191, 213–14, 219–220
rhetorical, 5–6, 25, 30, 33, 45, 47, 52, 60, 77–78, 117, 128, 133, 139–40, 146–48, 168, 170, 183–84, 188, 193–95, 198, 218
righteous, 48–49, 109, 110, 131, 152, 166, 203, 208, 210
righteousness, 3, 3n4, 4, 13, 13n40, 15n50, 15n52, 115, 131, 200, 206n17, 207, 207n18, 207n21, 208, 217, 217n38

scandal, 122–23, 125–26
   be/causing a, 125, 157
scandalize, 124, 156
   be scandalized, 124, 156, 197
scandalous, 212
Sermon (on the Mount), 5, 5n17, 6n21, 7, 13–15, 15n51, 30–32, 31n1, 44n37, 48n50, 52–53, 52n56, 54, 55n64, 55n66, 56–60, 117, 126, 128–29, 134n53, 137n64, 143n75, 144n78, 144n82, 145, 145nn84–85, 147, 187, 193, 195, 199, 202n7, 204–5, 207, 207n18, 208, 216, 218
significance, vii, ix, 5–6, 8, 13, 15, 17, 23, 27, 30, 33, 53, 79, 123n27, 150, 153, 165, 172, 179, 188, 205, 211–13
Sinaiticus, Codex, 50, 57n70, 130, 130n44, 130n46, 144
sins, 35, 96, 102–6, 109–10, 112, 115, 134–38, 151, 166, 186, 199, 205
   confession of, 4, 109, 136, 138, 147
sinner(s), 4, 19, 40–41, 85, 104, 123, 135–36, 152, 156–58, 159n33, 173, 199, 203–6, 211–12
slave(s), 90, 163, 168–73, 175–86, 201

fellow, 41, 143, 163, 168, 179–80, 185
wicked, 184, 186
slavery, 174–75, 182
source(s), 6, 28, 50, 52, 52n57, 55–57, 59–62, 118, 134–36, 146, 154–55, 190–92, 219–20
   four-source theory, 118
   two-source theory, 24, 118, 132
structure, 1, 10, 14, 24–25, 27, 30, 40n31, 45–46, 50, 57n69, 88, 117, 123, 123n28, 136, 192
   of Matthew/the gospel, 2, 53, 57n69, 60n73, 117, 126–27, 127n33, 127nn37–38, 128, 128n43, 129, 133, 149, 151, 176, 189
Synoptics. *See* gospel(s)
Synoptic gospels. *See* gospel(s)

talent(s), 161n45, 171, 171n67, 172
tax collector(s), 156
   and Gentiles, 157–58, 205
   and Gentiles, sinners, and prostitutes, 157
   and prostitutes, 157
   and sinners, 157, 204, 206
   and sinners, and prostitutes, 206
theism, 221
theme(s), vii, ix, 1–8, 11, 14–16, 23, 27, 30, 32, 37–38, 40, 49, 52, 54, 56, 60–62, 71, 74, 86, 88–89, 98, 100–101, 107, 109–10, 119, 123, 123n27, 129, 132–33, 136, 146, 149–150, 160, 163–64, 166, 177, 188, 190, 193–94, 196, 206–7, 212, 216–20
tolerance, 84, 86, 103, 105–6, 110–11
tradition(s), 11, 41n32, 50, 51n54, 127, 198
   biblical, 199
   Christian, 49
   Jewish, 101, 101n26, 107, 159, 203
   Johannine, 154n7
   Lukan, 9n27, 134
   Markan, 9n27
   Pauline, 9n27, 134, 153n7
   primitive, 58
   Q, 55

Stoic, 74
theological, 120
transgression(s), 1, 93, 109, 146, 218

unconditional, 21–22, 99, 116
unforgiving
   debtor, 149
   disciple(s), 33, 162, 168, 187, 192, 197
   person/people, 6, 11, 28, 35–36, 70, 73, 87, 97–98, 100, 116, 141–43, 147, 164, 170, 186, 192, 194, 219
unmerciful, 10, 35–36, 97, 162, 186
   debtor/creditor/slave, 12, 35, 41, 142, 180, 182–84, 186, 197, 200, 201
unrighteous, 48–49, 131, 199, 203, 210

Vaticanus, Codex, 50, 57n70, 130, 130n49
vengeance, 48, 94, 97, 113–15, 142, 165–67, 215
   God's/the Lord's, 11, 96–98, 100, 142–43, 192
vengeful person, 96–97, 100, 143, 166, 192
   spirit, 166, 215
violation(s), 66, 109, 134–35, 138, 147
violence, vii, 18, 56, 66, 112, 120, 178–79, 181, 212
   non-violence, 214

wrongdoer, 1, 19–21, 84, 138
wrongdoing, 1, 18, 21, 70, 84, 91, 104, 218

Index of Authors

Aarde, A. van, 119n5, 121n16
Abrahams, I., 9, 22, 22n75-76, 23, 142n73
Aitken, J. K., 101, 101n26
Aland, B. et al., 130n48, 131nA
Aland, K., 130n44-46
Allison, D. C., Jr., 48n51, 56, 57n69, 119n7, 127n38, 201, 201n5, 210, 210n28

Barth, G., 13n42
Bauer, D. R., 127, 127n33, 127nn37-38
Benn, P., 64n5
Bethune-Baker, J. F., 17, 17n60
Betz, H. D., 6, 9, 134, 137-38, 143-46, 217n41
Blomberg, C. L., 160
Boff, L., 138
Bonnard, P., 162
Borgen, P., 101n28
Boring, E. M., 121
Bornkamm, G., 119n7, 124, 154n8
Braund, S. M., 29, 76n50, 77n56, 79-80, 80n64
Brettler, Z., 201, 201n4
Brooke, G. J., ix, 96n18
Brown, J. K., 37, 37n19, 38, 38nn20-21, 39, 39n25
Brown, M., 3n5, 127n34, 217n38
Brown, R. E., 144n77
Bruner, F. D., 139-40

Carmignac, J., 8n26, 137, 137n63, 140, 140n68
Carson, D. A., 37n18

Carter, W. 6, 6n22, 7, 45, 45n41, 121, 121n21, 123, 123n26, 136, 136n58, 144, 144n76, 155n17, 156, 156n18, 158, 158n23
Copper, J. M., and J. F. Procopé, 74, 74n36, 76, 76n53-54
Couroyer, B., 31n2, 184n103
Crenshaw, J. L., 97, 97n22, 141, 141n71
Crystal, David, 26n84

Davies, W. D., and D. C. Allison Jr., 5, 5n15, 15, 15n51, 32, 32n4, 36n14, 45n41, 46, 46n43, 154n8, 158n25, 159, 159n26, 159n29-30, 162, 162n42, 167n51, 171, 171n67-68, 172n75, 173n78, 180n98, 185, 185n105, 185n107, 185n110, 186, 186n111, 207n19, 217n41
De Boer, M. C., 162n45, 171n67
Deines, R., 3n4, 4, 4n12, 217n38, 217n40
Deissmann, A., 174n82
Derrett, J. D. M., 162n45
Donahue, J. R., 38, 38n22, 40, 40n30, 42, 42n34, 123, 123n29, 174, 174n81, 175
Downey, G., 120n10
Downing, F. G., ix-x, 64, 64n6, 211, 211n30
Duling, D. C., and N. Perrin, 121n16, 146n88
Dumais, M., 48n50
Dupont, J., 207n19
Durham, J. I., 92, 92n12

Index of Authors

Ellingworth, P., 5, 5n14
Enright, R. D., 84, 84n78, 104, 104n36
Enright, R. D., and C. T. Coyle, 67, 67n10
Exline, J. J., et al., 16, 16n54, 36n15

Farrer, A. M., 118
Fensham, F. C., 9n28
Fiedler, M. J., 207n20
Fokkelman, J. P., 94, 94n15
Foster, P., 47, 47n46, 55n67
France, R. T., vii, ix, 3n4, 31, 31n2, 32, 32n3, 37n18, 44, 44n36, 45n41, 46, 47n45, 49, 49n52, 127, 127n38, 128n39, 157, 157n20, 158n22, 159, 159n27, 159n31, 159n33, 166–67, 167nn50-51, 167n56, 171–72, 172n70, 178, 178n93, 179, 179n96, 184n103-4, 187, 187n115, 207n18, 217n38, 217n41
Fromentin, V., 63, 63n1

Garland, D. E., 37n18
Giesen, H., 207n20
Gilbert, M., 47, 47n49
Goodman, M., 101n26
Gore, C., 31n1, 32
Goulder, M. D., 44, 44n38
Green, J. B., 26, 26n83
Grimal, P., 75n42
Guelich, R. A., 9, 44n37
Gundry, R. H., 40, 40n31, 121n17, 122, 122n23, 123n28, 154n8, 170, 170n64, 187, 188n116
Gundry-Volf, J. M., 39n26

Hagner, D. A., ix, 5, 5n16, 13n40, 15, 15n50, 15n52, 34, 34n11, 37n18, 119n8, 127, 127n33, 127n35, 151, 151n2, 154n8, 165n48, 167n51, 169, 169n58, 172n72, 176, 176n90, 185n108, 185n110, 206, 206n17, 207n18, 207n21-22, 217n41
Harrington, D. J., 119n7, 121n16, 146n88

Hatch, E., and H. A. Redpath, 90n1, 90n4
Hendricksen, W., 139
Hill, David, 31, 31n1, 32, 53n58, 207n19
Hill, P., 16
Hoehler, L., et al., 39n26
Holmes, M. W., 46n44
Houlden, J. L., 13n42
Huang, S. T., and R. D. Enright, 16n55
Huffman, N. A., 169n61
Hultgren, A. J., 37n19, 39n25
Hurtado, L. W., 2n2

Jastrow, M., 39n26
Jeremias, J., 171, 171n66, 171n69, 173, 173n79
Jones, L. G., 8n26, 18, 18n64, 19, 19n66, 152, 152n4, 152n6, 204, 204n15, 211, 211n29, 212, 212n31

Kant, I., 18, 18n62
Kilpatrick, G. D., 119
Kingsbury, J. D., 121, 121n15
Klein, R. W., 94, 94n16
Kloppenborg, J. S., 118n2

Liddell, H. G., and R. Scott, 29, 35n12, 91n8, 92n11, 93n13, 97n20, 102n31, 103n34
Linnemann, E., 163n46, 185, 185n106
Louw, J. P., 38n23
Luz, U., 3n4, 4, 4n13, 5–6, 6n19, 34, 34n10, 39, 40n28-29, 40n31, 47, 47n48, 54n60, 56n68, 119n8, 123n28, 127, 127n36, 128, 128n42, 136, 136n61, 144n80, 149n1, 153–54, 154n7, 154n9, 155, 158n25, 161n37, 162–63, 163n46-47, 166, 166n, 49, 167, 167n51, 167n53, 167n55, 168, 168n57, 169, 169n59, 170, 170n63, 174n83, 175n85, 176n89, 179, 179n94, 179n97, 180, 180n99, 182, 182n101, 188, 188n117, 207n19, 208n23, 217n38, 217n41

Manson, T. W., 162n45, 171n67
Marguerat, D., 44, 44n37, 45, 45n39
Marshall, H. I., ix
Martínez, F. G., 154, 154n10, 155, 155nn14–15
McCarthy, M., 27, 27n89
McCullough, E., S. J. Sandage, and E. L. Worthington Jr., 16
Meeks, W. A., 121n16, 146n88
Metzger, B. M., 51, 130, 130n47, 130n50
Michel, O., 39n26
Mohrlang, Roger, 10, 10n34, 13, 13n41, 13n43, 14–15, 122n25, 201, 201n6
Morris, L., 155n17
Morro, W. C., 8n26, 17, 17n59
Mortureux, B., 75, 75n42–43, 79, 79n59, 81, 81n70, 82
Moule, C. F. D., 9, 22, 22n74, 23, 23n77, 119n8, 142n73, 217n42
Mounce, W. D, D. M. Smith, and M. V. Van Pelt, 38n21, 39nn26–27

Neirynck, F. F., 127n38, 128n40
Nestle-Aland, K., et al., 51, 51n54–55
Nida, E. A., 26n85, 38n23
Nolland, J., ix, 6, 6n20, 45, 46n42, 55n61, 155n17, 156, 156n19, 161, 161n38, 167n51, 173, 173n78, 174n80

Oakes, P., viii, ix, 96n18
Oepke, A., 39n27
Osborne, G. R., 45n40, 47n48, 167, 167n51, 167n54, 175, 175n58, 176n90, 181, 181n100
Osten-Sacken, P. von der, 38n21
Overman, J. A., 3, 3nn4–5, 4, 4n9, 119n5, 119n7, 217, 217nn38–40

Plummer, A., 125, 125n31, 159, 159nn28–29
Pokrifka-Joe, T., 33, 33n6, 34, 140, 140n69, 141
Porter, S. E., 27n88
Powery, E. B., 118, 118n1
Préchac, F., 75, 76n45

Przybylski, B., 3n4, 119n8, 207nn18–19, 217n38

Quanbeck, W. A., 8n26, 9n28, 16–17, 17n58, 17n61

Rajak, T., 108n47
Reimer, D. J., ix, 7, 7n25, 8n26, 9, 9nn29–30, 10, 10n31, 10n33, 10n35, 11–12, 35, 35n13, 91, 91n7, 93, 93n14, 97, 97n21, 100n25, 142, 142n72, 160, 160n34
Repschinski, B., 119n5
Reynolds, Griffin, and Fantham, 74n35, 75n41
Richards, J. C., J. Platt, and H. Platt, 26, 26n86, 27, 27n90
Riches, J. K., 2n2, 52n57, 120n11, 209, 209n27

Saldarini, A. J., 119n5, 119n7, 209, 209n25
Sanders, E. P., 19, 19n65, 25n81, 152, 152n3, 152n5
Sanders, T. and J., 25
Schoedel, W. R., 120, 120n13
Schottroff, L., 161n40, 172, 172n74, 173, 173n76, 177n91, 187, 187n113
Segal, A. F., 121n16, 146n88
Senior, D., 2n2, 37n18, 121n16, 146n88
Sim, D. C., 2n2, 119nn5–7, 119n9
Skeham, P. W., and A. A. Di Lella, 97n19
Smallwood, E. M., and T. Rajak, 108n47
Snodgrass, K., 161, 161n39, 161n41, 162, 162n43, 167n51, 171, 171n65, 172n73, 186, 186n112, 187n114
Snyman, A. H., 26n87
Spicq, C., 182, 182n102
Spilsbury, P., 108n47
Stanton, N. G., 2n3, 3, 3n5, 3n8, 52n57, 119n5, 119n8, 203n10, 217n38
Stark, R., 120, 121n14

Index of Authors

Sternberg, M., 91n7
Stiewe, M., and F. Vouga, 51, 52n56, 145n84, 202, 202n7
Strecker, G., 55, 55n64, 55n66, 144n80, 207n18–19
Swinburne, R., 18, 18n63

Thompson, W. G., 122n24
Tuckett, C. M., 118, 118n4
Turner, D. L., 37n18

Vermes, G., 154n13
Via, D. O., Jr., 38n21
Volf, M., 8n26, 19, 19n67, 20–21, 212, 212n32
Vorländer, H., 8n26, 90, 90nn2–3

Watson, A., 137n62
Watson, F., 118, 118n3
Wenham, D., ix
Wenham, G. J., 91, 91n5
Westerholm, S., 8n26
Whiston, W., 29
White, L. M., 121n16, 146n88
Worthington, E. L., 15, 16, 16n53, 36n15
Worthington, Jr., E. L., J. W. Berry, and L. Parrott, 15–16, 16n53, 36n15

Younger, J. W., et al., 16, 16n56, 36, 36n16, 143n74, 214n33

Zerwick, M., and M. Grosvenor, 38n21

Ancient Document Index

HEBREW BIBLE

Genesis

4:13	90
4:15	165
4:24	166–67
18:26	90
32–33	9, 96, 99
45	9, 91
50:15–21	9, 89, 90–91, 98–99
50:17	90

Exodus

2:15	3
4:19	3
4:20	3
10:10–11	92
10:16–17	92, 95, 98–99
10:16–20	89, 91n10, 98–99
10:17	98, 134
21:24	56, 215n35
22:1–4	213
22:3	174
32:32	90
34:6–7	203n11

Leviticus

4:20	90
16	166
19:17	155, 155n16, 159
19:18	159
24:20	56, 215n35
26:18, 21, 24	166

Deuteronomy

12:5–7, 11–14, 17–18	102
15	136
15:2	90
15:11	136
19:15	155n16
19:21	56, 215n35

1 Samuel

8:6b–7	110
12:18–25	108
15:24–31	9
15:24–25	92, 95, 98–100
15:25	98, 134
25	9, 89
25:26–28	91n10, 93, 96, 99–100, 215
25:28	98, 135

2 Samuel

15:16	90
16:5–14	90
16:11	90
19:16–23	90
20:3	90

1 Kings

2:9–9, 36–46	10

2 Kings

4:1	174

1 Chronicles

29:4–2	171

Nehemiah

5:5	174
5:6	182

Esther

3:9	171

Psalms

17:14	90
25:18	203n11
32:1, 5	203n11
48:2	201
85:2	201n11

Isaiah

1:10–17	136
22:14	90
33:24	203n11
50:1	174
50:6	47
55:7	203n11
58:5–9	136

Lamentations

3:30	47

Amos

2:6	174
8:6	174

Jonah

4:4, 9	182
3:1–4	111

APOCRYPHA

1 Maccabees

13:36–40	89, 95, 98–100
13:37	90, 98
13:38	98
13:39	135

3 Maccabees

3:21	103
Sap	
14:26	103

Sirach (Ecclesiasticus)

5:4–7	10, 35
11:25	103
17:25–32	10, 35
18:8–14	10, 35
28:1–7	10–11, 35, 89, 96–98, 100, 142
28:1–4	10, 35, 100, 141–43, 145, 192, 200, 203n11, 204
28:1–2	10, 35
28:1	192
28:2	90, 97–98, 135, 205
28:4	10, 35, 100n25

PSEUDEPIGRAPHA

Testament of the Twelve Patriarchs

T. Gad

6.3–7	142
6.3–4, 6–7	214n34
6.7	187

T. Jos

18.2	142

T. Zeb

5.1–5	142
8.1–6	142

NEW TESTAMENT

Matthew

1:21	15, 158, 205
2:12	3
2:13	3
2:16	3
2:19	3
3:15	3
3:2	13, 19, 152
3:2, 8, 11	152
4:17	13, 19, 152, 201, 206
4:23	15, 121, 201, 206
5–7	4, 52–53, 58, 126, 128, 131, 195, 204, 208, 216
5:3–12	13, 53–54, 128
5:6, 10, 20	3
5:7, 21–26, 38–42, 43–48	7
5:17–48	3, 49, 53
5:20	14, 208
5:21–26	7, 19, 43, 45–46, 53, 55, 59–60, 125, 128, 143, 153, 195
5:21–30	14
5:22–26	14
5:22, 29, 30	14
5:22	11, 14, 44, 44n37, 45
5:23–24	5, 11, 45–46, 51, 61, 122, 216
5:48	32, 43, 48, 50, 56, 59–60, 122, 125–26, 162, 184, 195–96, 210–211
6:1–18	53, 56, 129, 131
6:1, 33	3
6:6–13, 25–30	15, 202
6:9–15	8, 11, 25, 105–6, 117, 129, 131–32, 201, 204, 220
6:12, 14–15	7–11, 15, 22, 24–25, 28, 31, 33–34, 45, 56, 59–60, 97, 100, 117–18, 122, 126, 128–29, 132–34, 142–43, 146, 151, 153, 164–65, 184, 189, 192–96, 198–99, 220
6:12b, 14–15	17, 36, 192
6:12, 14	4, 202–3, 210
6:12b	17, 36, 41, 139, 145, 162, 192, 199–200
6:14	5, 31, 57, 141, 145–46, 162, 199, 203, 205, 212
6:15	5, 10–11, 31, 35, 60–61, 126, 141–43, 162, 164, 186, 192, 197, 221
7:1–5	14, 49, 54
7:1–2, 12	7, 142, 187, 194, 196
7:7–11	15, 49, 54, 202
7:12–29	54
7:12	31, 48–49, 54, 58–61, 125, 184, 192, 194–95
7:12b	61
7:13–14, 21–27	14
8:12, 29	14
9:1–8	15, 205
9:2–8, 10–13	210
9:2–8, 13	202, 206
9:2–8	15
9:8	4
9:17	7
9:35	15, 121, 201, 206, 210
10:7	13, 201, 206
10:15, 26–28	141
10:20, 29–32	15, 202
11:20–24	14
12:31–32	15, 205
12:41–42	14
13:42, 50	14
16:19	4
18:3, 10	14
18:3–4	150
18:3	14, 41, 59, 124, 150
18:5	41–42, 150
18:6–10	14, 42, 125, 150
18:8–9	14
18:10–14, 19–20	15, 202
18:15–17, 21–35	7, 15, 45–46, 100
18:15–17, 21–22	165
18:15–17, 21	150
18:15–17, 33	50
18:15–20	12, 149
18:15–17	12, 41–42, 51, 60, 122, 125, 149, 151, 154, 154n10, 155, 155n14, 156, 158–59, 165, 194, 198, 200, 204, 216
18:21, 33	194
18:21	12, 41, 42n35, 163, 165, 200

Matthew (continued)

18:23–35	6, 10–12, 31, 33–36, 46, 59–60, 98, 100, 100n25, 118, 122, 126, 136, 136n61, 142–43, 149, 160–61, 161n36, 162, 164, 167, 188, 192, 196–98, 201–2, 204–5, 212, 214, 216
18:23–27, 32–35	15, 206
18:33	17, 31, 36, 41, 51, 200, 205, 210
21:28–32	14
21:31–32	157–58
21:31	15, 206
21:32	3
22:13	14
24:20	15, 121, 202
25:30	14
26:28	4, 15, 205, 211
26:36–44	15, 202

Mark

1:4	4
4:24–25	57
4:24b	50
9:33	58
9:34	58
9:36, 49	58
10:15	59
11:25–26	9n27, 105–6
11:25[–26]	11, 118
11:25	10, 12, 45, 57, 61, 97, 141–42, 146, 195, 205

Luke

6:20–23	55
6:27–38	49
6:28, 32–36	56
6:29–30	56, 61
6:31	58, 61
6:35–36	49
6:36	54, 6, 32
6:37–42ff	50
6:37	57
6:37a	57, 61
6:37b	57
6:37b–38	61
7:41–43	136n61
7:41	134
10:29–37	32
11:2–4	9n27, 11, 97, 105–6, 131–32, 142
11:4	97
12:57–59	55
12:58	181
11:14	10, 141
15:3–7	59, 61, 124, 157
15:1	157
15:3–10	152
15:11–32	152
16:1–8	136n61
16:1–2	172
16:5, 7	134
17:2	59
17:3–4	9n27, 59, 61, 151
17:3	59
17:10	134
18:9–14	10
19:1–10	21
19:8	213

John

3:24	181

Acts

11:26	120
16:23–24	181

Romans

4:4	134n52
4:7	9n27
4:14	134n52
8:12	134n52
12:17–21	212, 216
13:7–8	134n52
15:1, 27	134n52

1 Corinthians

5:1–5	153n7
5:10	134n52
7:3, 36	134n52
9:10	134n52
11:7, 10	134n52

Ancient Document Index   253

2 Corinthians

2:5–11	153n7
12:11, 14	134n52

Galatians

5:3	134n52

Ephesians

1:7	9n27
4:26	46
4:32	9n27
5:28	134n52

2 Thessalonians

1:3	134n52
2:13	134n52
3:14–15	154n7

1 Timothy

1:20	154n7
5:19–21	154n7

Titus

3:10	154n7

Philemon

18	134n52

Hebrews

2:17	32

James

2:13	10, 97, 141

3 John

10	154n7

Revelation

2:10	181

DEAD SEA SCROLLS

CD

7.1–3	154n12
9.2–8	154n12
9.17–23	154n12
20.4–8	154n12

1QS

5.24–6.1	154n12
5.25–6.1	155
5.26–6.1	154
6.24–7.25	154
6.24–7.25	154
9.16–18	154n12

RABBINIC WRITINGS

Babylonian Talmud

Meg.

28a	142n73

Sabb.

88b	142n73

Sabb.

151b	142n73

Yoma

8.9	92n10

Yoma

9b	142n73

Yoma

86a–86b	142n73, 166
86b–87a	92n10

Mishnah

'Abot

3.11	142n73

Tosephta

Yoma

5.6ff	142n73

Other Midrashim

Sifre

93b	142n73

JEWISH HELLENISTIC WRITINGS

Philo

Laws

1.235–36	103, 103n33, 106n39, 107n46
1.67	135n54, 102, 102n30, 107n41
2.196	102, 104, 104n37, 107n45

Punishments

166–67	105, 106nn38–39, 107n40, 107n43, 107n45, 107n46, 110n49, 203n12

Josephus

Antiquities

6.92–93	108, 109n48, 114nn57–59, 115n61, 115nn65–67, 135n56, 203n13
9.214	111, 111n51, 112n52, 114n58, 114n60, 115n61, 115n65, 135n57

War

5.376–78	112, 112n53, 115nn61–64, 115n68
5.379–81	113n54
5.394	113n55, 115n68, 215n36
5.415–16	114n56
6.103–7	111n50, 114n58, 114n60, 115nn61–62
6.104–7	110

GRECO-ROMAN WRITINGS

Cicero

Actio in verrem

2.5.44.115	80n68

Epistulae ad Atticum

14.19.2	80n68

De Inventione rhetorica

2.54.164	80n68

De officiis

1.25.88	80n68

Orationes

8.11.32	76n49

Oratio in Pisonem

41.98	76n49

Oratio pro ligario

3.10	80n68

Oratio pro rege deiotaro

15.43	80n68

De Partitione oratoria

37.131	76n49

Dionysius

Ant. Rom.

2.51.3	67n9
2.52.1–4	66, 67n8, 72n25
2.53	67n11
2.54.3	73n27, 73n30, 65, 65n7, 72
2.54.4	72n26, 73n27, 73n30
2.55.4–6	65, 65n7, 72n26, 73n27, 73n30
8.21.1	69n17
8.22.4	69n17
8.38	69n18
8.39.2	69n19
8.50.1–4	68, 68n12, 70n21, 72nn24–26, 73nn27–28, 73n34,

		1.9.11–12	84, 84n77, 85n81
	83n75, 84n79, 85n87, 143, 192, 200	1.9.11	85n82, 85n84, 85n89
8.50.1–2	69n16	1.11.4–13	76n53
8.54	71, 72nn22–23, 72n26, 73, 73n27	2.5.2	75n40, 80
		2.7.1–3	80
8.54.5	71, 72nn22–23, 72n26, 73, 73n27	2.7.1–2	85n82
		2.7.1	77, 77n55, 80–81
8.57.1	71, 72nn22–23, 72n26, 73, 73n27	2.7.2–3	78, 78n58, 85n82
		2.7.3–4	85n82, 85n85
		2.7.4–5	79, 79n60
		4.4–5–1	80n63

Ovidius

Metamorphoses

6.32	76n49
8.57	80n68

Quintilianus

Institutiones oratoriae

1.5.11	76n49
9.2.28	80n68
10.1.72	76n49

Seneca

De clementia.

1.1–9	75n39
1.2	79n61
1.3.1	75n44
1.3.2–8	76n51
1.5–6	81
1.6.2–3	80–81
1.6.3–4	85nn82–83
1.9–11.3	76n52
1.9.1–7	81–82, 85nn81–82, 85n86, 85n88, 99n24, 177n92, 214
1.9.3–7	81, 83n74
1.9.6	80n69, 82

EARLY CHRISTIAN WRITINGS

Clement of Alexandria

1 Clement

13.2	34n10

Didache

8.2	135

Ignatius

Polycarp's Letter to the Philippians

2.3	34n10

www.ingramcontent.com/pod-product-compliance
Lightning Source LLC
Chambersburg PA
CBHW050436240426
43661CB00055B/2407